The Allen Fisher Companion

The Allen Fisher Companion

edited by

Robert Hampson
& cris cheek

Shearsman Books

First published in the United Kingdom in 2020 by
Shearsman Books Ltd
PO Box 4239
Swindon
SN3 9FN

Shearsman Books Ltd Registered Office
30–31 St. James Place, Mangotsfield, Bristol BS16 9JB
(this address not for correspondence)

ISBN 978-1-84861-626-4

Copyright © 2020 by the authors.

The right of the persons listed on page 5 to be identified
as the authors of this work has been asserted by them
in accordance with the Copyrights, Designs and Patents Act of 1988.
All rights reserved.

Contents

Introduction: Robert Hampson / 7

Chapter 1: Siting Place / 25
Will Rowe

Chapter 2: Toward Health / 39
Pierre Joris

Chapter 3: Start Place in Flux / 53
Redell Olsen

Chapter 4: The poet, the document and the documentary / 65
cris cheek

Chapter 5: Chreods, Catastrophes / 83
Steven Hitchins

Chapter 6: Fractalising the Front Line / 98
Will Montgomery

Chapter 7: Apocalypse Then / 112
Robert Sheppard

Chapter 8: Reading 'Mummers' Strut' / 134
Scott Thurston

Chapter 9: Lines of Flight / 163
Clive Bush

Chapter 10: The New Complexity / 185
Pierre Joris

Chapter 11: Artefactu(r)al Logic in Allen Fisher's *SPUTTOR* / 191
Calum Hazell

Chapter 12: Imperfect Fit / 202
Allen Fisher, Paige Mitchell, Shamoon Zamir

Chapter 13: Philly Talks / 238
Allen Fisher, Karen Mac Cormack et al.

Contributors / 287

Bibliography / 291

Index / 294

INTRODUCTION

Allen Fisher is one of the most important figures to have emerged from the London innovative poetry scene of the 1960s and 1970s.[1] His sustained fifty-year project, across poetry, performance and painting, provides a model for practice as research. His talks, interviews and writings about his practice have been a significant resource for other practitioners.[2] His work as a publisher and his generous and informed encouragement of younger poets have also made him an exemplary figure.

Allen Fisher made his name in the 1970s, in the context of what Eric Mottram called 'the British Poetry Revival', as poet, performer and publisher.[3] Mottram describes Fisher in the early '70s as working in 'two different poetic areas' (41): first, as a member of the Fluxshoe group, with its focus on happenings and performance; secondly, as a page-based poet, developing a procedural and processual poetry out of the constructivist and open-field poetics of Ezra Pound and Charles Olson.[4] Mottram cites

---

[1] For an account of this scene, see Robert Hampson and Ken Edwards, *Clasp: late modernist poetry in London in the 1970s* (Bristol: Shearsman, 2016).

[2] See, for example, Allen Fisher, *The Topological Shovel: Four Essays* (The Gig Editions, 1999), which includes his important essay 'Necessary Business' This is also included in a more recent collection, *Imperfect Fit: Aesthetic Function, Facture and Perception in Art and writing since 1950* (Tuscaloosa, AL: University of Alabama Press, 2016). See also Andrew Duncan (ed.), *The Marvels of Lambeth: Interviews & Statements by Allen Fisher* (Bristol: Shearsman, 2013).

[3] See Eric Mottram, 'The British Poetry Revival, 1960-1975' in Robert Hampson and Peter Barry (eds.), *New British poetries: The scope of the possible* (Manchester: Manchester University Press, 1993), 15-50. This was the revised version of an essay originally published in 1974.

[4] It would be more accurate to describe Fisher at this time as already working in many overlapping cultures in London, in the UK and internationally. Interestingly, Doug Lang's novel, *Freaks* (London, New English Library, 1973), presents a version of him lightly disguised as Al Bass, 'as serious and as sensitive a poet and man as you could wish to meet' (56). He makes his first appearance at a book-launch in 'Belfy Books' in Soho, talking about 'water-divining and old roads built along the paths of ancient underground rivers' (57). Towards the end of the novel, he takes part in a reading with the protagonist, Calvin Longbow, at 'The Poetry Institute', where they are introduced by Will Dilling, 'a robust big grey-bearded man full of energy, with a sonorous voice, an authoritative manner, and a vast and impressive output of concrete and sound poetry to his credit' (115). Bass reads from his best-known poem, a long work called *Information Outlay*, 'which moved through its own language variants like a computer with a sense of humour' (116). He is last seen in conversation with two other poets, talking about 'conceptual poetry. Mathematical forms, Procedure. All that stuff' (117).

two early works: *Long Shout to Kernewek* (New London Pride, 1971), Fisher's first long poem, 'a collection of topological and topographical poems centred on Cornwall', and *Sicily* (Edible Press and Beau Geste, 1973), with its use of 'cut-ups, random and conceptual procedures' (41). However, Fisher's major work of the 70s was the ten-year project *Place*, which appeared in a wide range of small magazines and in successive volumes: *Place Book One* (London: Aloes, 1973), republished as *Place I-XXXVII* (Carrboro, NC: Truck Press, 1976); *Eros: Father: Pattern* (Secret Books, 1976); *Stane: Place Book III* (London: Aloes Books, 1977); *Becoming* (London: Aloes Books, 1978) and *Unpolished Mirrors* (London: Spanner, 1979). It was not published as a single volume until 2004, and this fragmented and complicated publishing history has probably meant that a work whose serial publication was excitedly awaited by its original readers has not had the sustained critical attention that it deserves, despite the work of critics such as Clive Bush, Peter Barry and Robert Sheppard.[5]

Fisher has been involved in writing and performance since 1962. His first publication was the elusive *Bavuska* (1969). He subsequently published *Thomas Net's Tree-Birst* (Edible Magazine Poisonous Edition, 1970), a subtractive or auto-destructive 'writing through' of the first book of the 1850 version of *The Prelude*, written between 1966 and 1970.[6] Fisher excavates from Wordsworth's long poem his own meditation on birth, sex and death; the relation of 'brain and eye'; the poet's role among living and dead peers; illness and health; discontent and ecstasy; the absence of myth and the present particularities of the natural world. His next publication, *Before Ideas, Ideas* (Edible Magazine, 1971), consists of three lunar meditations, written in 1967, and 'Play of Diction', added in 1970. It shows again Fisher's concerns with place and space, with the body and its relations, and with sex and

---

[5] The most extended critical engagement with Place is to be found in Clive Bush's *Out of Dissent: A study of five contemporary British Poets* (London: Talus Editions, 1997), 102-124. See also Peter Barry's engagement with *Place* in *Contemporary British Poetry and the City* (Manchester University Press, 2000), 179-85. Robert Sheppard has written widely on Fisher's work: in *The Poetry of Saying: British Poetry and Its Discontents, 1950-2000* (Liverpool: Liverpool University Press, 2005), he writes on *Place* (60-64) and on creative linkage' in *Gravity as a consequence of shape* (195-203); in *When Bad Times Made for Good Poetry* (Bristol: Shearsman, 2011), he writes on technique and technology in *Place* and *Gravity* (31-54); and in *The Meaning of Form in Contemporary Innovative Poetry* (Palgrave Macmillan, 2016), he focusses on *Proposals* (181-91.

[6] Subsequent volumes were to include *Tree-Bend* from *Book Second* and *Tree-Bird* from *Book Third*, but these seem not have been completed.

with health. He also produced in the early seventies a series of collage pamphlets in collaboration with Dick Miller: *My Bijou*; *All Horses have Feathers*; and *Shitwell Bernardo*.[7]

Perhaps his most important publications of the 1970s, besides *Place*, were *Paxton's Beacon* (Todmorden: Arc, 1976); his collaboration with Pierre Joris, *Fire Work* (Hebden Bridge: Hatch Books, 1977); and *The Apocalyptic Sonnets* (Durham: Pig Press, 1978). *Paxton's Beacon* is extracted from a larger work, 'The Art of Flight', which Fisher describes in his Introduction as a 'formal treatise' on 'the usage in ideas and in language of the terms "light and dark"'. The title, 'The Art of Flight', alludes to 'The Art of Fugue', Bach's unfinished exploration of the possibilities of counterpoint. Fisher used Bach's Contrapunctus I and III as the basis for sections I and III of his own work, translating Bach's notes through his own system of verbal equivalents for these sections. Other sections are less strictly procedural and introduce the process of Fisher's own writing patterns. This attention to procedural and processual practices has obvious affinities with *Place*. The title, *Paxton's Beacon*, references Joseph Paxton's Crystal Palace, a cast-iron and plate-glass structure originally erected for the Great Exhibition of 1851, designed by a distinguished gardener and garden-designer, drawing on his interest in glass-houses and inspired by the water lilies at Chatsworth. In addition, as *Paxton's Beacon* registers, the Crystal Palace, after its move to Sydenham, was also the location for John Logie Baird's 1930s experiments in developing television. This constellation of natural and man-made structures, of technologies of light and glass, of patterns of sound and colour, provides the matrix for Fisher's procedural and processual project with its investigation of light through a characteristically wide range of informations – optics, photochemistry, visual arts, heliotropic plants, lighthouses among others.

The Apocalyptic Sonnets were similarly part of a larger project, *Faust Undamned*, and Faust and Marguerite, from Goethe's version of the legend, re-appear throughout the sequence. *The Apocalyptic Sonnets* are actually double sonnets, set out as seven quatrains with the final quatrain indented, like the final couplet in Shakespeare's sonnets. These final quatrains offer a recurring address to 'Technology', exploring good and bad understandings of technology – and the relationship between technology and art – which are recurring concerns throughout Fisher's work. The

---

[7] *My Bijou* (London: I. B. Held Books, 1971); *All Horses Have Feathers* (London: I.B. Held Books, 1971); *Shitwell Bernardo* (London: I. B. Held Books, 1972).

sonnets follow Dürer's woodcut series 'The Apocalypse', with almost every sonnet referencing one of the prints and with each sonnet dedicated to a current cabinet minister. Although the titles of individual poems bring in references to a range of books, films and art-works, the sequence engages with embodiment in a recognisably contemporary London – a characteristically Reichian engagement with energy, eroticism, health, and violence within the 'tight social noose' of contemporary capital. As in Goethe's *Faust*, however, this is a story of redemption – of undammed energies – and, as Robert Sheppard puts it, the tenth sonnet ends with an 'unalienated interaction and interpenetration of place, body, and utterance'.[8] The sonnets were accompanied by seven etchings by Robert Clark and were described as 'scores': in performance, Fisher engaged in an element of improvisation, extemporising from the text.

Fire Work bound together *Fire-place* by Allen Fisher and *Hearth Work* by Pierre Joris. Both works responded to a comment by Jonathan Williams on the presence of 'warming particles' in the word 'hearth': 'hear, heart, ear, earth, art'. This led directly to Joris's extended birthday meditation on fire and the multiple origins of civilisation. In Fisher's case, a section of *Place* addressed to Peter Maxwell Davies and the Fires of London music ensemble and engaged with Alexander Pope's *The Dunciad* took a 'second spread' from Williams's words. *Fire-place* figures fire as both creative and destructive: on the one hand, fire figures as inspiration and as Wilhelm Reich's orgasmic energy; on the other, fire appears (as in *The Dunciad*) as the pyre on which the dunces' books are sacrificed, but also as the source for the inherited fear traced through the Great Fire of London, building regulations, insurance companies, and the fire-bombing of cities in the Second World War.

In 1982, Fisher began his second large-scale project, *Gravity as a Consequence of Shape*, which was completed in August 2005. The first volume, *Gravity*, was published by Salt in 2004. The second volume, *Entanglement*, was published by *The Gig* in the same year. The final volume, *Leans*, had its first appearance, when extracts from it were published by Barque Press in 2006 as *Singularity Stereo*. *Leans* itself was published by Salt in 2007. As with *Place*, Fisher has published versions of *Gravity as a consequence of shape* during the period of the project in magazines and as pamphlets. These showings include: *Boogie Break* (Torque, 1984), *Brixton Fractals* (Aloes Books, 1985), *Buzzards & Bees* (Microbrigade, 1987), *Convalescence* (Wiwaxia, 1992), *Dispossession &*

---

[8] Robert Sheppard, *When Bad Times Made for Good Poetry*, 47.

Cure (Reality Street, 1994), *Civic Crime* (Sound & Language, 1994), *Breadboard* (Spanner, 1994), *Fizz* (Spanner, 1994), *Now's the time* (Form Book, 1995), *Pulling Up & Quasi Queen* (Spanner, 1996), *Fish Jet* (Torque Press, 1997), *Ring Shout* (Equipage, 2000), *Sojourns* (2000). The complete *Gravity as a consequence of shape* was published by Reality Street as a single volume in 2016.

The title of the overall project sets it firmly in the world of quantum physics – just as the title of the first section 'Brixton Fractals' gestures towards twentieth-century mathematics. However, the life and culture of Brixton are as important to 'Brixton Fractals' as the various kinds of theoretical reading that Fisher draws on. The poems register the built environment of walkways and balconies, local place names like Electric Avenue and 'The Windmill', and the fire-crews and helicopters of the Riots. In the same way, after Fisher's move to Hereford in January 1989, the poetry is then informed by this new environment and turns to ecological concerns. The individual poems, at first glance, appear to be organised by an alphabetical sequence of jazz-dance titles running from 'Banda' to 'Yanayallow'. However, this pattern is disrupted: at the start, 'Banda' and 'Ballin' the Jack' are out of sequence, warning the reader against relying on such organising principles; and, at the end, Z is missing. The penultimate poem in *Leans* was 'Zigzag', but this was followed by 'Mezz Merround', a play on the name of the jazz-musician Mezz Mezzrow, a name with plenty of zzzs but none at the start. Neither of these appears in the Reality Street edition. Instead, in his Preface to this edition, Fisher points the reader to 'ZIP' as the 'last poem in the sequence', which is only available online as a sound performance.[9] In fact, as Robert Sheppard notes, 'Zigzag', which looked like a conclusion in *Leans*, was actually written for an earlier project, *Ideas of the Culture Dreamed Of*, so that any sense of linear development was undermined.[10] In the Reality Street edition, this effect is achieved by a literal endlessness as the reader is directed beyond the borders of the book. At the same time, 'ZIP' itself is a reworking of 'African Boog', taking is back to the start of the sequence. Significantly, both poems foreground a cyclist (the German mathematician David Hilbert) making a figure of eight – the mathematical symbol of eternity.[11]

---

[9] Fisher gives the following addresses: http://utterpsalm.blogspot.co.uk; http://writing.upenn.edu/pennsound/x/Fisher.php; and www.allenfisher.co.uk.

[10] *When Bad Times*, 186.

[11] For Hilbert's 'mathematical bicycle rides' around his two rose-beds, see Benjamin H.

As this suggests, mirroring is one of the devices to which Fisher has recourse in his practice. In an interview with Ken Edwards and Peter Barry (January 1976), Fisher talked about the mirror structure of *Place*: 'Book III is a partly distorted mirror of Book I, and Book II again acts as a mirror to the other two, and Book IV again is a mirror, so that Book V is a composite mirror if you like'.[12] In *Gravity*, for example, the final sequences mirror the opening sequences. I have mentioned how 'ZIP' reworks 'African Boog'; in addition, 'Wobble' mirrors 'Ballin' the Jack' and 'Winging Step' mirrors 'Banda'. In each case, the later poem revisits and reworks the material of the earlier poem in what Fisher terms 'reconfigured repetition'.[13] Thus, the opening line of 'Banda' ('Took chances in London traffic') is referenced at the start of 'Winging Step' ('Initial engagement recorded risk in London commerce'), while 'Wobble' repeats the form of 'Ballin' the Jack' (four sections of thirty-two lines) with certain horizontal thematic correspondences – most evident, perhaps, in the lines, in each section, attentive to healthy eating. From a different perspective, that opening line of 'Banda' introduces the bicycle which re-appears as a motif through subsequent poems as part of another pattern of echoes and repetitions.

In addition, appropriately for fractals, this large-scale mirroring has its smaller scale equivalents. Thus, in 'Ballin' the Jack', the second section begins ('painted blue') with a variation of the final words of the first section ('painted green'); the 'flat' (apartment) in the third line from the end of the first section becomes the 'knees flat' for Tantric sex in the third line of the second section; the 'tropical independence of miasma frame' in the fourth line of the second section reworks the 'topological dependence of plasma membrane' in the fourth line from the end of the first section. As this suggests, the second section is an inverted (and distorted) image of the first section. Section three is an inverted (distorted) but only partial mirror of section two: the final line of section two ('a tiredness from exposure'), for example, becomes the opening line of the next section ('wired up from explosion'). Fisher then

---

Yandell, *The Honours Class: Hilbert's Problems and their Solvers* (New York, NY: CRC Press, 2001), 17.

[12] 'An Interview with Allen Fisher', *Alembic* 4 (Winter 1975 / 76), 49-57; reprinted as 'Interview for *Alembic*, January 1976' in *The Marvels of Lambeth*, 29-37.

[13] 'Of Mutabilitie: Interview at Roehampton University' (February, 2005), reprinted in Andrew Duncan (ed.), *The Marvels of Lambeth* (Bristol: Shearsman Books, 2013) 104-27, 104.

reworks the latter half of section two for the first half of section three. Similarly, in section four, the first half of section three is inverted as the final half of section four, but with new concluding lines, which are themselves re-worked in later poems. Through these repetitions, Fisher encourages the reader to experience connections between different poems (and different sections of the same poem) as part of a larger project of transforming damage into creative activity.[14]

This device of mirroring through the transformation of individual lines recurs throughout *Gravity*. In 'Dispossession and Cure', for example, adjacent poems reveal similar sonic and or syntactic patterns. For example, 'Horse' begins 'For sometime the Architect was unprepared for understanding'. The resemblance to the opening line of the next poem, 'Hubble', ('Suddenly the sleeper listened intensely') is not striking. However, the next stanza of 'Horse' begins: 'Not rich enough to buy cheap things', and the second stanza of 'Hubble' begins 'No itch rough but stinging nettles'. Similarly, stanza three of 'Horse' begins 'Zoned into separate conditions' while the third stanza of 'Hubble' begins 'Cloned as desperate renditions'. At this point the reader recognises how 'Hubble' is reworking the previous poem. In his Introduction to *Entanglement*, Fisher observed that 'several methods have been used to guarantee overlap in spatio-temporal imperfect fits'.[15] The ideas of 'overlap' and 'imperfect fit' are evidenced in the examples above. For Fisher, it is important that things should not be resolved in order to energise the reader: expectations should be challenged; structures subjected to change.[16] (This stands in contrast to Fisher's own reading experience of the poetry of R.S. Thomas: 'the level of predictability goes up through the entire book to the point where you can't even read a poem, because you know exactly where it is going to go.')[17] From the writer's perspective as well, as Fisher notes, 'the complex of the work is never fully realizable' and 'each new part to the work deconstructs and potentially damages what has been written' (61).[18] Later in the Introduction to *Entanglement*, Fisher observes: 'Distribution

---

[14] See 'Of Mutabilitie', 104-13.

[15] *Entanglement*, 9.

[16] See 'Interview with Scott Thurston' (1999), reprinted in *The Marvels of Lambeth*, 63-76, 65.

[17] 'In One Side and Out the Other: Lulham Interview 2', *The Marvels of Lambeth*, 165.

[18] 'Interview with Adrian Clarke', *Angel Exhaust*, 1987, reprinted in *The Marvels of Lambeth*, 53-62, 61.

of entangled states between distant locations is essential for quantum communication over large distances'. What Fisher refers to here is the meaning of entanglement in quantum theory: namely, how quantum particles mirror each other's behaviour even when far apart. However, as he goes on to say, 'Owing to unavoidable decoherence, the quality of entangled states generally decreases exponentially with length'.[19] Again, in quantum theory, decoherence refers to when one quantum of energy experiences interference from another. These ideas of entanglement and decoherence underwrite the patterns of distorted and partial mirroring, of damage and transformation, present in *Gravity*.

Fisher's work from an early stage, has consciously resisted totalization – whether through the complex cross-referencing of the poems in *Place* or through the singular mixes of material for particular readings – or through the complex mirrorings outlined above. Fisher has described 'self-interference' and 'transformation' as two key terms for the *Gravity* project, and added that 'ordering and disrupting would be a second set'.[20] The handling of the alphabetical ordering of *Gravity* signals Fisher's need to 'make and break sets', a habit which he derives from Blake's injunction to make your own system or be enslaved by another man's.[21] Indeed, an important element in *Gravity* is Fisher's meditation on Blake's *Notebooks:* the radical South London poet, painter and publisher is an important precursor, and Blake's Notebooks are part of 'the schema' of the project.[22] In addition, Fisher has also noted in interviews that the Fibonacci series was 'the directing principle of *Gravity*'.[23] He began with a diagram using the arithmetic of Fibonacci and the Golden Section, which he made into a cylinder – and then he bent the cylinder in order to inflict damage on these orders as the basis for a positive transformation.[24] In *Gravity*, appropriately, Newtonian order gives way to quantum mechanics, chaos theory, chance operations, and the acceptance of mistakes, and radical discontinuity is

---

[19] *Entanglement*, 10.

[20] 'Interview with Adrian Clarke', 61.

[21] Simon Collings, 'Necessary vulnerability: an interview with Allen Fisher', *Journal of Poetic Research* 07.

[22] 'Interview with Scott Thurston', 69.

[23] 'The Curve of Increase or, On Growth and Form', in *The Marvels of Lambeth*, 93-103, 93.

[24] 'Of Mutabilitie', 106.

produced through entanglement (mirroring) and decoherence, the juxtaposition and overlapping of multiple discourses. This multiplicity of discourses, with their individual and competing truth claims, points to the impossibility of any single coherent narrative. This relates to Fisher's expressed need 'to develop a new set of conditions' for thinking and being.[25] And this, in turn, has political implications – not least, an opposition to 'totalitarian capitalism, which tends towards the extinction of life on earth'.[26]

Since 2005, Fisher has continued to be productive – indeed prolific – as poet, painter, and performer. His major publications from this period are *Proposals* (2010), *Sputtor* (2014) and *loggerheads* (2018). *Proposals* dates from Fisher's move from Roehampton to Manchester Metropolitan University and begins from Fisher's new travel arrangements and working conditions. The volume consists of a series of 35 'Proposals'. Each 'Proposal' takes up a single opening and consists of four elements: a poem on the left-hand page (which might, in fact, be the 'Proposal', since it carries the title); two visual images side by side (which might represent the opening of a sketch-book – a smaller represented opening within the actual opening of the codex) on the facing page; and a short passage of prose underneath the visual images, which is situated as if it were a gloss on the images, but isn't. The OED defines the primary meaning of a 'proposal' as 'The action, or an act, of putting before the mind; setting forth, propounding, statement'. Each opening certainly places something before the reader, but what is placed before the reader is not a statement. Instead, *Proposals* foregrounds the discontinuity of the component parts: not only is there a non-coherence of poetic text, prose text and visual image, but the visual image is itself composed of two parts, whose relation to each other varies, and the prose text is sometimes a statement and, at other times, some form of collaged prose or series of discontinuous sentences. Furthermore, since many of the left-hand images involve fire and industrial processes, there is also the sense of a vertical (but incomplete) linkage through the successive pages of the book pulling against the horizontal display of the opening. In short, the volume foregrounds discontinuity in multiple ways. It repeatedly suggests relations and simultaneously disrupts expected connections.

---

[25] 'Necessary vulnerability'.

[26] 'Necessary vulnerability'.

Sputtor was created from Andrew Wilson's *Space Shuttle Story* (1986), which, in Amazon's words, 'traces the history of the Space Shuttle from the early days of rocketry to the destruction of the Challenger in January 1986'.[27] Fisher's title is derived from Wilson's in the manner of Tom Phillips's treatment of Mallock's title *A Human Document* to produce *A Humument*.[28] However, Fisher's treatment of his source text is quite different: rather than revealing another narrative within the source text through a process of redaction (as Fisher had done early on in *Thomas Net's Tree-Birst*), he rather overlays his original with other verbal and visual materials, including a sequence of his own poems. Fisher's neologism 'Sputtor', while suggesting *sputnik* (traveller), the Russian name for first man-made object to be placed into the earth's orbit, summons its homonym 'sputter'. The primary meaning of the noun 'sputter' is 'a state of bustling confusion or excitement'. In more general use, this is a verb meaning 'to spit out in small particles and with a characteristic explosive sound', which might have more obvious relevance to rocketry. However, 'sputter' is also associated with candles (or flames more generally) in the process of going out, thus anticipating the Challenger disaster. Although he uses little of Wilson's text, Fisher picks up on a contradiction inherent in Wilson's book: the celebration of the science that made space missions possible, a narrative of steady progress ('an outstanding series of successes'), and the conclusion of this narrative in failure with the destruction of the Challenger. Fisher accepts the format and pages of Wilson's book, but he interferes with and redirects the original text by pasting over other materials in a complex verbal and visual collage.

In an interview in *Sugarmule*, Fisher described the themes of the original text as the idea of 'getting off the planet'. *Space Shuttle Story* offers adulation of the space race which started with that surprise launch of Sputnik 1 in 1957 and was a component of the Cold War between Russia and 'the West'. Fisher's intervention uncovers alternative possibilities that emerge from the contradictions in the original narrative. Thus, an early intervention isolates a section of Wilson's text ('New products and services will emerge from spacetime that living on Earth will make less sense for human beings, than more') in a way that links the story of space travel to the current dream of the super-rich to escape

---

[27] *Sputtor* (London: Veer, 2014); Andrew Wilson, *Space Shuttle Story* (Random House, 1986).

[28] Tom Phillips, *A Humument* (London: Thames & Hudson, 1980).

from Earth ('getting off the planet') once it is rendered no longer inhabitable through the processes from which they derive their wealth. Early references to 'tipping points' (16, 18) intimate the ecological disaster of the Anthropocene within which Fisher re-situates Wilson's celebration of space travel. David Miller observes, in an online review of *Sputtor*, that the book is positioned 'at the very end-point at which a plan for the resuscitation of human history will ever emerge'.[29] However, in introducing readings from the work, Fisher has been more pessimistic and has emphasised that the 'tipping point' for human survival on Earth has already passed.

Sputtor begins by turning Wilson's monologic Foreword into Fisher's own multi-voiced 'Forewords'. This initial opening juxtaposes two narratives: Mary Shelley's account of finding in the Sybil's cave the writings which she has turned into her dystopian novel, *The Last Man* (a title which has some resonance in Fisher's ecological context), and Wilson's account of 1986, which 'promised to be a bumper year of space achievements' (7). Wilson's boosterism is set against Sybelline prophecy and Shelley's vision of catastrophe. Two further fragments are set in dialogue with these narratives: an extract from *The Coming Insurrection* by The Invisible Committee (on mobility as uprootedness, isolation, exile) and an extract from an extended article on the British 'New Age' composer, Daphne Oram (about bringing diverse disciplines to bear upon wave phenomena).[30] With this reframing, Wilson's celebration of technological advancement has its relation to state power and 'the war machine' foregrounded, while Oram's commitment to multi-disciplinary research and improving 'the conditions of human life' provides one of the parameters for Fisher's own work. (A coloured version of the photograph of Oram in her studio, which had appeared in *The Wire*, appears, subjected to some damage, later in he volume.) Oram's connection to science-fiction through providing the music for *Dr Who* is perhaps also not irrelevant.

---

[29] See the series of perceptive blog essays by Korea-based David Miller that were put up between February and July 2015: http://www.urbananxieties.org.

[30] 'The Invisible Committee' was the nom de plume or nom de guerre of a group of post-Situationist French radicals. A translation of *The Coming Insurrection* was published by Semiotexte in 2007. 'The Woman from New Atlantis' was published in *The Wire* (August 2011), 29-35. Oddly enough, the extract Fisher cites also appears in a June 2016 blog, 'Sound Morphology', as part of a review of a piece by Bill Smith, 'ImmunoRadio Dramatique' for Orchestra, Voices, Archival Shortwave Radio Broadcasts, Resynthesis and Particle Pluriphony.

One of the concerns in *Sputtor* is with truth and truth-telling. In an interview with Andrew Duncan, Fisher described one of the issues with which he has been engaged for some time as: 'what are our criteria for truth, for certainty, for lacks of truth, for lacks of certainty'.[31] This follows on precisely from his engagement with numerous disciplines with their different truth-claims. In *Sputtor*, Fisher initially fixes on *parrhesia*. In classical rhetoric, this signified speaking candidly – or asking forgiveness for speaking candidly. Fisher's *parrhesia*, however, is Foucault's, where the parrhesist is someone who takes risks by speaking truth to power as part of non-violent political action.[32] In *Sputtor*, Fisher's engagement with (lacks of) truth and (lacks of) certainty focusses on an examination of his own method of juxtaposing texts and images through bringing in Walter Benjamin (whose *Arcades* project is the great precursor), Theodor Adorno's critique of Benjamin's 'dialectical image', and Fredric Jameson's critique of the dialectic.

From the start of his career, Fisher has been very conscious of the performative aspects of poetry reading. His early career involved Fluxus-style performance pieces and one-man fugal pieces involving reel-to-reel tape-recorders in series.[33] As mentioned above, performances of *The Apocalyptic Sonnets* in the late seventies included improvisation on the printed text. These performances, rather than asserting the authority of the poet, exposed the vulnerability of the performer, using the possibility of failure to energise the performance.[34] Fisher's early performance work was directly related to Fluxshoe. Fluxshoe was conceived around 1970 as a show that would travel around the UK.[35] It was conscious of such precursors as FLUXFESTS (Amsterdam and Copenhagen, 1963), FLUXCONCERTS (New York, 1964; London, 1968) and FESTA

---

[31] 'Of Mutabilitie', 109.

[32] Michel Foucault, *Fearless Speech* (Semiotexte, 2001), edited by Joseph Pearson. These six lectures were given in English in 1983.

[33] For more on Fisher as performer, see the chapter, 'You Are Invited to Perform: Process, Mutation and Participation in Allen Fisher's *Blood Brain Bone*', in Juha Virtanen's book, *Poetry and Performance During the British Poetry Revival 1960 1990. Event and Effect* (Palgrave, 2017).

[34] See Tony Lopez, *Meaning Performance: Essays on Poetry* (Cambridge: Salt Publishing, 2006) for a discussion of similar engagements with anxiety through improvised performance in relation to work by David Antin and Steve Benson (73-81).

[35] See Kyosan Bajin, *Introduction to Fluxshoe* (Cullompton, Devon: Beau Geste Press, 1972), 3.

FLUXORUM (Düsseldorf, 1963; Berlin, 1970). It followed in the Fluxus tradition of games, instructions, riddles, and performances in galleries and public spaces.

One survival from this period is *Creek in the Ceiling Beam* (London: Aloes, 1973). The published text provides documentation of an investigation into a creak in the ceiling beam in Fisher's flat in Hayes Court in the summer of 1972. After a notation of occurrences and a graphing of occurrences to produce a procedure for selection of textual material, Fisher follows various lines of inquiry (including water-cisterns and plumbing, possible stress concentrations on welded joints, and the location of the flat both locally and in relation to the planets) to produce the contention that there is a connection between the creak in the ceiling beam and multiple factors including 'the migratory patterns of pigeons, their sex cycle' and 'the influence of geodetics on this pattern'. He also includes a list of lines of inquiry not pursued (including geological influences, temperature and humidity, electrical factors, the history of architecture). In addition, the book also includes material that demystifies its own method of production. The project thus includes the potentially endless inquiry into the complex of causes, a display of the procedures by which work is produced, and a display of the processes of inquiry and production.

Fisher has also been actively involved as a publisher – primarily through his *Edible Magazine*; as co-publisher of Aloes Books (with Jim Pennington and Dick Miller) and of New London Pride (with Elaine Fisher); and through *Spanner*, which has published what Fisher would term 'pertinent work' since 1974. *Edible Magazine* and Aloes Books provided outlets for Fisher's own early work. Two sections of *Place, Stane* (1977) and *Becoming* (1978), for example, were first published by Aloes. In an early interview, Fisher mentioned 'the need to carry the work process across into book production'.[36] This not only provided 'autonomy in production' (and the possibility of doing things with typefaces and colour that a commercial publisher wouldn't countenance), but also the opportunity to engage with 'the "communities" of artists similarly involved'. New London Pride published volumes of poetry by numerous poets including Clayton Eshleman, Bill Griffiths, Pierre Joris, Tony Lopez, Barry MacSweeney and Bill Sherman. Each issue of *Spanner* has been devoted to a single author or topic. In addi-

---

[36] Allen Fisher, quoted in G. Soar and R.J. Ellis, 'Little Magazines in the British Isles Today', *British Book News* (December, 1983), 728-33, 732.

tion to volumes of poetry by Eric Mottram, Ken Smith, Ralph Hawkins, John Welch, Ulli McCarthy, early issues included John Cage and Eric Mottram in conversation (1974), Clive Bush on Muriel Rukeyser, Mottram on Ginsberg (1978), 'Speech Poetry' (1980), Clive Meachen on Charles Olson (1983), and Fisher's own influential essay, 'Necessary Business' (1985), which has recently been republished in his collection of essays, *Imperfect Fit* (2016).[37]

Other Spanner publications included *Fool's House* (1980), *January 1981: A Painting* and Fisher's own *Convergences* (1976), *Blood Bone Brain* and *Unpolished Mirrors*. In addition to publishing some of his own work, Fisher has also made available a wide range of English and North American experimental poetries, as well as various forms of critical engagement with these poetries. These latter remain an under-used resource for understanding one aspect of Anglo-American literary relations in the late twentieth-century. More importantly, they also evidence and underline the sustained attempt on Fisher's part to develop an aesthetics of innovative practice.

Fisher has also been active as a visual artist since the start of his career.[38] Subsequent to the visual collages produced in collaboration with Dick Miller in the early seventies, Fisher published three of his own 'visual presentations' through *Spanner*: 'Reich', 'Combs' and 'Kessingland Studies' (1978). The last of these consists of a series of 6 studies made at Kessingland Beach, near Lowestoft. Site-specificity has been (and remains) an important part of both his poetic and visual art practice.[39] Over the last thirty years, Fisher has had several individual shows including 'Dispossession & Cure' in the Old Mayor's Parlour, Hereford (1991); 'Tools & Traps or Damage', a retrospective exhibition at the Hereford Museum and Art Gallery (1994), and 'Engaged Embrace' in the Apple Store Gallery, Hereford (2013). His work has also been included in numerous group shows including 'Fluxbrittanica', Tate Gallery, London (1994); 'El Arte de Los Libros de Artistica' at the Instituto de Artes Gráficas de Oaxaca (1998) and at the Biblioteca México,

---

[37] For a fuller account of Spanner, see Wolfgang Görtschacher, *Little Magazine Profiles: The Little Magazines in Great Britain, 1939-1993* (Salzburg: University of Salzburg Press, 1993), 32, 148-9, and 194.

[38] Fisher was appointed Professor of Poetry and Art at Roehampton University in 2001. He was subsequently Professor of Poetry and Art at Manchester Metropolitan University.

[39] His current project, 'Black Pond', is a site-specific visual art and poetic project.

Mexico City (1999); and the MIRIAD touring China Show in Beijing (May 2007), the Gallery of Chinese Profiles, Xiamen (October 2007) and the Art Museum, Guangzhou (November 2007). His work is held in private collections in the UK, USA and UAE and in various public collections including Hereford City Museum; King's Archive, University of London; the Tate Gallery, London; and the Living Museum Reykjavik, Iceland.

The essays in this collection cover the range of Fisher's career. Redell Olsen and cris cheek discuss Fisher's relations to Fluxus and the documentary. Will Rowe approaches *Place* in terms of the large-scale poem as a heuristic device, a 'practice of knowledge'. Pierre Joris addresses the important topic of health in Fisher's work. Will Montgomery considers Brixton as a 'sounded space' in the work of Allen Fisher and Linton Kwesi Johnson, while Steven Hitchins tackles one aspect of Fisher's significant engagement with science: fractals as a way of negotiating the discontinuity and noise of everyday life. Robert Sheppard discusses *The Apocalyptic Sonnets* as the link between Fisher's two large-scale projects, *Place* and *Gravity as a consequence of shape*; Scott Thurston offers a close-reading of 'Mummer's Shout' (from *Gravity*) in terms of its compositional procedures; Clive Bush engages with 'Philly Dog' and the political limitations of Deleuze and Guattari; and Calum Hazell explores *Sputtor* in terms of collage, quotation and poetic knowledge. The volume closes with two collaborative pieces: an interview between Fisher, Paige Mitchell and Shamoon Zamir and a selection of documents relating to *PhillyTalks #19* with Karen Mac Cormack (17 October 2001).[40]

---

[40] PhillyTalks#19 is available online at http://writing.upenn.edu/pensound/x/Fisher.php.

Allen Fisher : Siting *Place*

WILLIAM ROWE

The large-scale poem as heuristic device, in which procedures of construction are worked out in the process of its writing, a process that takes place in historical time and includes transformative rewritings and re-readings of itself, had become, by the time Allen Fisher began in 1971 the project called *Place*, one of the most demanding and exciting challenges that a contemporary poet could take up.[1] One mode of this self-reflexivity, and a particularly important one for reading *Place*, concerns the long poem as practice of knowledge: more accurately, as a site for testing different types of knowledge, in their relationship to desire, will, politics, and truth.

Place includes a number of passages where its own motivations and decisions are (re)considered, for confirmation or modification. These include the pieces written 'To Pierre' (Joris) and to Eric Mottram, fellow poets living in London, strongly committed at the time when *Place* was being written to expanding the resources of poetry in English, in particular through the study of Charles Olson's work. The first piece responds to the deaths of Pound (1972) and Olson (1970) by considering what possibilities their work might generate in a British context and what responsibilities it might confront one with: 'in front of us / a flow of field spiralling out... not through him or me except THRU me via US to / a collective... we are left not to close the shop' (86-87).[2] The 'Letter to Eric Mottram', whose essays and teaching already constituted a major onslaught on parochial anti-modernism, takes on a double challenge: first, how to study history, not merely as 'the historical pleasure palpitant' ('find the paths in the graves of their absence'), but as source of possibilities generated by 'the men that lifted

---

[1] A brief indication of the landmarks, by the time Fisher began *Place*, would include Ezra Pound's *Cantos*; William Carlos Williams's *Paterson*, which began to appear in 1946; Charles Olson's *The Maximus Poems*, the first series of which was published in 1953; Robert Duncan's *Passages*, a series which begins in *The Opening of the Field* (1960); Roy Fisher's *City* (1961); Basil Bunting's *Briggflatts* (1965); Lee Harwood's *Cable Street* (1964).

[2] Page references given in the text are to Allen Fisher, *Place*, London: Reality Street Editions, 2005.

/ the sense of this to here… in our / land we no longer know.' In other words, how to be responsible to the energies of the past, which could not be done without achieving a practice of knowledge that would be non-alienating, 'not directed by commodities' (174-5). The second challenge is to carry out the work ('this narrative   or research') such that it 'becomes a synapsis   pairing the body's / colours / interposing the nerves' (176): that the finest and most complex of the body's capabilities be included in the mapping that as it traces the past and present city called London also projects a possible city, one that is not assigned a single name or nature but acquires a variety of inflexions: 'a coming English Revolution', 'the garden,' (quoting Blake) 'the Auricular Nerves of Human Life,' (after Beuys) 'soft control,' or (after Henri Corbin) 'mundus imaginalis' (366, 368), to mention some but by no means all of the key phrases in this respect. Alongside these ideas of positive transformation are ranged a series of diagnostics of alienation and damage, as for example 'a system of cruelty and selfishness / as natural /… for a nation of bankers and banked' (403).

However, a major part of what *Place* offers as challenge and excitement to a reader is the inadequacy of any dualistic reduction of its language into fixed oppositions such as utopia and damage. To move away from abstracted semantic oppositions towards a historical sense of language, necessarily means locating utterance spatially, emplaced within the lived sites of the city, and temporally, within actions of selective remembrance and obliteration. Thus a reader is offered not a unidirectional unfolding but language traversed by space and time: a writing that receives traces and in the same act tracks itself. The impulses towards such a reflexive architecture include the power of such a prospect as well as the criticism of power. But what is the relation between the will to power and the criticism of power within the project of *Place*?

It is in the final section, 'Unpolished mirrors', that the book most insistently holds up a mirror – more accurately, several intersecting mirrors – to its own production, which makes this part of the work the best evidence for a detailed discussion of the question I have outlined. It is here that *Place* goes furthest to dramatise its own impulses and thereby to open itself to the outside: the outside, not in the sense of what the past did not know, but of what the present does not know of itself, except through inquiry into its composition. The method makes particular use of dramatic monologue, where the characters that speak are historical (Wren), fictional-historical (Doll), and fictional-allegorical (the Artist, the Gardener). In fact the distinctions between history, fiction, and allegory blur and overlap, so that referential frames such as 'past', 'present', poem, and author are complicated and overlaid. The use of figures or *dramatis personae*, drawing on Blake's approach as well as on twentieth-century works such as Olson's *Maximus*, makes it possible to consider will inside history.

A recurrent scenario is the mutual reflection of the senses and spatial construction, 'building by giving / psycho-physiological well-being to the occupants,' 'in "scent and mirror-deepened rooms"' (405), where the mirroring action generates expanse and prospect towards joyous space, which would mean the body in space, upheld and not subjected. The impulse includes (here acknowledging Hart Crane) 'dream synthesis in bridges' (384), a statement whose critical edge shows in the idea that the 'unconscious... desire' at stake might (via a Reichian hypothesis) include sexual violence ('I build a brick arched roadway / under this foul Thames / between Wapping and Rotherhithe / a phallus joining two bodies at the drilling' [383]). Thus, while for the architect, mythically, the work might signify 'a rebirth into the nerve tank... the plebs at the work site say otherwise / say the tunnel is terrifying toil' (384).

The last phrase brings into location the labour that's invisible in Sinclair's imagination, in *Lud Heat*, of will that crosses time and space in the shape of London architecture. The architect in *Place* is Wren, both historical personage and figure of the artist shaping the scene of the contemporary. The 'dream' as projective synthesis traverses the work of both, where history and imagination meet to produce 'a collective,' an 'us' that until now has been purchased at the cost of sacrifice (the two World Wars, via Reich's 'emotional plague', a palimpsest of the 'Great Plague') and through authoritarian coercion, of the kind that the monologue entitled 'Watling's Way' displays: a myth of stars ('My Via Lactea') plotted as rectilinearity and stratification onto the city out of 'the passion to control,' 'Roman and Victorian.'

Contrary impulses surge in the rewriting of Baudelairean luxury as scenario of Blakean and Sufi imagination, i.e., an encounter between spiritual geography and the historical city. The full title of the section in question, 'FIRST RELEASE / Homage to Charles Baudelaire', brings the splendour and misery of the bourgeois city, 'Perfume's tonic toned fragrance / on wasted ground' (367), mingling excess with repetition ('tonic toned') and linearity ('sickly syrup lining respiration'), the pleasure of complete surfeit ('I glut myself with this cosmos') with damage ('an inhaled fever'). The possibility of the self transported and upheld ('senses transport a moving sea') in calm equilibrium of inside and outside ('calm pulses coasting grades of light'), without damage, has the power to hold its historical antagonist ('mindless consumption gardens flesh') in a complex embrace.

Thus the 'Homage to Charles Baudelaire' works as a threshold to 'The gardener's fourth monologue', where Langland and Blake are rewritten, with calm mastery of voicing, upon late twentieth-century surfaces:

> I have come to garden and plant seeds
>   of the coming English Revolution
>   whose man-made blossom requires many to make it bloom
> after the seeds have passed from it
>   only its reverberations will recollect this polluted space.
>
> I approach the garden in a sweve
>   the auricular nerves of human life (369)

The slowly cascading open rhythm, without wilful imposition of the tonic, contrasts sharply with Watling's monologue, which sounds like the power-driven insistence of the Thatcher-Blair voice.

The poem rewrites the Baudelairean sensual luxury but without stasis:

> About the garden that appears without boundary
>   darts a scent of semen and cultivated poppy
> Again given movement
>   movement enough to change

Change is embodied in the changes of rhythm, where the background trochaic pattern, heard as the more recognisable order of spoken will ('I have come to garden... I approach the garden'), is cut across by variation that transports the ear into complexity ('many to make it... only its reverberations... the auricular nerves... without boundary... cultivated poppy'). There seems to be a suspension of will as the rhythm departs from the central tonic that characterises Watling's voice ('I have come to quell the revolution / to centralise the call chains... many bridges carry my knowing' [377]), with its display of the insistent stress of ego as phantasy of collectivity, the stressed syllables sounding the authoritarian rigidity that came to characterise Thatcher's voice. By insistence on single measure, that voice diminishes the availability of the senses to experience. As Nietzsche wrote: 'Man... wants to find formulas so as to simplify the tremendous quantity of his experiences.'[3] Prosodic formulas reduce the range of sound, where sound is the phenomenic bridge between the material world and the knowledge produced by the poem.

The interweaving of large and small scales of movement, embracing the 'English Revolution' and 'darts a scent', is part of the mastery of this writing, its capacity to resist grand design imposed through selective data. Over against the authority of citation (a temptation of the poetry of knowledge), it invites a reader to test the power of language to produce the not-known: a different proposition from the power of the Idea to become, through Will, history, since the Idea in this sense works, like theories, through exclusion. The poem embraces an opposite movement:

> What I do not know of myself
> prevents my becoming
> What I am frightened of as artist
> This incoming
> this sea welling inside
> inside shields
> it has penetrated
> broken the dream's crystal
> the needed body boundary penetrated (382)

There are various ambiguities of sense: is it that not to know prevents becoming, i.e. transformation? Or is it, specifically, the lack of spontaneous knowledge, what I know 'of myself' and not by external means, that does this? In which case, would non-spontaneous (or counter-intuitive) knowledge have the opposite result? That type of knowledge includes, in the context of the book as a whole, a large range of scientific ideas, such as those of J.Z. Young about the nervous system (170). But how would that knowledge permit 'my becoming / What I am frightened of as artist'? To become 'what I am frightened of' is an imaginary identification, and is not the same as imagining what I am

---
[3] *The Will to Power*, New York, NY: Random House, 1968, 341

frightened of. Or is 'becoming' itself the thing that 'I am frightened of'? Either way, the turning point is given by the imaginary boundary of the body 'penetrated' by something else. The complexity of the book, at this point, hinges on its decision to juxtapose the phenomenological imagination with history and science. Phenomenology is itself dependent on a reduction, and thus scientific knowledge can enter as the excluded outside. But then scientific functions are not translatable, phenomenically, into poetry if poetry is 'lines of sound drawn on the air', as in Bunting's formulation. A different poetics becomes necessary. Here *Place* touches its own limits and presents the context of Fisher's decision to move to a different, conceptual, type of poetics in the later books. I would argue however that scientific data, in the later work, compensates its lack of 'inscape' (if we take Hopkins's term as principle of equivalence between sensation in nature and sensation in the poem) by acquiring an imaginary concreteness and that what is problematic about this tendency is its similarity to the pseudo-immediacy of popular science. Although the poetry criticises the power-effects of scientific discourse, it relies on a projected immediacy (broadly, a fetishism of data) in order to do so. This is not to say that the other way, the phenomenological approach to sensation, whose model is the isolate individual, is any better at bringing counter-intuitive knowledge into poetic language. These are rifts that run through Olson's poetics and remain unresolved.[4]

Section 66 of *Place* negotiates those complexities ('my mind shuttles through Robert Duncan's music / weaves a weft of dream in day time' [169]) as they arise in the confrontation of inner life ('woman of my light / receive my cock-sperm first sacrifice of manhood' [168]) with those non-symbolic processes that are its physicality ('the nerve transmits the commands of the brain that / responds to the nerve'). And once again the book touches its limit: 'chance gives the correspondences between me and / the external' (170). How is that outside to enter the poem – if it is random? 'Putrid breath that does not awaken brain image / agitates chaotic dance' (168). There is a similar moment in William Carlos Williams's *Paterson* where measure, the process of transposition of the

---

[4] Olson's comments on Melville show his desire for a direct transposition of 'physicality' into writing. Thus he links the 'penetrations of physical reality', where 'the unconscious is the universe flowing-in, inside,' to the principle that 'methodology is form', which takes its shape in the notion of topology as the link between non-Euclidean space and writing. (*Collected Prose*, Berkeley: University of California Press, 1997, 116-118, 183).

physical world into writing, breaks down, into smell, mere 'granular stench'. With *Brixton Fractals*, the theory of fractal mathematics offers a way of conceptualising those types of non-regular relationship.

In *Place*, what destroys 'the dream's crystal' is not just what is outside the 'dream' but outside culture: 'the needed culture / making jewel.' If 'crystal' and 'jewel' are figures of knowledge where knowledge is made equivalent to transparency and light, and the poem is here emphasising what is damaged or 'repressed' by the type of analysis of the visible that such knowledge would imply (the Newtonian implications of 'a pyramidal city / separating light as prisms / dividing love into colours… / alienating life'), then the challenge laid down is to discover other ways of knowing. And so it is surprising to find that the lines that follow state, 'So at least type here direct / Magnesium limestone / the first Westminster bridge / 1750 by Labelye,' as if such presentation of data held some unmediated positivity ('direct') and were not itself selective, and a power-effect, once one acknowledges that the conversion of space into data is the territory of the State.

That statement needs qualifying: the book does expose critically a number of programmes of knowledge as power in the history of London. Thus 'WATLING'S WAY' shows a schema of spatial operations ('my cardinal line') recurring from Roman to Victorian times, offering 'security' within the 'unknown', recurrent ideas – to place one's reading in the present – in Donald Rumsfeld's speeches: the long duration of ideas as mentalities (to use the *Annales* historians' term). If Rumsfeld inherits the subordination of the symbolic to logistics (which is actually the conversion of logistics into the symbolic: the usurpation of language by war), via the development of Operational Research in the Second World War, the integrative operations of Fisher's Wren are geometrical and astronomical: 'Gibbons and Wren… view dome of panorgum astronomicum,' (383) 'the day after the break up of Great Frost': Wren's will to clear and shape the city is contrasted with chaotic materiality. The critical dramatisation of territory (territoriality, in fact) has similarities with Iain Sinclair's *Lud Heat*, which *Place* responds to in a piece called 'To Iain Sinclair, on the publication of his book "Lud Heat" in 1975' (152). The engagement centres on energy and measure:

> It is, you maintain, on these lines, or because of these lines of energy, that certain situations occur… It remains outside of your concern to give measurable determinations of these forces.

> It might, however, be pertinent to note that the presence of William Blake's house in Hercules Road, Lambeth... presents a psychical as well as a physical presence for you.

Should we read 'measurable determinations' ironically, after the criticism of Newton's alienating method and after the adumbration of chaos ('chance gives the correspondences')? What would Blake have made of that phrase? And does it not fail to acknowledge the *absence* of chaos in *Lud Heat*? *Place* does not register the extent to which Sinclair's geometric mapping is driven by the ghastly prolongation of the past in malign will (or magic), a metaphor of British power and politics of the late twentieth century. It offers a reading of *Lud Heat* in which the fusing of the psychical and the physical is bought at exactly that price: the alienating form of the writing acknowledging and pointing to the (unconscious) outside that drives it. That impulse is not registered in Fisher's optimistic reading of *Lud Heat*. On the contrary, he redeems Sinclair's terrain and its vocabulary: 'Your territory is your possession purchased by your care and your work' (153). Isn't the redemptive impulse ('purchase... care') more that of *Place* itself?

The difference between the two writers shows itself in their respective attitude to found materials. These, in *Lud Heat*, are 'A sequence of heated incisions through the membranous time-layer' or 'Dead geometric persistence. What the masonry holds beyond decayage. Compressed, the fear of form'; and are confirmed in the sick body of the author: 'Disease... is a form of pure message.'[5] Acquisition of form, via compression, key process of the lyric, is reversed. It's not the poet who produces significant form, through compression of materials; rather, the forces (power) within the materials compresses them, inscribes them on the body of the poetic self. Compression into singleness is the alienating form of the language. *Place*, on the other hand, generates a multiphasic language, to use Robert Duncan's term, for example by exhibiting the names of 'ICI Metallichrome' colours (375), making a probe into technological/cultural/perceptual interfaces, or offers an inventory of 'TWENTY-FIVE MEMORY JARS' (391), which echo Beuys's display cabinets, offering the materials of consciousness without the mirror-effect that produces the identificatory 'I'.

Not so 'THE ART OF MEMORY', where decision is placed as will inside history: 'I want to hold the crystal of / the Revolution / I don't

---

[5] *Lud Heat*, 6, 67, 51

want to / change / the garden want / to tend it' (389). The mirror here held to the will of the book as a whole is of course partial, the image is partial, yet the type of decision involved in its representations seems not to leave a trace upon it. Walter Benjamin's distinction between truth and knowledge is perhaps relevant here: 'Truth, bodied forth in the dance of represented ideas, resists being projected, by whatever means, into the realm of knowledge. Knowledge is possession. Its very object is determined by the fact that it must be taken possession of... For knowledge, method is a way of acquiring its object.'[6] *Place* traverses this dilemma. It includes incompleteness as part of its method, in order to elude possession; yet what exceeds knowledge does not penetrate to the level of form.[7]

On the other hand, *Place* includes reflection upon the limits of knowledge as project, so as to 'Move from knowledge to unknown / yet possible joy,' though precisely at that point the writing moves once again into useful data ('I pulled out the oldest patents / engraving, printing, maps, places /... construction of locks sluices cranes') before returning to 'the crystal of the Revolution... which will never leave me' (389). One of the differences between reading 'Move from knowledge to unknown / yet possible joy' and 'I pulled out the oldest patents' is that in the first there is an unfolding or suspension of sense-making, in the duration of the phrase being read,[8] and in the second a degree of subordination to goal, of separation of reason from pleasure. As Theodor Adorno wrote in 1944, 'He alone who could situate utopia in blind somatic pleasure, which, satisfying the ultimate intention, is intentionless, has a stable and valid idea of truth.'[9] Once again, the problem is the relation between data and truth: how to move from data to the embodiment of truth.

Previously, 'crystal' had been exposed to an understanding of analytic optics as 'alienating life.' The section ends with:

---

[6] Walter Benjamin, *The Origins of German tragic Drama* (London: *New Left Review*, 1977), 29

[7] For a contrastive approach, see Michael McClure's sense of writing as exclamation in the face of the radically contingent, or Olson's grappling, in 'Human Universe', with the problem of how to achieve a non-selective relation with 'physicality'.

[8] See Bataille on knowledge as project, and thus excluding expenditure.

[9] *Minima Moralia*, London: Verso, 2000, 61

>   westward moving
>   with you my love   through
>   an unhinged garden door
>   the dreamscape remaining beyond (390)

How does this, within the larger movement of the book, differ from an uncritical alternation with the form of knowledge that alienates life? The section 'Unhinge 2' takes up some of the implications of 'unhinged' as apprehension of emergent shape: 'edge of the dawn / dream / blur / of day's movement / an intentional shape / giving / the sensed a / meaning / as a new morning / spread.' This is located as occurring between imagination and cognition: 'if cognition / came from shape / then what seemed imagined… / remains new… yet shape / becomes recognition / in the imagined process of deconstruction' (396). The first statement is of the new, what comes from outside, as active inside imagination; the second, that analysis has as its object the already-known (the usual meaning of knowledge), and that that reduces imagination to recognition. In that case form in poetry would be reduced to recognition patterns: the repetition of inherited knowledge in inherited forms. One way of breaking that is to write poetry that requires active, participatory reading: '-a participating reader / - re / cognises / their shape violates / their initial dwelling.' Participation produces new meanings, their vehicle the phonic drift of language: 'violets' become 'violates'.

The book states one of its core tensions, between data and imagination, and proposes that neither is given without the other. Yet a question remains: who is the knower, who is the subject of knowledge? What makes for their continuity, which is the continuity of the poem in the relation of its parts. Or, to say it differently, what type of subject do the specific acts of knowing, the particular forms of knowledge, so important in the poem's composition, imply? The shape of those acts, their limits, can begin to be outlined by contrasting the process of *Place* with Sohrawardi's narrative of the process of knowledge in his Sufi recital, 'Occidental Exile,' where the subject has to pass through 'the great disaster'.[10] This cataclysm, catastrophe, calamity is the measure of the transformation required: 'they imprisoned us in a hole of infinite depth.' '*C'est le secret sur lequel fut fixé le site des soufis es des visionnaires*,' comments Meddeb. Transformation whirls the seer, the intention, and the language outside the territory. Or, to introduce a further marker,

---
[10] Abdelwahab Meddeb, *L'exil occidental*, Paris: Albin Michel, 2005, 58-59.

it is Rimbaud's 'disordering' of the senses that makes knowledge, in poetry – i.e. the knowledge specific to the poem – possible. The project of *Place*, by contrast, rests to some extent upon a narrative of knowledge as redemption whose subject remains in possession of himself.

Nevertheless, the book signals how 'possessive individualism', in the shape of consumer choice, feeds alienating power structures ('purchasing power is the license to purchase power controls' [175]), and, in the context of nineteen-seventies urban redevelopment, produces a non-participatory society ('were you asked what you wanted / tenants of these houses'). A key counter-proposition is the inclusion of the body (its 'auricular nerves') in space dreamed of. Yet that conjunction of space and desire needs to include measure, and intuition is insufficient for understanding measure ('local regularity / is deeper than intuition' [351]), an example of which is given in 'a map of south London showing relationship / between underground rivers and pneumonia outbreaks.' Thus a knowledge other than that afforded by intuition is required, other than that afforded by the phenomenology of the senses. And so the territory of poetry is redefined by the incursion of an outside, a physical unconscious, that it had not grappled with until the mid-twentieth-century long poems of Williams and Olson.[11] What *Place* does is bring to a particular threshold of contradiction the difficulties involved. On the one hand there is the confidence in measure and sense data: 'we are part of a measurable spiral trajectory /... through a field of motion / electromagnetically and by / generative energies / tied to the microcosmic / geometric limits' (149), i.e. a confidence in the 'measurable determinations' mentioned in the paragraphs addressed to Iain Sinclair. Later, however, in 'Unpolished mirrors', measure and sense do not necessarily coincide, 'giving / the sensed a / meaning,' since there can be occasions 'where magnitude and timing of cracks is beyond calculation / the pattern and topology of their joining / the indeterminate' (350). The writing here begins to open up the territory of Fisher's later work, from *Brixton Fractals* onwards, where, for example, the traditional opposites of ordered and chaotic space interpenetrate, and incompleteness as aesthetic decision is brought into dialogue with uncertainty as objective principle of contemporary science.

The singularity of 'Unpolished mirrors' is that it makes the decisions

---

[11] I do not include Hart Crane's *The Bridge* because there engineering loses its physical import within metaphorical language.

in the writing of *Place* apprehensible within a field of power relations, as acts of will inside historical time, something that Fisher's later work no longer does, though I say this to stimulate critical debate, not pre-empt it. 'Wren's monologue' perhaps works the best because the character's optimism of the will has a historically discernible programmatics to it, a profile visible against the background of everything that did not, over time, correspond with his will, and discernible as in league with oppression, historically interpreted. Thus Wren's geometrically oriented rebuilding of London is shown to have entailed the breaking of tombs and clearing of exposed burial ground as a form of production of capital through deterritorialization (399-400). As in Sinclair, architecture can be malign ('Night shifts up the hill   the tower block's / shadow' [401]), nature made malign in 'second nature', a Marcusian notion that the book acknowledges elsewhere: 'a hydrocarbon dawn numbs the questions.' (402) The reconstruction of London represses the past 'beneath insurance foundations', and Wren's works ('financial backing making my decision') via montage effects of composition are cut into the violence of Roman invasion, nineteen-seventies public architecture, the expansion of multinationals ('City Lead Works purchased by Shell Petroleum' [402]), and the Thatcherite Docklands Development Corporation.

All of this gets placed as 'a system of cruelty and selfishness / as natural / a mnemotechnics of torture / for a nation of bankers and banked' (403). What happens if one compares the confidence in being able to encompass damage through knowledge with Sinclair's early work? The terrain of *Lud Heat*, *Suicide Bridge*, or *White Chappel Scarlet Tracings* may seem phantasmagoric in comparison: diminished in its interpretative power, since it includes 'magic' in its data. And yet, is there not a will to power in *Place's* deployment of knowledge? And in Sinclair's work, don't the insistences of the past occur in the present, its tracings, less easily encompassed and controlled given that they penetrate the senses and the intellect and mingle with the very means (signs) by which any collective struggles to grasp where 'we' are. Knowledge does, in Sinclair, imply disaster. 'We survive the dead... until we can remake the past, go into it, change what is now, cut out those cancers – we are helpless. We are prisoners, giving birth to old faults,' as *White Chapell Scarlet Tracings* puts it.[12]

---

[12] 112-3

'Wren's monologue continues' turns Wren into Benjamin's 'angel of history' (of the 'Theses on the Philosophy of History') but does not include Benjamin's emphasis upon the great catastrophe of paradise become progress:

> His face is turned toward the past. Where we perceive a chain of events, he sees one single catastrophe which keeps piling up wreckage upon wreckage and hurls it in front of his feet. The angel would like to stay, awaken the dead, and make whole what has been smashed. But a storm is blowing from Paradise…[13]

In Benjamin's dialectical image,[14] it is the force of 'paradise' that prevents the angel from redeeming the past but at the same time the catastrophe of the past that orients him towards paradise. *Place* has Wren renounce history ('I have been the historian too long / immersed in wreckage hurled at my feet' [404]) and embody progress ('trampling burnt memorials… drilling and carving the land'): i.e., in a linear resolution that eliminates the force of paradise and makes Wren the agent of the wreckage that Benjamin's angel 'would like to… make whole.' Nevertheless, 'I… act as agent for light, space and supports / continuous membranes', makes the architect/poet a conduit for habitable if not paradisal – space. And the Gardener's 'garden first placed… the garden of a coming English Revolution', receives a certain reflux of the wind blowing from paradise, as the body mapped onto space by 'tracings' that 'continually move / the entrance / love changing the boundary' (342), in an action capable of 'building by giving / psycho-physiological well-being to the occupants' (405). Within these orientations, Wren's reveals itself as a project for social amnesia ('where spaces no longer read the locality / makes space by clearing the place'), accentuated in the twenty-five years since 'Unpolished mirrors' was first published, enforced clearance as Wren's neoliberal ambition, and whereas Benjamin's angel 'would like to stay' but for the 'storm… blowing from Paradise,' where the Klee painting places the viewer at the same place as the 'catastrophe' the angel is

---

[13] Walter Benjamin, *Illuminations*, London: Fontana, 1973, 259

[14] On the Benjaminian dialectical image, see Susan Buck-Morss, *The Dialectical Seeing: Walter Benjamin and the Arcades Project*, Cambridge, MA.: MIT Press, 1991, where it is defined as an arrangement 'of contradictory terms, the "synthesis" of which is not a movement toward resolution, but the point at which their axes intersect.' (210)

gazing at, Wren's resolution, translated to the nineteen fifties ('from bombed out framing / to mobile consumer chromiums / obliterating memory and place'), places a reader at a different type of intersection, where the elevated gaze of Wren meets its limit in a version of the future as 'existence ... / gratified of basic needs / freed of guilt of fear / the arena of constraints collapsed / into a cooperation' (407).

Fisher's Wren works somewhat like Blake's Newton (who both sits upon and turns his back to the seething of matter in time), a protagonist of knowledge, whose neoclassical gaze sublimates Roman and subsequent historical violence, yet does not find a counterpart in a figure of reason entangled in its own linearising will, in its own capabilities, as happens with Blake's Urizen or Sinclair's James Hinton.[15] Thus when Wren makes 'technoskills substitute devalued motifs / of historicisms with form,' the phrase 'devalued motifs / of historicisms' seems to partake of the same Urizenic intellectual abstraction that, in a reading informed by Blake's books, it would need to criticise. So too with Wren's 'changing the tongues of the economic charade', in that the intellectual ease of the phrase, running talk into motion, would seem to underestimate the sheer dead weight of history, dissolving the dead hand of the past, or the dead labour of capital, into optimism of the intellect, something not to be found in Blake.

The writing does at times move towards that zone, as with Wren's 'sublimity of tranquil terror / awed in contemplation with extreme antiquity and decay,' where lack of sensual engagement with his own project and lack of affect find their counterpart in his fascination with the machinic production of energy, anticipating steam power as engine of the industrial revolution:

   gradually manipulated by hallucination

   thudder loss of nearness
      restored from impoverished intimacy
   cupping my hands around
      invisible steam (407)

Here opposing forces move without intellectual abstraction. Wren's and the book's project merge for a moment in 'what I could have / deliberately unfinished,' where the line-break introduces a syncopation,

---

[15] See *White Chapell*, 92-3

and ambiguities as to whether it means that what could have been done as deliberate decision remained, because of external forces, unfinished (the case of Wren), or that there was a choice not to finish the project as a whole, or that what could be held as possession ('have' here applying to knowledge) is the unfinished. The latter, more exciting, possibility keeps the sense unresolvable.

If not to complete is a decision of the author's, but an accident of Wren's project, then 'unfinished' can be read as characterising the limits of intellect in history, and thus 'unfinished' as including 'unpolished' in a cognitive gain. What is certain is that Wren's 'loss of nearness', 'impoverished intimacy' and blurring of the ear ('thudder') by willed emphasis, all carry a critique of willed order. The final section of *Place* displays the difficulty of avoiding that type of blur, while also retaining the productive indefinition of the 'unfinished'. 'Wren's monologue' locates 'deliberately unfinished' as an artistic decision not to appropriate space into the segmentations of 'Taylored time'. In this case, 'unfinished' or 'unpolished' makes an equivalence between aesthetic and ethical refusal (like Blake's, of 'single vision and Newton's sleep'), but this refusal of 'distinction' does not cease at the same time to be an ideological gesture, the action of a sort of 'covering cherub',[16] which encompasses the negative (Taylorism and by extension capitalism) and appears to resolve it ('gratified of basic needs / freed of guilt and fear / the arena of constraints collapsed / into a cooperation') by refusing its language, when that refusal also preserves what it denies. Thus

> the mind as energy and raw material
>   larger than the self
> open to an infinity of measures (407)

can be read as enshrining the division of matter and measure, force and form, object and labour, while also transcending it: the separation of empirical, unimagined 'raw material' and idea, which allows intelligence to drift above the real in abstraction, making this also a 'bad' infinity of

---

[16] 'The covering cherub is the final error, the last enemy to be slain... The ultimate meaning of the Covering Cherub is the Selfhood, that self-seeking which is the root of all the Christian errors. But error is prophetic: it preserves concealed the very thing it denies. The truth becomes petrified into dogma and relegated to ritual.' S. Foster Damon, *A Blake Dictionary*, Hanover, NH and London: University Press of New England, 1988, 93-94.

endless proliferation, so that the beauty of calm mastery also alternates with a thinness of intellectual abstraction, and a similar ambiguity traverses the last two lines of the book,

> to change this city
> > join the dances of that without pain (407)

insofar as 'without pain,' while affirming pleasure, might also mean without pleasure, preserving what it denies.

Allen Fisher: Toward Health

PIERRE JORIS

Later I'll call it a poetry of use. But I want to go back to first takes, circa 1973-75, while Allen Fisher was producing the first books of *PLACE* and the performance work of BLOOD BONE BRAIN. A line, not underground, no ley line as such, but of simple, i.e. complex human interchange ran from my place in Tooting Broadway over to Allen Fisher's Streatham flat ('The name Streatham means the "Hamlet on the Street" – Street Ham. This shows the origin of the town as a small cluster of houses along the ancient trackway that now forms part of the A23 London to Brighton road.') and on to Herne Hill and Eric Mottram's house (where Allen Fisher & I spent many evenings being instructed by Eric Mottram in twentieth-century classical avant-garde music). We walk a fair amount around Lambeth – Fisher is exercising the maps that serve him in *PLACE*.

We never open other doors than those of the body. The cosmic labyrinth is in us as we are in it. It forms and deforms the texture of our carnal substance. The religious forgery conceived its Gods in the core of an evolutional matter to whose power, omnipresence and omniscience we now lay claim to – because they belong to our human specificity.

Summarizing what he is concerned with, Fisher says that it 'has to do with the idea that mathematically for instance, as Gödel has shown, truth cannot be demonstrated. That also led on to the fact that the only witness to truth is using a confidence curve or using some kind of statistical analysis which is what science's main mode is. And it drops off either side of it elements that have nothing to do with the truth I'm after, even though they are actually there in the experiment. And then I connect that to some of the ideas in biochemistry I'm reading at the moment, in cell biology, where aspects of electro-chemistry, electro-magnetic chemistry are … making clear that the cell so to speak is making decisions about quantum level phenomena and within that discussion it talks about freedom free will of the cell as being entangled. Now, what I really ... pull that directly into the experience we all have, of the brain's consciousness – the brain is full of cells essentially. This is therefore an inherent structural position we're already in. We are already biologically in a particular free will situation. That is to say in an entangled situation. I want to add that to the fact that following quantum mechanics' observations it's recognized that reality as such can't be local; it's a non-local condition, reality, which is kind of shocking in many ways, if we take reality in one sense, that is to say in the sense that my perception is a construct – that might be well on the way to summarize some of the things that still shock me into writing, that it is necessary to confront two of the issues I first mentioned: truth and freedom. (59:27)

<u>I say I bring thee Muse to-day and here,</u>
  <u>All occupations, duties broad and close,</u>
  <u>Toil, healthy toil and sweat, endless, without cessation,</u>
  <u>The old, old practical burdens, interests, joys,</u>...

Poem as energy enactment, or even as act (not re-action), so that despite the extremely complex structure of the overall work, the benefits of the poem (energy at both physical and cognitive levels) can easiest be gathered by hearing (& seeing, if at all possible) the poet read, enact her work. To do it alone in front of the printed page is more difficult, one has to expand energy to begin with in order to bring oneself to the place of the poem and tap its energy-spirals. Once one has achieved that (& a good starter help is given by knowing – for having heard, seen, witnessed – readings of that specific or other poems by the poet himself), one can swing along.

<u>A healthy presence, a friendly or commanding gesture, are words,</u>
  <u>sayings, meanings,</u>
  <u>The charms that go with the mere looks of some men and women,</u>
  <u>are sayings and meanings also.</u>

Land of the herd, the garden, the healthy house of
    adobie!

1974 walks in London in joy Allen Fisher tracking ley lines, underground river & stream lines, now hidden, now dead, of a psycho-geo-topography of South London, the idea of energy sources to be reawakened possibly, re-kindled – or that by being walked in consciousness could effect even buried, even today a sort of personal *Feng Shui* – maybe rid one, or at least learn control, of migraines, if possible to map temporal migraine maps with geographical maps of ley lines (that's my thinking now, not exactly Fisher's back then necessarily – though it's the idea: an ecological reorganizing of energy flows and patterns to make the body (of/and) the city an energy household that is dynamic system of interchanging, *malgré* the obvious and necessary negentropy. And a new poetry the place, the space to map said travels & travails.

AFOOT and light-hearted, I take to the open road,
Healthy, free, the world before me,
The long brown path before me, leading wherever I
    choose.

A healthy presence, a friendly or commanding ges-
    ture, are words, sayings, meanings;

The charms that go with the mere looks of some men
    and women, are sayings and meanings also.

Throbbing pain
caused by swell of blood
outer cover of brain dura
embedded in vessels and sensitive
nerve fibres release
compounds awaken receptors and
vessels
swell again.

Crowd-Out: A phenomenon whereby new public programs or expansions of existing public programs designed to extend coverage to the uninsured prompt some privately insured persons to drop their private coverage and take advantage of the expanded public subsidy. Ex:

Crowd-Out in the State Children's Health Insurance Program (SCHIP): **Incidence, Enrollee Characteristics and Experiences, and Potential Impact on New York's SCHIP** (2008). Laura P. Shone, Paula M. Lantz, Andrew W. Dick, Michael E. Chernew, and Peter G. Szilagyi

The extent to which the State Children's Health Insurance Program (SCHIP) displaces or 'crowds-out' private insurance whereby individuals drop private insurance coverage to obtain public insurance coverage remains a topic of interest for many policy-makers. Researchers studied the incidence of crowd-out, and whether enrollee characteristics were associated with crowd-out, in the New York SCHIP program. Crowd-out was relatively modest in New York SCHIP: only 7 percent of SCHIP enrollees were deemed enrolled due to crowd-out. Crowd-out was associated with some enrollee characteristics including income but not health status. Researchers conclude that most movement from private insurance to enrollment in New York SCHIP was not the result of crowd-out. States are encouraged to implement ongoing, detailed monitoring methods to determine crowd-out in SCHIP. For more details, see the 2008 issue of the *Health Services Research* 2008 Feb;43(1 Pt 2):419-34.

Crowd-out also occurs when such programs act as an incentive for employers to contribute fewer dollars to employees' health insurance coverage, or altogether drop coverage in an effort to prompt employees to enroll their children in the new program.

What health, and why?

Mapping headaches, really migraines, i.e. a deeper structure of repetitive physiological occurrences via, with, or against the occurrence of repetitive creaks in ceiling beams on a space & time system of coordinates. Analogical thinking escapes the oversimplification of cause-&-effect.

Tracing such maps on paper can offer structures that become poems. And may heal the initial impulse. Or so we would like to believe. We have to believe again against the linear oversimplifications, against the materials offered by industry & commerce. I seem to remember such trackings from the early seventies Streatham days, but Fisher remembers only 'a computer-like card system for migraine checks but it may never have come to anything in the poetry.'

***

Nietzsche used Julius Cesar's remedy for migraine: 'long walks, a sober life, long sojourns in the fresh air, assiduous work.'

***

E p. 20:
For nearly three minutes he listened to the headache
Felt hair growth each second sudden swells
White light hits the wall reflections
Too many ways to skin a cat
From inner forward in the free the corrupt
A constant shudder
Storm in the forehead in the teacup
Through any day's token like that

---

fractal (fràk'tel) noun

A geometric pattern that is repeated at ever smaller scales to produce irregular shapes and surfaces that cannot be represented by classical geometry.
/
a given fractal may have a finite area but an infinite perimeter; such shapes are considered to have a fractional dimension – for example, between 1 (a line) and 2 (a plane) – hence the name fractal.
/
Michaux speculated that all this drug-induced eye candy constitutes an amplification of brain-wave activity, especially that of the visual cortex. The fact that some migraine sufferers see similar patterns – known as the migraine aura – suggests that in certain extreme states, the internal link MS/DOS and subroutines of the brain can be apprehended by

consciousness. 'Some people can get the aura effects without the pain of migraine,' says Plant. 'It's happened to me about three times in my life, at times of extreme exhaustion. This almost kaleidoscopic stuff kind of creeps across your visual field from one side to the other. It's really quite stunning, and not at all scary. The fact that there are "natural" equivalents to drug-induced experiences suggests the possibility you are in some sense observing what's going on in the brain.' Noting the similarity between these psychedelic hallucinations and the self-similar patterns of Mandelbrot's fractals, Plant characterizes the drugged or migrained brain as a cranked-up biochemical computer capable of picturing the self-organizing behavior and nonlinear dynamism at play within normally staid reality.

fractals and migraines?

To yours. To your health. To write health. I write to yours. You write health. No, but you can write toward health.

But we do not yet know what health is.

Which is why writing health is explorative, experimental mappings. And has nothing whatsoever to do with writing-as-therapy. The latter being a vomiting of psychic indigestion into the landscape of the reader. Who needs it? Certainly not the reader, except for a perv who is into vicarious vomiting. And the writer of such stuff is continuously looking inside with eyes revulsed – meaning the French *révulsés*, translatable as 'disgusted,' though I heard a revolution/turning/backflip of eyes in that word – to see when evacuation is done, when the inside is emptied into the scape and the feeling of empty can be mistaken for health.

    Health, and trying to write health is a mapping of possibilities not yet achieved, unrealized: health is not the homeostasis of a finite system – this or that individual human being. Health is a relationship – unstable, constantly to be evaluated, tweaked, re-engaged ('will you dance with me world'), invented, calibrated, worried over (it's a bone, not a boner).

    The aesthetics of the poem-as-therapy can only be ego-flood with first person vomit with eyes revulsed (I'll keep that word) – i.e. not seeing the outside, not caring for it, the *Umwelt* only there as dumping ground for self's detritus. The poet as that absolute bore at the bar telling the bartender (but he is paid to listen, or is he?) and everyone else in voice-reach how sad he is, how sick he is and that if only he could get it off his chest, seat of his soul & mind, he'd feel better.

And feeling better is mistaken for being healthy again. As if we ever were healthy. As if health had been some primal condition from which life has estranged us via childhood illnesses, cigarettes, bad food and love experiences, bad sex and war wounds. If only things were that simple.

My health is the condition of the world. It runs both ways, i.e. all ways, all channels are open. How then do I block those that could kill?

What's the point of discovering who I am if it isn't to know who I want to be?

… We are the prisoners of an ontological image whose cogs move thought, physiology, and behavior simultaneously. We have donned, all the way to our unconsciousness's full-sails-ahead navigation, the en-soi being of a sophisticated machine.

Now, this body mutilated in its live exuberance, what if we redesigned it according to the will to happiness from which it emanates and whose exigencies we sense? If we conceived of it not – falling into the trap – as a desiring machine, but as a creative power, a poetry of beings and things capable of breaking the causal chain, the power of wondering, inherited from childhood and resolved to rewrite the world according to the language of correspondences and analogical signatures?

The attempt exists, it is even frequent judging by the approach of certain sick people, such as the woman who, telling of her fight against cancer, insisted that her healing had been helped by her insistent visualization of her tumor-gnawed uterus as a smooth, pink organ that radiated vitality. She used every second to polish this image. She cleaned it in a way, as one polishes a precious piece of furniture and cajoles it so affectionately that the caress absolves the effort.

The example, I hasten to add, sins by omission. Although it distances itself from it, the patient's vision tends to stay inside the field of influence of a stereotypical representation, and escapes with difficulty the metaphorical identification of the body with a machine.

It remains weighed down by the fear of dysfunctioning, threatened by the guilt of subtracting oneself to that medical vigilance outside of which, tradition has it, there is no salvation. For the laborious function which denatures /alters the body and vows it to endemic state of morbidity, pertinently demands the help of a medicine of mechanics. I do not underestimate the importance of such a recourse, I do think, however, that a therapy of illnesses must not occult the art of reinforcing one's health by treating the body like the singular manifestation of a living totality, by being careful to strengthen a symbiosis that mechanization dismantles continuously.

Against the frozen representations that inhabit and haunt us, we need to rediscover this genius of analogy the child possesses before geometric knowledge robs it of poetic knowledge.

Blood Bone Brain took my interpretation of an ancient Egyptian hieroglyph of wholeness (a jug containing a heart; a bone; a bird of prey). I found my cancer to ward off pathological collapse in an obsessional concern with love, logos and creativity (the highest point a bird of prey reaches in the sky is known prior to attack to be its 'place'..."

Health and energy lines. Ley lines. We were all reading *The Old Straight Track* by Alfred Watkins. (the preface of which is signed by the author in 1925 in Hereford – the city Fisher will move to in the 80s & is still based in today. Says the book:

> Some churches in London appear to have been placed along alignments, such as St Martin-in-the-Fields, St Mary-le-Strand, St Clement Danes and St Dunstan-in-the-West in Fleet Street.

Watkins notes:

> London church alignments are many, but should not be accepted as final until the structural history of each church is verified as being on an ancient site.

Alexander Thom (1894–1985) was a Scottish engineer most famous for his theory of the Megalithic yard.

Two British dowsers, Captain Robert Boothby and Reginald Smith of the British Museum, have linked the appearance of ley lines with underground streams and magnetic currents. Underwood conducted various investigations and claimed that crossings of 'negative' water lines and positive aquastats explain why certain sites were chosen as holy. He found so many of these 'double lines' on sacred sites that he named them 'holy lines.'

Mapping ley lines, according to New Age geomancers, can foster 'harmony with the Earth' or reveal pre-historic trade routes. John Michell's writing can be seen as an example of this. He has referred to the whole face of China being heavily landscaped in accordance with the laws of Feng Shui. Michell has claimed that Neolithic peoples recognized that the harmony of society depended on the harmony of the earth force. And so in China, ancient Greece and Scotland, men built their temples where the forces of the earth were most powerful.

The necessity to adapt to the surrounding environment for survival is an animal behavior. The primary human action consists in creating an environment that is favorable to the development of life.

The cosmic myths and initiation legends suggest the existence of worlds that a timeless fluidity entangles, superposes, locates in hidden recesses where the most certain laws of our Aristotelian sciences and of our geometrical apperception, as inherited from the Great Watchmaker, are abrogated.

[As I write in the *Nomadic Poetry Manifesto*:] We will take the whole of the new century to finally read Allen Fisher's vast investigation into all our knowledges, the great serial constructive *dérive* he calls *Gravity as a consequence of shape*. From his Introduction to *Brixton Fractals*: 'Imagination and action. My knowledge of the world exists validly only in the moment when I am transforming it. In this moment, in action, the imagination functions, unblocks passivity, refuses an overview. Discontinuities, wave breaks, cell divisions, collapsed structures, boundaries between tissue kinds: where inner workings are unknown, the only reliable participations are imaginative. The complex of state and control variables. The number of configurations depends on the latter: properties typical of cusp catastrophes: sudden jumps; hysteresis; divergence; inaccessibility. Boiling water's phase change where the potential is the same as condensing steam. Random motion of particles in phase space allows a process to find a minimum potential. What is this all about? It's a matter of rage and fear, where the moving grass or built suburbia frontier is a wave prison; where depth perception reverses; caged flight. With ambiguous vases it's as if part of the brain is unable to reach a firm conclusion and passes alternatives along for a decision on other grounds. The goblet-and-face contour moves as it forms in your seeing.'

Our ideas, our imaginary games, our wild dreams, our most unreasonable speculations sketch out in us a plurality of inhabitable worlds. We own only meteoric fragments of them, repertoried by common sense into the drawers of the nonsensical.

The reality that imposes the economic management of beings and things is the lie that engenders all the other lies. Where is the truth of the living in religion, philosophy, ideology, culture, science, art, ethics? We have it but the mirrors of its negation.

The result of which is a poetry of use, though the uses be not your usual aesthetic jouissance and/or socio-political alibis: '**Brixton Fractals** provides a technique of memory and perception analysis. It can be used to sharpen out-of-focus photographs; to make maps of the radio sky; to generate images from human energy; to calculate spectra; to reconstruct densities; to provide probability factors from local depression climates. It becomes applicable to reading; to estimate a vector of survival from seriously incomplete or hidden data, and select the different structures needed. It can provide a participatory invention different from that which most persists.'

Even now, I submit, the question of health is present. One of Allen Fisher's recent concepts is the Notion of **crowd-out:** it involves issues of damage and recovery. The recovery I see achieved by Cubism, for instance, – 'negative crowd-out': a political disaster one has to confront, and it is that disaster (it might be a censorship, it might be information you don't get inadvertently for some other reason, it might be information that you get that is incredibly focused to the point of crowding out other information. …say something about genetic damage   it seems to me that what we are trying to do (on the cell-biological level he is speaking about) is to crowd-out genetic diseases, crowd out all sorts of problems that we would have by trying to exist – it is very simple issues like that which are obviously political at the same time.

I just feel astonished… that I've been dropped, not here, but on the planet and I say, wow, how did this happen? Honestly, I spend a lot of time in that state of delighted alienation and then not too delighted about it, flipping in and out of that experience really…

From Allen Fisher Interview 10/13/07:

PJ: The notion of "health" in your work.

AF: Now that you say it, it is obvious. I can see it right the way through. It's got different levels, if that's the right way of saying it – different intensities, different details, like it has to do with the health of walking the streets, and the lost atmosphere, the poisons and stuff that crop up in the early *PLACE*, say, it talks about Epsom Salts, for example, … in Lambeth which is clearly gone for a long time – and then, jumping around a little bit, and as I remember things, in *BECOMING* I get very interested in human physiology. It was not the first time I was interested in physiology but it become much more intense and focused – I took an Open University course at that time, part of that was work with the physiology of plants and I found that very rewarding. At the same time I was interested in the technology of dialysis, on how it worked, on a kind of metaphorical level, if that was what it was, where you could talk about notions of boundaries, between the blood and the outside of the body, between internal and external, between thinking and action, between being where you are and being who you are, so that being with that whole idea of more than one reality, of simultaneity – of you and I talking here and realizing there is someone on the outskirts also involved or being aware of a buzz in my head and all sorts of things going on at the same time, realizing that perception isn't singular at any given moment .

PJ: Listening to you this other idea just came to me that health is in fact the imperceptible – you perceive illness, not being well, but being healthy you are not normally conscious of.

AF: You do, don't you! And then there is another – a figurative, a rhetorical issue to do with civilizational health, with what that prognosis is, or what your propositions are, your projections, that kind of health issue, it is metaphorical in the sense of the political health – I think as a consequence of the Open University work I got interested in some other issues, I was looking at the biological work that was being done by C.H. Waddington, René Thom, by work being done in Edinburgh in those years and so forth, in physiology generally and how it acts with our existence, with our way of being and that's sort of philosophical on another level as well, which isn't really quite health really… but it is difficult to separate and extract it, it is actually a false intrusion, a false intrusion in a sense, it makes a false set of boundaries which doesn't fully appreciate or take into account all our notions as a need or health as we recognize our need for separating out and having to make a prognosis on the basis of fragments but when we do that we know that we are in fact damaging. And that is reminding me, using vocabulary that is quite late for me, that later on I get into a whole set headed 'tools, traps and damage'. It's traps *or* tools, *and* damage. What that takes on board is the recognition that damage is actually an essential part of our health, an essential part of our renewal, that we can't possibly sustain and that we need to be selective. And realize how damage then becomes this discarding of cells that the brain is involved in but also this whole traumatic idea that rhymes for me with your dream or your vision or thoughts about potential which are linked to potential in the sense that damage is involved in doing away with or transforming some things. Therefore, the vocabulary that in the first place, like traps, like damage, values, is of immediate value, you can see needn't be at all, might actually become necessary, might become something you work on as necessary or as positives. So that's at least three points I'm bumping across, from place to dialysis, to debate, but, in a sense, like a Venn diagram, they overlap with each other. But there could be something else here – but I've lost it for a second – a gap between the eighties and nineties – yes, it might have to do with my interest in Joseph Beuys at that time, as well as homeopathic ideas that are in him, ah, figurative, that is to say they are metonyms, or allegories... a huge range of questions, human kind, for example, or for him larger issues for example how deal with having been a German in 1945 – how to deal with this now – he went through a whole range of analyses and difficulties and, I think, solutions effectively, and with some of his students – or Kiefer's say – how they deal with that, ill health, say, and the levels then become multiple and huge between one's singular being as a person, and the whole community nexus, and then how this affects your ideas of a polis, or your ideas of a network or nexus. People aren't necessarily geographically in the same place, but a nexus of sensibilities of some order, which, say, you and I don't lose in the panic, though it is not necessarily there geographically because you moved, we are migrating nomadic people. So that's actually the four I would, doing it quickly, I would look at.

One is quite undemanding, if you walk in the street and have tetrachloric lead rammed into your lungs, that's a straight forward issue, a multiple issue, but nonetheless straightforward not particularly a poet's concern or an ecologist's concern, and then secondly dialysis, which is very very particular, but that at another moment I am trying to shift into other areas of interest for me, to do with osmosis, to do with boundaries, inner and outer bodies etcetera. And thirdly Beuys, as an exemplar for me, as someone I would aspire to be – without being pretentious, and fourthly, this idea that I am still in the process of developing, *the traps or tools and damage* sequence – the title of a lecture for a professorship, but in fact it is much bigger than that – it included a whole range of sets of research I did for investigating how image and meaning were not always related and how you can have an image and that would have a multiple range of meanings depending on which part of the Mediterranean or which part of the world you were in. And I got involved in the serpentine form around a rod, in how the serpentine and the straight, the linear, enter into European, Italian, Germanic, Celtic areas – it is so massive. But I recognize links between the serpentine form and health, serpentine form and spiritual matters isn't just Mesopotamian but is also Celtic, early Celtic I mean, Bronze Age, not Christian Celtic. And then the whole business of the alchemical comes in through that because it picks up from the hermetic ideas – all of which I am still researching, I am still reading Asclepius, or Asclepian texts, Hippocrates and so on. For obvious reasons this is all related to health, and how that links across, strangely but not so strangely, and into ideas of beauty, how being becomes alert, because I am aware – this discussion of health is coming together somehow under something called ethics or ecological ethics or something. I haven't developed that yet, and don't know if I'll manage to… So I recognize more and more talk about planet and singular being, a person's existence in a social nexus, which may not be geographically the same place, then the nexus being the planet. Then this talking about health has to entail… though the word health then maybe becomes too small a word to talk about it, but it isn't actually… though it might be if you only used this word without encouraging some activity of nuance around the word though that it enlarges and complexes.

Legend

bold: Allen Fisher's words
<u>underlined</u>: Walt Whitman citations
italics: Raoul Vaneigem (*Imaginary Journal*)
Roman: Pierre Joris's words

Start *Place* In Flux:
Allen Fisher and Fluxus 1970–1977

REDELL OLSEN

The development of Fluxus in Britain in the early 1970s coincides with Fisher's writing of *Place*. During this period Fisher was exploring a range of methodologies for writing that span from John Cage and Jackson Mac Low's chance-operational and procedural poetry to the more intuitive and process-driven writing of Charles Olson. Fisher's Fluxus-inspired performance events and texts in this same period provided him with a mode of working and thinking through which to develop the writing of what would eventually become *Place* (2005).

Any reader approaching *Place* rapidly becomes aware of many different contextual affiliations and networks of contiguity that the poem negotiates and proposes. In response to just one of these affiliations, this essay explores some of the Fluxus materials of the 1972 *Fluxshoe* tour, materials directly relevant to the strategies of writing and making in *Place*.

In his essay 'Poetry, a priority: being some notes on my relationship with the work of JACKSON MAC LOW', Fisher distinguishes between poetry that is produced through procedural means and poetry which is written through 'processual' techniques (Fisher, *Prosyncel*, 36). Procedural writing is identified by Fisher as poetry which is produced according to systems, such as Mac Low's *Stanzas for Iris Lezak* (Barton, VT: Something Else, 1971) and *Asymmetries* 1-260 (New York: Printed Editions, 1980), which were constructed through acrostic reading-through text-selection procedures. Fisher identifies processual writing with Charles Olson's emphasis on composition by 'field' and with a writing practice that necessitates the ongoing modification of material according to more intuitive criteria.

The early writings of *Place* (*Place; Book One*, 1974 and 1976; *Stane, Place Book Three*, 1977, *Becoming, Place Book Four and part of Five*, 1978) and the related sequences associated with *Blood Bone Brain* (1982) which include *Ffacece* (1972), *Creek in the Ceiling Beam* (1973), and *Sicily* (1973), embody Fisher's struggle to reconcile these two elements, a struggle to 'incorporate process-SHOWING procedures' into processual writing (*Prosyncel*, 37):

By 1973 I knew that I needed to find a method of writing processually that could incorporate process-SHOWING procedures and systems where it wished to and yet still allow me to go, to be on-going, rather than the "closed field" that systems alone inevitably would lead me into (*Prosyncel,* 37).

CONVERGENCES / IN PLACE / OF THE PLAY (1976) (written in June 1973) synthesises these two different models and allows the reader to read syntactically 'across ten columns of different informations' and 'separately down them' (*Prosyncel,* 37). As Fisher points out: 'The system is inherent in the poem so that the poem is process-showing and procedure showing. It is both a process poem and a poem incorporating strict procedures' (*Proscyncel,* 37). The struggle to synthesise otherwise distinct methodologies is mediated by Fisher's interest and participation in the performance activities of *Fluxshoe* that took place in Britain in 1972.

The European context of Dada and the activities of the Cabaret Voltaire are clearly an important influence on the aesthetics of Fluxus. More immediate influences can be traced back through, on the one hand, the experimental Black Mountain College pedagogies of Olson, and on the other, the writings and teachings of John Cage.[1] These different modes of practice correspond to the importance of both processual and procedural strategies of writing in Fisher.

Charles Olson visited Britain in 1967. He performed at The International Poetry Festival at the Albert Hall and made connections with British poets such as Tom Raworth. This led to a number of publications from Raworth's Goliard Press (London), which included *West* (1966) and *Maximus Poems IV, V, VI* (Cape, 1968) (*A Charles Olson Reader*, p.x). Dick Higgins and Jackson Mac Low had been students of John Cage at the New York School for Social Research during his 1958/59 seminar, and his ideas influenced their directions in performance, writing, multimedia and publishing activities. Fluxus also has shared tendencies with what Allan Kaprow defined as 'Happenings' (1965), as well as the Auto-Destructive art made by Gustave Metzger in Britain (1959-61). Like Kaprow and Metzger, Fluxus artists blurred the

---

[1] For an account of Black Mountain College see Vincent Katz (Ed.), *Black Mountain College: Experiment in Art*. Cambirdge, MA: MIT Press, 2003. For a discussion of John Cage's ideas see Joan Retallack (Ed.), *Musicage: Cage Muses on Words, Art, Music*. Hanover, NH: Wesleyan UP, 1996.

boundary between art and life, and foregrounded the making of art along with the processes of breakdown and destruction of materials.

During the early 1960s Fluxus emerged in the US as a 'varying community of individuals' who made work as a part of a series of collective activities that included mail art, performance and the production of multiples in the form of ready-mades, boxes and bookarts (Smith, *History*, 226).[2] Owen Smith divides Fluxus into three phases which he calls: the 'proto-Fluxus period 1961-64', the period from 1964-70, and the late Fluxus performances from 1970-78 (Smith, 'Avant-Gardism', 4). The first phase involved concerts and events at the Washington Square Gallery in New York, the AG gallery and in May 1964 the 'Fluxus Symphony Orchestra' at the Carnegie Recital Hall. The period from 1964-70 was characterised by the publishing of multiples. The anthology publications *Fluxus 1* (1964) and *Flux Fest Kit 2* (1970) occurred during this period and Higgins's publishing venture, *Something Else Press*, published nearly one hundred titles before going bankrupt in 1974. Titles from *Something Else Press* such as Alison Knowles's *By Alison Knowles* (1965) and Jerome Rothenberg's *Ritual: A Book of Primitive Rites and Events* (1966) opened up cross-overs between performance and avant-garde writing and publishing. At the same time this period saw a move away from performance towards the production of objects and bookworks which existed as limited editions and which quickly entered the art market as collectable items.[3] The final phase of Fluxus marked a return to performance but on a much larger scale. 'Flux Mass', 'Flux Divorce', 'Flux Tours,' and 'Flux Games', as their names suggest, blurred the distinctions between audience and participants in highly ritualised group activities (Smith, 'Avant-Gardism', 5).

Through *Spanner*, Fisher was actively in correspondence with Higgins, Mac Low and other Fluxus artists. He published Higgins and Mac Low as well as an interview between Eric Mottram and John Cage.[4]

---

[2] George Macunias's 1963 Manifesto called for Fluxus artists to react against the commercialisation of culture and to 'Promote living art, anti-art' which would 'FUSE the cadres of cultural, social & political revolutionaries into united front & action' (Smith, 'Developing,' 4).

[3] These included George Brecht's *Water Yam* (1964) and the anthology *Fluxkit* (1964).

[4] See *Spanner* 1, 'The Pleasure of Chaos' (John Cage and Eric Mottram in conversation), London, 1974. pp. 2–15, and *Spanner* 9, 'Call It "Something Else": Dick Higgins in conversation with Eric Mottram', pp. 157–184. Both interviews are collected in *Spanual*, Vols. 1 and 2, issues 1–20. In 1978 Fisher published Jackson Mac Low's, *21 Matched Asymmetries*. London: Aloes,1978. Fisher was similarly interested in the work of George

Fisher's emerging inter-disciplinary practice coincided with Higgins's revival of the term 'intermedia' (a term first used by Coleridge in 1812) to describe work that seemed 'to fall between media'; a characteristic that Higgins found prevalent in the 'best work' of his contemporaries (Higgins, *Intermedia*, 18). Higgins's definition of 'intermedia' not only concentrated on work that fell formally between genres such as painting or sculpture, or writing and the visual arts, but also on those works which suggested 'a location in the field between the general idea of art media and those of life media' and which often used found or ready-made objects in their construction (20). The term coincided with Fluxus performance works which were '"concerts" of everyday living' in which 'everything was itself' (Higgins, *Intermedia*, 88).

There are affinities here with Fisher's practice during the 1970s which often incorporated found material as well as structures and rhythms from daily life into its make-up. Fisher's interest in the relationship between the procedural production of work and performance was already in place through his readings of John Cage, Jackson Mac Low, Daniel Spoerri's *Topology of Chance* (1966) and the writings of the Situationist, Raoul Vaneigem. For Vaneigem 'the new artists of the future' would be those who were 'constructors of situations to be lived' (Vaneigem,149), a description that mirrors the call for the dissolution of the boundaries between art and life.[5]

Fluxus events began to reach London in the early 1960s. *The Festival of Misfits* at Victor Musgrove's Gallery One in 1962 included work by Arthur Køpcke, Daniel Spoerri, Robert Filliou, Gustave Metzger, Emmett Williams, Robin Page and Ben Vautier. Vautier lived in the gallery window for fifteen days and nights, labelling everything as a work of art and offering himself as a 'living sculpture' for £250 (Glew, np).[6] A *Little Festival of New Music* at Goldsmith's College in London

---

Macunias, Nam June Paik and Joseph Beuys as well as the concrete poetry of Emmett Williams and event scores of George Brecht whose work he 'occasionally performed' (E-mail to Redell Olsen, 22nd November 2006).

[5] Other influences on his developing sense of procedural aesthetics included: Christopher Butler and Alistair Fowler, Steve Reich, Terry Riley, Vito Acconci's *0-9* and Stockhausen's *Die Rie*. Fisher, Allen. "Re: Fluxus." E-mail to Redell Olsen, 22nd November 2006.

[6] Subsequent performances as part of the exhibition by Dick Higgins, Alison Knowles and Emmett Williams similarly merged the boundaries between life and art in ways which were not entirely popular with the public. As Higgins recalls: 'We did a performance at the old Institute of Contemporary Arts on Dover Street, which tho-roughly shocked the Londoners, gentle as it was, and turned off Britain to Fluxus for another ten years –

in 1963 featured works by George Macunias, La Monte Young, George Brecht, Emmett Williams and Nam June Paik. The *International Concrete Poetry* exhibition at King's College, Cambridge in 1964 and the *Destruction in Art Symposium* in London in 1966 featured Fluxus tendencies.[7] Indica Gallery and Lisson Gallery presented shows by Yoko Ono in 1966 and 1977, and in November 1970 – January 1971 The Whitechapel Art Gallery presented an exhibition of *New Multiple Art* which included Fluxus works (Glew, up).

In 1972 the *Fluxshoe* tour took place in Britain. The touring exhibition consisted of a variety of performances, films, objects, texts, readings and spontaneous events and began at Falmouth College. It visited seven places over a period of nine months between 1972 and 1973 and involved over sixty different artists and groups.[8] Some of the artists and writers who appeared at various events included: Allen Fisher, Helen Chadwick, David Mayor, John Wilkinson, Genesis P-Orridge, Ben Vautier, Alison Knowles, Ian Breakwell, Robin Crozier, John Gosling, Opal L. Nations, Stuart Brisley, Carolee Schneeman, Eric Anderson, Henri Chopin, Felipe Ehrenberg and Sandy Nairne.

The tour was principally organised by David Mayor, who ran Beau Geste Press with Felipe Ehrenberg. Mayor was a post-graduate student of Mike Weaver at Exeter University. Weaver had begun a correspondence with both Macunias and Ken Friedman, who was the American co-ordinator of *fluxus West* (initially in relation to the work which he had seen in the International Concrete Poetry exhibition in Cambridge). What was originally intended as a travelling exhibition of Fluxus works expanded to include a range of European and American performers and artists many of whom were not associated with the original Fluxus members. They coalesced around overlapping interests in the possibilities of what Craig Saper has in retrospect termed 'networked art', a term which includes postal art, small-press publishing and the widespread interest in works of art that took place outside the gallery system (see Saper, 2001).

---

frightfully English to react that way' (Higgins, 'Minesweeper', 32).

[7] At the 'Destruction in Art Symposium', Bob Cobbing (one of the principal speakers and organisers) contributed a repeatedly mimeographed version of the programme of events that presented its gradual obliteration as a series of pages collected together in the form of a book (Wilson, 106).

[8] The tour was funded by Exeter University, the Arts Council of Great Britain and S.W. Arts Association.

Spanner, the magazine still edited by Fisher, was highly influential in the distribution of Fluxus ideas and works of art in the UK. In an interview with Eric Mottram on February 19th 1973, Doug Lang referred to *Fluxshoe* as 'a spanner in the works' of poetry, and less than a month later Fisher wrote to David Mayor expressing his intention to change the name of his magazine from *Wooden Shoe* to *Spanner*: 'everything happens so fast the above heading [Wooden Shoe letterhead] now becomes SPANNER (spanner to throw in works / spanner to span time / life / spanner a tool to make use of etc)'.[9]

Performances at the *Fluxshoe* festival included the staging of various Fluxus event scores by artists and writers such as La Monte Young, George Brecht and Jackson Mac Low as well as participatory events which included large audiences.[10] In Exeter and Falmouth, buildings were tied up with string by David Mayor, while Martha Ehrenberg 'sewed the audience together'. In Falmouth, Eric Anderson invited members of the public to follow directions and meet him at various venues with the promise of 'FREE DRINKS—FREE MUSIC—FREE SEX', and Alice Hutchins invited the audience to make poems with her from a game involving words and a dart board. In Blackburn texts were placed in the adverts section of the local newspapers. In Oxford a pre-recorded tape loop of street sounds was dragged through the streets before being played back in the gallery. In Croydon Helen Chadwick cast chocolates and agar-jelly in a mould from her own face before inviting the audience to join her in eating it. At many of the venues people danced to the music of the Taj Mahal Travellers who played music in front of projections of the sea.[11]

According to Anderson, *Fluxshoe* 'generated a set of hilarious and libertarian ideas which were passed from hand to mouth – or from mailbox to mailbox – across the provinces of the coca-colised world,

---

9 See Eric Mottram, *Interview with Fluxshoe group (Opal L. Nations, Allen Fisher and Doug Lang)*. The Poetry Society London, 1973 and Allen Fisher, 'Letter to David Mayor 5th March 1973' (David Mayor collection, Hyman Kreitman Research Archive, Tate Gallery, London).

10 For a selection of Fluxus Event Scores see the *Fluxus Performance Workbook* edited by Ken Friedman and Owen Smith (with Lauren Sawchen) published with 'On Fluxus', *Performance Research*. Vol.7, No.3 (September 2002). Available to download at http://www.performance-research.net/pages/epublications.html

11 See Mayor, David, Felipe Ehrenberg, Terry Wright. Eds. 'Add End A', *Fluxshoe 72-73*. Beau Geste Press, 1974 and Allen Fisher eds. 'Fluxus: Notes, diary, gaps'. *Spanner*, Vol. 1, no. 3, May 1975.

mostly on a level that generated no more objective evidence than a fading mimeographed flyer, saved for posterity by accident rather than design' (Anderson, 22). His comments underline the ephemeral qualities of *Fluxshoe*. Even its organisers suggest that *Fluxshoe* was perhaps more about 'the attitudes which most of the fluxshoe artists share' (Mayor, 'Add End A') than about the production of specific works. Many Fluxus and *Fluxshoe* performances replaced the art object (and even the artist) with ritual and group participation, and, as a result, the documentation of the involvement of many of the individual artists and participants in *Fluxshoe* has remained difficult to trace.

As noted earlier, a number of Fisher's projects are contemporary with the *Fluxshoe* tour and related events. These include *Spaces For Winter Solstice* (1972), *Blood Bone Brain* (published in 1982 but performed during the early 1970s), and *Taken The Days After We Had Beef Curry* (1974), *Creek In The Ceiling Beam* (1973) as well as *FFACECE* (1972) and *Sicily* (1973). Simon Anderson also credits 'the obscure *Spanner*' (along with publications such as '*Art Press, Source, Canal* and *AQ*') as extending the audience for Fluxus (Anderson, 26). However, it is the documentation of Fisher's actual role in *Fluxshoe,* rather than anything in *Spanner*, which is 'obscure'. At times this lacuna in the history of the development of British Fluxus has seemed to suit Fisher's occasional playful projection of his own role as an artist and writer.

The Fluxus Reader (1998) includes Fisher as one of the participants of *Fluxshoe* but under Fluxus Sources he is listed as:

> Fischer, A, 'Fluxus', Spanner, no.3 (June 1975).

Fisher seems to have been conflated with the next entry:

> Fischer, Hervé, ed, *Art et Communication Marginale*, Paris, Editions Balland, 1974.

Elsewhere, he is again listed under Fischer in the list of Fluxus works: 'Fischer, Allen, *Taken the Days After We Had Beef Curry Between 28.7.72 and 28.10.72,* Cullompton, Beau Geste Press, 1975'. Similarly, despite the fact that on the *Fluxshoe* tour, Fisher read extracts from *Collision, Blood Bone Brain, Place, Creek in the Ceiling Beam, Winter Solstice* and *Sicily*, none of these other works appears on the list as part of the Fluxus canon listed by *The Fluxus Reader*.

As if in anticipation of the *Fluxus Reader's* mistake over his identity, the cover of *Prosyncel* (1975) has a picture of 'Allen Fischer on coach outing commemorating his retirement'.[12] To confuse matters further, Fisher also published under the pseudonym Thomas Net and signed some of his letters to David Mayor as from 'Aleister Fissure'.[13] Ephemeral broadsheets such as Mike Dobbie's 'Mugshots' (1976) mystified his identity further by leaving a space blank for signing by the author.[14] Mistakes in the bibliography of the *Fluxus Reader* emphasize the play characteristic of Fisher's involvement with *Fluxshoe*. This attitude is continued in a number of works by Fisher which approach the making of visual art, publishing and writing as provisional acts, or performances which necessarily call into question the role of the writer or artist.

For Eric Mottram there was a direct connection between the role of the artist in performance and the role of the poet in the procedural text. In an interview with Fisher he remarks that 'what these *Fluxshoe* performances are doing is concealing the artist inside in a very similar way' to the way in which the poet is also concealed in the 'relationship between systems and interferences of the systems' in the [procedural] poem.[15] 'Now you don't know if an artist is involved' Fisher remarks in response. His answer highlights Fisher's interest in the use of performance and writing to efface rather than to promote the figure of the artist in relation to the work. Similarly, many of Fisher's early works seek to deny their own copyright: 'This edition is not copyright the author and director of co-ordination who is Allen Fisher' (Fisher, *Sicily*). Others replace copyright with the possibility of a gift to the participants of the performance: 'Anti-Copyright: a copy of the resulting poem will be sent FREE to anyone leaving their name & address / this poem may be repeated at anytime with different rules without rules…' ('Milk in Bottles', Performance Flyer, 1973). This strategy is in keeping with the explicit intention of many contemporary Conceptual and Fluxus artists to remove art from the commodity system by dematerialising its status as an object that could be bought and sold.[16]

---

12 On the back cover is an extract from *The Listener*, 26th April, 1973 which records a Dr. Fisher's contribution to the study of 'the biology of the female orgasm'.

13 See the David Mayor Collection, Harvey Kreitman Archive, Tate Gallery, London.

14 The copy I have is signed Allen Smith.

15 Eric Mottram, *Interview with Fluxshoe group (Opal L. Nations, Allen Fisher and Doug Lang)*. The Poetry Society London, 1973. Tape Cassette. Kings College London.

16 See Lucy Lippard, *Six Years: The Dematerialization of the Art Object from 1966-1972*.

This distancing of the poet or artist from the authorship of the work is often at odds with the fact that this authorship is made explicit again in the body of the performer at a live-event. Andreas Huyssen identifies this trope as a major contradiction at the heart of Fluxus. For Huyssen 'The high-modernist notion of individualised artistic expression based on a transcendent vision' is replaced in Fluxus with 'a focus on the *évenement trouvé*' only to find itself "caught" in the "paradox", that 'the "found event" from everyday life still needed the artist as a medium to stage and perform it' (149). The goal, however, for Fluxus artists was not that these *évenement trouvés* should be taken out *from* everyday life and performed by the artist but rather that they should continue to exist as events within the everyday, as Raoul Vaneigem described, as 'situations to be lived' (Vaneigem, 149).

In Fisher's work the exploration of these 'situations to be lived' involves strategies of durational performance both in the writing and in the live reading of the work. Each informed the development of the other. During the period of *Fluxshoe* Fisher's performances followed two broadly distinguishable methodologies. The processual accrual and superimposition in performance of the sequence *Blood Bone Brain* is in marked contrast to the procedural operations of 'Milk In Bottles', which he performed as part of the *Fluxshoe* tour in Croydon in January 1973. At this event Fisher invited each participant to drink from a milk bottle, the contents of which was then measured 'to the nearest centimetre (or number of fingers laid horizontally)' and 'the resulting number' became 'a CODE used to extract a WORD from the newspaper'.[17] These words were then compiled on a blackboard until the board was full. Participants continued to add and subtract from the words on the board through further milk drinking and measuring to create a poem. Fisher determined to record the poem 'in multiples of 5 minutes multiplied by the number of letters in the first word at the top left'.[18]

In its reliance on chance operations in relation to a limited range of data available for recombination as a poem or as a final text, this performance

---

University of California Press, 1997. Fluxus itself was in a contradictory position in relation to this because many Fluxus artists made objects and multiples specifically to be sold. For many, especially British artists, the 'obscurity' that Simon Anderson identified was the price paid for remaining outside the art market.

17 Fisher, Allen. *Milk In Bottles*, Performance handout, Edible Magazine, 1972.

18 Ibid.

echoes some aspects of the procedural works of Jackson Mac Low and John Cage. This procedural performance is in marked contrast to the organic evolution of text in performance that was occurring in Fisher's work throughout the *Fluxshoe* festival in the performance of his linked poem sequence: *Blood Bone Brain*. The performance of *Blood Bone Brain* combined and recombined a variety of texts that included: *Creek in the Ceiling Beam, Sicily* and *Ffacece*. The first performances and writing cycle of *Blood Bone Brain* began in 1972 and continued for 39 weeks on the Fluxshoe tour (*Blood Bone Brain*: London Performance 'A', Programme Fragments, 1974). Every Sunday, Fisher recorded 'various subjective estimates' of his brain, heart and bone condition 'together with what he felt were related factors, such as temperature and place' (*Blood Bone Brain*: London Performance 'A', Programme Fragments, 1974). The texts were performed at *Fluxshoe* as communal and participatory events for multiple voices in which Fisher also made use of recording technologies, slides and music:

> …next, allen, felipe, paul and his wife Judith, read from al's poem CREEK IN THE CEILING BEAM as part of his BLOOD BONE BRAIN for four voices and a backing tape loop of piano notes, F.F.A.C.E.C.E., voices changing in loudness according to suit turned up on a pack of cards (spades=quite soft, etc., Felipe is handed a joker . . . !) . . . the voices are recorded for 23 minutes, then the recordings are re-recorded while Steve, aged 8, urges everyone to play 'snap' with him and al's pack of 1920's nude lady cards (Mayor, 'Add End A').

The performance of *Blood Bone Brain* included selections from 78rpm records chosen to evoke 'nostalgia', slides of 'local sites' and of various objects preserved in jars, and word 'accumulations' from John Buchan's novel *39 Steps* (*Prosyncel*, 16).

The slides of objects include the following titles:

Sentimental Jar One, Tulse Hill, potato, 1965
Norbury Ironwork, found in hen house, 1964
14. 'Money I can't spend', 1970-73
17. 'Boiled Clock', *Creek in the Ceiling Beam*, 1972
28. Reversal Jar, hair rollers immersed in shampoo
31. Light switch bulb with candle and torch, for Jackson Mac Low,

1973.
37. Shagjam, 1972

The lists of titles form subsequent texts for performance that might exist with or without their original objects.[19] In Blackburn in July 1973 Fisher incorporated the recordings of his earlier performance of *Blood Bone Brain* into a new performance and combined it with a reading from *Sicily* (published in the Autumn of 1973). The audience were invited to participate: 'The performers will be reading from the sheets from the as yet uncompleted book event "Sicily". The audience may read from the sheets "Creek In The Ceiling Beam"' (Mayor, 'Add End A'). Rather than the occasion for a static and finished poem, the performance of *Blood Bone, Brain* at *Fluxshoe* extends and shapes the emerging page-based text that will later evolve into *Place*. Throughout *Fluxshoe* his multiple works on the page exist in fluid relation to one another and offer different possibilities for recombination, superimposition and layering in a live context.[20]

Other performances for the *Fluxshoe* tour find their way into the synthesis of materials that make up *Place*. 'The author's preface' in *Unpolished Mirrors* has some conceptual similarities to a performance / bookart project carried out by Mayor and Chadwick at the *Fluxshoe* event in Croydon. Chadwick and Mayor produced a book of photographs that combine two sequences of images that run from the front of the book to the back and from the back to the front on alternating pages. Each sequence of 1–15 images is a record of the walk by the

---

19 *Blood Bone Brain* was eventually published in 1982 as a series of texts that were accompanied by images of the slides on microfiche inserts. See *Prosyncel* p. 16: 'BLOOD BONE BRAIN is the most eclectic of the projects encompassing book and environmental work; process and systems; documentation; writing, sound and graphics; printing and filming. It is the product of earlier work & conceived as such. The book work forms "D" in what I called "a series of three lettered 'ABCD'". The first sets were: A. *Ffacece*, dealing with graphics, printing, system and process; B. *creek in the ceiling beam*, covering documentation, process, system, writing, filming, printing, graphics and conceptualising; C. *Sicily*, covering system, process, printing and writing. The environmental work extended out of the live performance of the Musics made from A & B, and the writing out of B & C, and the system-concepts and processes used in ABC (and its recycling)'.

20 There is a characteristic fluidity to the directions at the beginning of *Plans: Blood Bone Brain, Documents One '72-74* (Spanner, London, 1981) which reads '…included also may be the tapes of Sicily readings as underlay to all three sets'.

photographer across a courtyard with a door at either end. Chadwick stands in front of both doors as the object in focus common to the two different records of perspective. In a possible echo of this performance bookwork in *Place*, in 'The Author's Preface' Fisher describes:

> the notion
> to draw knowledge
> afforded of a room by mirrors fixed on opposite walls
> which reflect each other
> without being parallel

> then move

> suddenly

The poet, the document and the documentary about documentation

CRIS CHEEK

Allen Fisher's body of work, which is to say his life, as a publisher, a teacher, an essayist, a poet, a painter and a performance writer, can be productively understood as a network of speculative creative praxes, generating overlapping domains of documentary resonance and layers of documentary evidence through a prolific output of visual art, poetry and performance, both on and off *the page*.

Fisher's way of working through evidence of engagement with documents, in such ways that hold some of the earth around the root, is obvious from an early publication such as *Thomas Net's Tree Birst*.[1] The title page provides its frame, 'a cold Auto-Destructive Text of Helen Darbishire's Oxford Edition William Wordsworth's 1850 version "The Prelude – Book First".' One text has been *found* inside another text, a poeisis broadly contemporary with other document-redaction projects such as Tom Phillips's *The Humument* and Ron Johnson's *Rad Ios*. Choosing the pseudonym of a character named Net, working through the image of a decentered variable margin text understood visually as a burst tree 'objecting this life,' Fisher produces a network of spatially broken stanzas, drawn from the well of another poet, that foregrounds framing elements often taken for granted, such as 'publisher,' 'edition,' 'author function,' and 'version' as integral to its compositional intent.

Without explicitly using the term document, this found poem, as with all found poems, projects a documentary poetics. One document is indebted to another document and openly acknowledged to be so. Were it an isolated instance in Fisher's earlier work we might remain less certain of his commitment to performing acts of writing through performances of reading, but other significant works from this period, *Creek in the Ceiling Beam* (1972) and *FFACECE* (1972), contain almost everything, barring full dietary disclosures and suchlike, that you might need to know about the production of the document, including production material costs and location, working notes, drafts, comments from other readers during the process of composition included as part

---

[1] Fisher, Allen. *Thomas Net's Tree Birst*. (London: Poisonous Edition, 1970)

of the composition, contextual observations, and product information that might and might not be pertinent; in other words the document includes documentation as an intrinsic component of its composition.

Almost all of his poetry since that time appears alongside lists of sources and resources. He openly acknowledges his indebtedness, the aforementioned *Thomas Net's Tree Birst* is partly in homage to the auto-destructive artist Gustav Metzger, for example, as well as to the work with the found in William Burroughs's cut-ups. And what we can now call an inter-textual poetics is extended to include a dialectic tension among his poems in extended sequences, alongside an interest in unconventional rhyme, as a formal device to achieve versioning within the poems themselves, among stanzas, and among lines within and between stanzas.

*

I want to begin with a little bit of personal recollection that might provide a useful way into Allen Fisher's ludic work, his prolific output, and his importance as a hub of influences and references within British poetry over the past sixty years. I will continue by transcribing and engaging with video documentation from a performance given in tandem with an exhibition at Froebel College in 2002 and conclude with some thoughts about how we might use such a document to understand his documentary poetics.

It might have been in 1976 or '77 and I'd been invited over to Allen Fisher's house in south London. I have no clear memory what the occasion was. In all likelihood it was just a typically friendly and generous gesture on Allen's part. He was in many ways an instant friend and peer, also a mentor, a teacher, who has amplified his lifelong work in the broadest possible sense of pedagogy. He was living on a London Borough of Lambeth council housing estate, just off Brixton Hill, tucked away behind the prison, a handful of miles south of the Thames. I think it might have been that he was keen to share some d.i.y. perfect book-binding techniques he had developed for a series of beautifully rendered Exclusive Mimeographed Masterpieces by fellow poets such as Bill Griffiths, Bill Sherman, Eric Mottram, Barry MacSweeney, Tony Lopez and Pierre Joris, in the series and that he was publishing under a New London Pride imprint. The series remains an exemplary, perfect-bound, public-housing industry; 1970s mimeo books at their finest.

London Pride is the name of a distinctive, champion, *best bitter*, brewed by Fullers, that 'gives the sensation of angels dancing on the tongue,' not a bad way into Allen's work itself. The quotation is courtesy of the beer critic Stephen Cox, but it's not exactly *New* London Pride. On the other hand, the imprint's name might have been a reference to Noel Coward's lyric 'London Pride has been handed down to us, London Pride is a flower that's free' – perhaps a pithy summary of Allen's lifelong commitment to political, social and cultural affiliations and variant philosophies of the commons. New London Pride then ought no longer be handed down to us as a stultifying binding of ancestry so much as the subject of something that we would continually refashion to contemporary purpose and renew as part of an urgent and never complete discussion about *human freedom*.

In any case it was tough not having books as one focus of conversation, since there were piles of these publications among various imprints in varying states of construction and completion around the apartment, books gifted by fellow poets, books he was reading in earnest as part of his often autodidactic poetic research, books he was referencing in overlapping domains of poetic composition, and it's important once again to catch this body of work that Allen Fisher has been producing for the past fifty years as an extraordinarily interwoven mesh of attentions led by acts of reading and performances of interpretation. The ground-breaking handwritten wheeling page of notes lifted out of Charles Olson's *Maximus Poems* with the phrase 'This is the Rose' almost at its epicentre hung framed on the wall. I have partly and inadequately produced a reductive transcription: 'the completed picture./Consciousness Mind/always invades/opposes successfully/the Previous./The <u>other</u>/location./This is the Rose/of the/World' circles the phrases at the hub of Olson's poem.[2] Fisher was at that time enmeshed in sequences of open field poems, combining processual documentary and procedural compositional flights and constraints, gathered under the sky of one title, *Place*, clearly in open conversation with Olson's documentary project.

There were precarious stacks of vinyl 45s; part of an extensive collection of and enthusiasm for the *blues*, an important fire source not just for the *British* '60s blues boom from the Graham Bond Experience

---

[2] Charles Olson, *The Maximus Poems* (Berkeley, CA, Los Angeles, CA, & London: University of California Press, 1983) p.479

to Cream, but more importantly an influence on his compacted turns of poetic phrase. There were materials related to painting and paintings in process and progress, partly constructed frames, and sketches for what he was working on at that time. Fisher has been increasingly recognized and exhibited as a fine painter, making it unsurprising that in the poems he is frequently an astonishing image-maker. Prominent in my memory are several large screw-top glass jars, the kind of display containers used to hold loose candy in corner-street convenience stores at that time. Except these jars were not holding conventional sweets. One I remember well was at least halfway full of sardine cans. The cans were opened and the fish usually preserved inside in olive oil had been eaten, or so I presumed for Allen doesn't have a tendency to want to waste anything. And now those sardine containers were inside a further container, and floating like stuffed empties behind glass, in engine oil. Not oil cans but cans in oil. The can and cannot of which marry the bureaucratic and the literary. The fish consumed, the containers filed, and yet that subsequent filing has taken place through a material associated with movement, with locomotion. Vernacular forms between the containers and the contained have moved on, some form of consciousness remains.

I am going to propose that we think about those sardine cans in oil that I saw at Allen's flat in 1976-77, piled on pile into a glass jar, held together higgledy-piggledy with their adjacencies and ordering proximities determined by gravity's shape, as documents. I need a little help to make that claim viable, and I lean on two important names connected with the European modernist documentarian group that foreshadow information science in beginning to do so.

Firstly the Belgian documentarian Paul Otlet included objects as documents in his 1934 *Traité de documentation*, to the extent that they could be considered to capture an expression of human thought in any form, using any media. Why is it the case, he asks, that when a person's work is archived, their papers and the objects from their life are separated out. Why are objects not considered texts, correspondences, forms of thinking, and why are texts not considered as objects perhaps. Objects themselves ought to be understood as documents, and the idea of housing such a complex of documents alongside each other, exemplified in his proposals for a *Mundaneum*, anticipate the hyperlinked network of things in vogue eighty years later. Secondly, in overlapping orbit with Otlet, the French modernist documentarian Suzanne Briet published

What is Documentation in 1951, and her document quietly contests the positivist advocacy of information science by bringing *valid knowledge* into intimate dialogue with *empirical evidence*. In what is also now heralded as a prescient publication she proposes that a definition of documentation include:

> all concrete or symbolic indexical signs [indice], preserved or recorded toward the ends of representing, of reconstituting, or of proving a physical or intellectual phenomenon.

She continues:

> Is a star a document? Is a pebble rolled by a torrent a document? Is a living animal a document? No. But some documents are: the photographs and the catalogues of stars, stones in a museum of mineralogy, and animals that are catalogued and shown in a zoo.[3]

Briet challenged orthodox limitations as to what might and what might not be considered an object of study, but her "No" here, to me, seems almost quaint in the contemporary moment. It has, I think, been contested by forms of indirect testimony (the tape recorder for example) and more thoroughly by new and emergent media that enable the documentation of a living animal or a star to be studied. Even a pebble rolled by a torrent might be examined for before and after evidence; even a pebble rolled by a torrent leaves another kind of mark in its wake, and that mark is a document of its rolling. A cave can be mapped by millions of data points for further study and so on.

Through both Otlet and Briet we can begin to understand the sense of conscious documentary poetic intention in Fisher's objects. Further examples I remember around Allen's apartment include a jar holding a rotting pear labelled *Lumb Bank Pear* and *Tulse Hill Potato* (1965) that he calls a *sentimental jar*,[4] leading to the idea that these are bottled things paradoxically intended to keep a memory open. They can be considered as prompts for conversation, as souvenirs of the moment,

---

[3] Suzanne Briet, *Qu'est-ce que la documentation?* (Paris: Éditions Documentaires Industrielles et Techniques, 1951) p.7. A translation into English by Ronald E. Day and Laurent Martinet is hosted at: http://ella.slis.indiana.edu/~roday/briet.htm

[4] Allen Fisher, *Prosyncel* (Vancouver, BC: Strange Faeces Press, 1975) p.15

as *objets trouvés*, as documents of events, as metaphors for something elsewhere, as *aides de mémoires*, as embodying technologies for knowing something; all in a clear tradition of the art object, stretching back at least as far as the *Wunderkammern*, except that these pieces were not gathered in a discreet cabinet so much as integrated with an open field of the creative everyday in the sense of a home not as a museum but as a living archive. Such objects occupy a place in that 1960s international industrialized nation-state network of interdisciplinary artists known as *Fluxus*, and indeed Allen's work is partly housed among and grounded in such artistic company. Fluxus foregrounded demotic performances, through which objects became both material and inspiration for composition; object-object juxtapositions and object-title interrelations generated strangeness, objects changed status through time.

They were objects in flux, and they brought perspective to the flows of human attentions. Poems and paintings and sound compositions understood as presenting objects of study to be referenced, but also occasions of aesthetic engagement combining into flows of emergent composition. The poem is an object in flux; it is neither completely stable nor completely unstable. The poem is a visual object, and it can be a sound object. The poem documents the ongoing struggles to apprehend syncretic links using processes of proprioception. The poem embodies the illusive curiosity and immersion of the quest.

*

The following transcription is from a documentary video, whose documentarian is Paige Mitchell, presenting a behind-the-scenes glimpse into Fisher conducting an archaeological study on his own practice followed by a live drawing performance, a reading, interventions and re-reading. I was unable to attend the event and my account is wholly dependent upon the document. Para spaces I have inserted approximate breaks in the spoken.

VOLE VOLESPIN: an installation and performance by Allen Fisher at Lulham studios, Froebel College, 7th May 2002, published by Root & Branch videotape in 2003.[5]

---

[5] VOLE VOLESPIN: an installation and performance by Allen Fisher at Lulham studios, Froebel College, 7th May 2002, published by Root & Branch videotape in 2003.

[transcription begins]

Fisher: D'you think?

Mitchell: Tell me about it.

Fisher: Well the show is trying to bring together two sets of studies, which will culminate in single sets of paintings

and the two sets of studies are the watercolour studies, done in correspondence with Clive Bush's poems and Nicholas Poussin's paintings

and the other studies are trap studies, they're drawings which I'm going to integrate across these images . . or some of these drawings already are destined to be integrated into technical drawings of traps, and you'll see elsewhere in the exhibition actual traps that I'm using as the basis for drawings, like the badger trap, mouse trap, rat trap that you see elsewhere in the space

and then I'm also trying to reconcile the fact that all of these subjects, both traps and their different interfaces are cropping up in different ways, metonymically and actually in the poetry that I'm writing and you'll see exhibitions of some of the poetry also as a consequence

and also I'll show some of the drawings that were made of four trap studies which overlap so to speak the technical drawings

and to get a full visual explanation of these concepts one would need a show about four times bigger than this

but that's the position so far. So it's just a sample, a set of samplings.

And I'm going to open at least one bottle, I know of at least two people that are going to come.

—The camera tightens into a close up of a rectangular slip of paper instruction headed 'TRIP TRAP,'

'kind to your fingers
even kinder to your mouse'

with instructions for baiting and setting, checking and release, alongside an actual baited snap trap for mice made by VICTOR, painted with a sculpted shape of yellow cheese onto the wood.

—*We hear a cork being pulled from a bottle.*

Mitchell: In what way are these trap drawings?

Fisher: They're drawn of situations of trapped visual imagery. A city traps images, for instance. Certain shaped streets don't change much or certain shapes of window or certain shapes of structures of that kind trap image shapes, image forms, and image potentials. They're all cityscapes. There are many more trap studies of figures.

—*The video jump cuts, into activity in front of a seated audience later that evening.*

Fisher is preparing, hovering at the edge of the screen with his back to the audience moving behind a blue cord hung over an easel with the cord acting like a fourth wall, creating a studio as a stage bringing witnesses into a recreated site of his process. The layout of the stage with multiple easels reminds me of a scene from Tony Hancock's movie *The Rebel* in which Hancock has been taking evening art classes and when his landlady knocks on his door to collect his late rent he opens it to reveal a room jammed higgledy-piggledy with easels. The landlady asks him with some consternation what he's doing in there, eyeing a painting on the wall. 'That is a self-portrait' he replies, 'who of?' she utters in hilarious confusion and dismay.[6]

—*There is a cut in the video to the opening performance for the exhibition, and the playback of Fisher's recorded voice reading a text which functions as a prologue to the overall performance has already begun. At the moment of this cut, which I think is an in-camera cut, the performance document exhibits a recorded discontinuity of his*

---

[6] Robert Day, *The Rebel*. Associated British Picture Corporation, 1961. The film was released as *Call Me Genius* in the USA.

voice, so that we do not hear the beginning of him speaking, unless the recording of him speaking has been deliberately cut so as to stage an entry *in media res*. Attempting an accurate transcription of the short text that follows there are potential layers of noise in play, such as the quality of the recording and the quality of the sound relay into this new audio space. We hear the effect of the quality of the microphone on the camera, the additional impact of DVD copying on overall resolution and the quality of the laptop computer speakers from which I am attempting the transcription. I hear something close to:

one end [or the other end] secured to the bank. The poultry of the few branches hid a small end to prevent the railings coming off

cold water animals when caught in traps plunge into deep water immediately and the rear of the trap chain slightly down the hole as it's impossible for the captured animal to again regain the shore

in order to make this outfit more certain that our generals such as otters and beavers a stone of six or eight pounds should be tied firmly to the chain but not to interfere with the trap to the action of the circle

—The idea of the trap is one way of considering performance, particularly when viewed through the lens of the spectacle. (Raoul Vaneigem from the Situationist International lurks with glittering menace here). The performer can be understood as a captured animal, subjugated to the gaze of those seeking to evaluate performative activity against forms and norms of competence measured against competitive criteria, and the structure of the spectacle can be understood as a trap in which both performers and spectators are caught and complicit.

—The voice of Fisher performing the function of a prologue on tape falls silent and the pre-recorded sound of a person drawing begins. Unless the sound has been programmed we are listening to a person and not a machine drawing. The sonic embodied, even though it could be adroitly programmed to *sound* embodied. The sound of chalk or charcoal making sweeping rhythmic strokes, big and quick open gestures; the kind of gestures that might be used for filling in an existing outline. But Fisher has not turned towards the audience, except that he is busy behind the nearest easel to his entrance and clearly also working on the far side of that easel. The audience cannot see what kinds of marks he's also making. The sound of pre-recorded drawing and of drawing occurring in the room form an overlapping domain, with awareness of being a watcher or a witness to what we think we perceive.

— The camera widens its focus, and we can see now that there are six easels, all in portrait format literally strung across the space. They might be understood both as an entrapment of the audience and / or as a trap for the performer Allen Fisher and or an entanglement of both. He moves most of his body beyond the frame of the easel he has been working on, standing alongside it but with his left arm and hand still drawing. He stops drawing live but the pre-recorded sound of drawing carries on.

— Fisher shifts to the adjacent easel and performs a similar sequence of actions. He is looking at the audience as if he might be attempting a portrait of an audience. The rhythm of his drawing is more open, as if he is attentive to and responding to a rhythm of thinking and observation and reflection. He is hearing the sound of drawing whilst drawing. He might be depicting something else such as an internal state or a state of observing or a state of not seeing in order to see in another fashion. He repeats this concentration from left to right along the line, across the sequence of easels.

— The camera moves behind the easel line, and we can see he is making marks. He is using charcoal on white paper. Each easel is marked with a fresh charcoal stick and he's using thick charcoal, about half an inch diameter. The drawings take form around a vertical axis, an asemic line moving from top to bottom almost in a column but jagging out and flowering around that notional column into striking totemic gestures and figurative features that strike out and pose before being drawn back in. Fisher is looking at the audience as a subject and ostensibly not *looking* at the marks he is making and breaking the habits of tracing as he makes them. These are a highly energised and compelling set of drawings.

— The blue nylon cord (thin blue line) vibrates between the easel he is working on and its closest neighbour. He subsequently moves back along that line using a graphite pencil to add a further mark to each drawing. All this while we are hearing the sound of recorded drawing actions, and now that resonance has moved from the tone of charcoal to graphite. He moves back along the line of blue rope again, using thinner charcoal (I think). When the pre-recorded tape of the sound of drawing stops playing he stops drawing, wipes his hands. Still standing in a roped-off area behind the blue line between himself and those witnessing his performance he addresses his audience, offering an introduction to the poems he is about to read:

'It comes out of Nietzsche, it's the burglar that steals your consciousness and might send you to sleep if you like but it's also the burglar that might start interfering with your dna. You might catch some notions of paradise, which are quoted from *Moby Dick*, and the idea of a ploughman is somebody who used to live down the road from me, that is to say *Piers Ploughman*, William Langland's 11th–12th century work. Needless to say i wasn't around at the time. The Moorman is the writer of a work on trapping from the 19th century and i need to say that in case you think I'm talking about religious persuasion. And i think trapping gravity comes into this discussion because I'm interested in the discussion that critiques the ideas of coherence and comes much more fully into a critique of the concept of the idea of completion or uniqueness. The third piece has interruptions and those interruptions are designed in a part of the earlier part of the work. And all of these works link, rhythmically or visually or in other ways of rhyme, with earlier parts of the sequence, but you don't need to worry about that, unless you've read the earlier parts.'

Beginning with a classic storyteller's rhetorical device 'There was once a town...', he reads *Vole*,[7] in its entirety, printed oversize on loose A2 sized sheets instead of read out of a bound volume.

The poem contains, or threatens to release, many themes already familiar to readers of Fisher's work: the idea of the garden, the figures of *a* burglar and *the* blacksmith, the tension between *free will* and *the commons*, the impossibility and undesirability of completion.

Vole is organized through four sequentially numbered sections in the

---

[7] Allen Fisher, *Entanglement*. (Willowdale, ONT: The Gig, 2004). All of the texts Fisher reads and rereads during this performance are from this volume.

form of long sentences. Sentences run across breaks between chunks of lines we might call stanzas but there is no regularity or overall pattern of length for these stanzas. Some punctuation is providing by line endings, but within and among those lines both a reader on a page and a listener in a room must navigate their own sense of where to pause and how to place emphases. In his live version Fisher extemporizes commentary, inserts asides into the printed text. He plays the tempo of the poem like an instrument and performs a live reading, a living interpretation. He breaks the frame of the printed document somewhat, including and embracing occasional mis-readings that bring their own additional meaning, for example 'Employment' corrected to 'Enjoyment' that completes the line at the start of which it appears ('Enjoyment of activity enslaves') quite differently.

Vole is followed by a variant *Volespin*, and once more asides are inserted and the titles make kinship adamant. However, there is an important difference in the way that the personal pronoun is used. *Vole* stages a self through quotation, 'In no Paradise myself/I am impatient of all misery …' whereas *Volespin* includes personalized observation from its first line, 'Flew from my bike,' projecting a self, thrown into the empirical. Besides being linked by their titles the two poems are imbricated, and in dynamic tension, with this second poem projecting a more deliberatively lyric persona, tending towards an immersive swoon.

The final poem is a sequence called *X-Buckle*. Fisher introduces that by saying 'and it has these interruptions.' Immediately the screen goes blank. We see screen static, a brief glimpse of him turning a page, more screen static and an announcement:

We regret that we are unable to bring you X-Buckle at this time. We will restore normal service as soon as possible.

A break in proceedings follows, an intermission for wine and conversation, during which Fisher's voice can be heard reading a prose discourse on traps broadcast from a self-contained speaker amplifier in the space amongst the conversing audience. Foreground and background are being smudged here, attention and awareness being teased. The camera roves from one drawing produced during the initial section of the sequential performance to another drawing to another drawing. They are complex drawings and my own sense of figuration and energised portraiture remains. The drawings catch the occasion and his perception of the witnesses to this occasion. The idea of both a drawing and a text AS a trap and a snare persists here. Traps of habitual engagement, traps of linguistic limitation, traps of compositional trope, consistent with one of his daily practices in which he makes a small drawing to start the day, without looking at the drawing as he is making it, but drawing something out the moments of his emergence from sleep.

After the interval Fisher re-emerges wearing headphones. In the tape edit he is caught mid-flight talking about the performance of reiteration, listening to a recording of himself reading a text and the consequence of trying to keep pace with them, replace them or ignore them at the same time as listening and at the same time as repeating what he is hearing. 'The consequence is improvisation,' he says, 'although some people might argue about that definition.'

He begins to read, speaking aloud as he listens to himself through the headphones reading, and the videographer documents the subtle differences as we are taken on a tour of speculations by which material forms of poetry, the interpretative strategies and the circulation of poetic texts *can* become stable and authoritative tools for perceptual analysis. I am ignoring line breaks in my transcription of what follows:

So this is Vole, no it's not this is Volespin flew from my, this is Volespin flew from my bike lilac crimson gold semi-circles of petals beneath dahlias with twelve inch blossoms severed raw hymn simply fragrance frozen refuse root canal connection to ph of bacterial population

sitting in the garden is wonderful we are surrounded by pears and hedge sirens motor roars and bees everyone talks of rest here but seems very busy (audience laughter) freedom and truth seem to be the discourse analysis of mesmerized desire is escaping here gravity theatre introduces another dapple medley takes the cedar out of contemplation's garden storm field William Blake takes a tracing grinds it to his head pain irritation redefined as a row of alternative solutions

(the most divergence between what is printed/published, previously read as part of this event, and what is spoken, occurs around these following three sections)

i open my mobile instead of a packet of pills an apple falls it turns into plastics golden coins become

another narrative another burn of busses and beans before the cloud shifts another crowd-out give me air another breath

begin construction begin formalities spade into soil soil mixed with sandstone patches of root growth decomposed animal behind choices sheened a gardener weariness above the choice raft showers into the earth torns watch the responses to light there hesitates crumps rainfall into crevices dried burn there in sunshine the creation of new presence a refreshed humanity

my eyes started to water i smelt a sweet fruity odour thought it was harmless tears of pectin the pitching of two singularities pushed through my eyelids caught in a tear trap

to make probability judge to make correct probability judgments relations among concepts a truth statement about degrees of confirmation as a matter of rules linked to language

you can wash your clothes you can't wash your lungs…

Fisher is caught largely in the trap of repeating the majority of his own poem verbatim. And yet there is a shift in phrasing and line ending brought about by the intervention of listening and of temporal context. Potential line endings wobble between speaking and listening, between trying to repeat and keeping up to the speed of what has become now a form of secondary witness, a spoken original on tape being treated as a text to be reread. All manner of interplay with discourses well rehearsed by commentators such as Ong, Havelock, and McLuhan on the borderlines among forms of orality and forms of textuality as technologies for documentation and communication are being danced around.

Fisher reads *Vole* in the same format. The entire event is being worked as a quasi mirror form, although the texts are not moving backwards towards a mirror of the beginning.

The gambit places an enormous amount of pressure onto the act of listening. His own performance of listening alongside performances of audience attention, speaking both to a specific cultural moment of composition as well as to the present revisited; listening for subtle deviations, listening for bumps and swerves in his performance, listening for rephrasing, listening for detailed replacements of emphasis. The whole explores the stability of his texts. He is over-writing them, our collective and biologically individuated memories of them, our sense of how they flow in our bodies. He is re-writing them, live on live, recorded on live, and live on printed; he is making a version, he is mediating and remediating the scene of writing. He is testing them and he is also emptying them out of their potential meanings, somewhat reminiscent as a tactic from Fluxus events perhaps.

The event ends, Fisher's performance is greeted enthusiastically by extensive applause.

But the video enters a final batch of footage:

Thanks to help from the future, we are now able to bring you

X-Buckle

"a poem in 19 stanzas

read against 19 drawings

by allen fisher

Each stanza is read juxtaposed with a different drawing. The drawings are not the same drawings as shown onscreen during the Froebel College event. A further temporal shift is in play.

[end of transcription]

*

In retrospect the sequence of events represented through the documentation of VOLE VOLESPIN does not occur in the chronological order that would seem to have been intended. Linear temporality is punctured, and teleology arrives damaged. Human-machine memory remains incomplete, partial and faulty, subject to interruption, significantly intangible.

Performance overlaps with exhibition to such an extent that the video document does not have a clear conclusion. Something is missing, either through the kind of accident that is not accident or else exhausted, as out there in the darkness, beyond the constraints of the Froebel studio, regrouping for another day.

Generative questions about the material status of documents and documentation are posed during the course of the filming and postproduction of this event. We are left with a composite of performances, as a form of complex document, offering no closure, and transmitting just one framed point of view. The decision to produce documentation of the event is obviously preconceived, and Paige Mitchell's presence as documentarian is integral to the productive tensions between that which was planned and that which actually occurs. The entire process of production offers a kind of drill into Fisher's practice, and an enormous amount of data about poeisis is networked through its editing and presentation as a publication. Diverse documents have been witnessed being produced live, the process of their fabrication made evident. Indicative archival materials have been prepared in advance; tapes of pre-recorded reading of printed texts, as well as the carefully devised staging and site-specific constraints of the whole. Momentary drawings, and recordings of Fisher's situated reading, and the re-reading of printed texts whilst simultaneously listening to his initial sited reading, are layers of imminent action. Reading as a performance of interpretation, even of mediation on the threshold between what are conventionally considered the process and the product, the doing and the done, the saying and the said, the writing and the read, construct place.

The base text of *Vole* includes lines that suggest meta-narrative observations that help clue and cue us into ways that both the performer and the audience might navigate this event as a document, and how its composition plays into discourses concerning discontinuity and continuity, closure, variation and stable order. For example:

The Moorman uses nonlinear analysis
to examine recorded succession

. . .

Each object's information demands
deaccession, broken egg shells
to analyse connection residues between

. . .

Actions are partly indeterminate to
which becoming clings to distinct moments, condensed
matter digested into movements of
response passed through the meshes
of natural necessity, free from the particular
rhythm which grades the flow in such a
way that sensible qualities, in memory-perception,
particulate aspects of successive reality.

. . .

They watch the collision again
and watch account of its repetition
in a pie chart, a Boltzmann truth
a prediction of text before it is read

. . .

Juxtaposition of dialectical statements held in tension among lines to create a wobble between senses of scale is one important source of pleasure in Fisher's poems. Readers are thrown into gaps among productive affects. Seeking to learn more about Bolzmann, for example, I am connected to the following seemingly 'tell it like it is' quotation attributed to him, 'if you are out to describe the truth leave elegance to the tailor.' Fisher's spectral fashioning of truth accumulates resonance through a joyful and dizzying proliferation of uncertainties. Both within each aspect of each piece of work, at the level of compositional detail, as well as among the works and the aesthetic disciplines they contest on a larger scale, I experience his work's embodiment of a passionately humorous engagement with the concept of the search, and with the inevitability of, not finding absolute answers, so much as generating additional questions each of which has specific context. Although both a writer and a reader, a painter and an improvisatory performer can be considered as technicians, something is missing, and or ghosted as linked to between the document and the documentary. The poetry of Allen Fisher seeks to apprehend variant imperfect forms through which he tunes in to that incompletion.

Chreods, Catastrophes and Fractals: 'The Mathematics of Rimbaud' and *Brixton Fractals*

STEVEN HITCHINS

In 1982, Allen Fisher began work on *Gravity as a consequence of shape*, the long poetic sequence which would be published in separate editions or 'showings' as it developed over the next 25 years. The first showings appeared in 1983 with the publication of 'African Boog' and 'Banda', both subsequently collected in *Brixton Fractals* in 1985. Prior to these earliest showings from the sequence, Fisher's essay 'The Mathematics of Rimbaud' appeared in *Reality Studios* in 1980. It has since been reprinted in *Future Exiles* (1992) and *The Topological Shovel* (1999). This essay provides an insight into Fisher's thinking around the time when he began working on *Gravity as a consequence of shape* and introduces many of the key scientific concepts which would later appear in *Brixton Fractals* and throughout the *Gravity* sequence.

Fisher conceptualised the overall procedure of the sequence by constructing a 'Fibonacci cylinder', a tube of cardboard from a kitchen roll marked off into ratios according to the Fibonacci series, and then crushing it in a vice. The crushed cylinder offers a way of visualising the structures of the seemingly random or chaotic forms of the poems. Fisher takes the ideal form of the Fibonacci series, long used by artists, architects and poets as a set of 'perfect' proportions, and fractalises it. The Fibonacci cylinder is an image of symmetry, the crushed cylinder an image of randomness. It shows that even as random an act as crushing a cylinder produces a set of mathematical proportions. By considering catastrophe theory, we will see that even the apparently random shape of such an irregular object is determined by numerous minute variables. The shape could have turned out in many indeterminate ways depending on such variables as the force with which it is squashed, the weight applied, the angle, the surface. The use of such notions from science might allow us to consider seemingly random poetic forms as structures. This essay seeks to suggest some possible analogies or models for these poetic structures by considering some of the scientific concepts discussed in 'The Mathematics of Rimbaud', before ending with an attempt to apply these in a close reading of two poems from *Brixton Fractals*.

'The Mathematics of Rimbaud':
understanding chreods, catastrophes and fractals

Fisher's main complaint in 'The Mathematics of Rimbaud' is that 'too much mainstream art and poetry of this century' has been made 'inside of neo-Platonic resolutions'.[1] 'Neo-Platonic' stands for ideals of order and harmony, both in the universe and art. The neo-Platonic artist orders the work under the illusion of determining what its meaning will be for the audience and the reader is expected to find certain meanings in the text.

Fisher finds alternative orders to these neo-Platonic resolutions in the mathematical theories of fractals. Benoit Mandelbrot explained how the ideal shapes of classical geometry do not resonate with the way in which nature organises itself. Classical geometry presents an image of harmony but the world contains discontinuity, noise. Instead of claiming that these discontinuities were accidental blemishes distorting the classic shapes, Mandelbrot claimed that they carried meaning. He decided to investigate those forms of nature usually considered 'formless', developing the 'morphology of the amorphous' which he called fractals.[2]

In contrast to deterministic models of the text as fixed, stable, a complete product, Fisher conceives of poetry as process: 'It is a requirement of this art that, to answer Olson's 1962 'A Later Note on Letter No. 15', the poetry is always "yet to be found" in the process of its making, and that making continues to take place through the physiology of the reader'.[3] For Fisher 'the reader is not simply an observer but a participator and thus affects what is read'.[4] In contrast to neo-Platonic assumptions, then, here the artist renounces control over the meaning of the work. This art provides the reader with a process at work, not just an end product. The reading is part of the process of the poem, another stage in its morphogenesis.

Viewing the poem as process enables us to consider the work in terms of structural stability as in catastrophe theory:

---

[1] Allen Fisher, 'The Mathematics of Rimbaud', *Future Exiles* (London: Paladin, 1992), p. 42

[2] Benoit Mandelbrot, *The Fractal Geometry of Nature* (New York: W. H. Freeman, 1982), p. 1

[3] Fisher, *Future Exiles*, p. 42

[4] Fisher, *Necessary Business* (London: Spanner, 1985), p. 235

In any process there may be regions that are well determined and structurally stable, being Waddington's chreods – the canals of consistent memory – and instabilities or indeterminisms – the generalised, unformalisable changing topologies – the poetries of the inventive memory...[5]

The concept of chreods was developed by the biologist C.H. Waddington. A chreod is defined as a canalised pathway of change. This can be visualised as a channel which a process follows, like a river through a valley.[6]

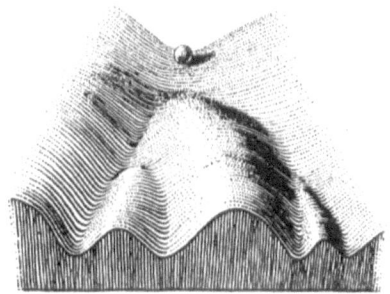

Figure 1: Epigenetic landscape of a chreod
Source: http://www.springerimages.com/Images/
LifeSciences/1-10.1007_978-1-4020-9650-1_11-0

Topology allows us to visualise a process in time as a shape in space. This shape, which often resembles a landscape, represents all the possible states of the system. As James Gleick explains:

A single point on such a surface represents the state of a system at an instant frozen in time. As a system progresses through time, the point moves, tracing an orbit across the surface. Bending the shape a little corresponds to changing the system's parameters...[7]

When a chreod is stable, after being displaced by a slight perturbation the system will return to the canalised pathway. This can be visualised as the point moving up the side of the valley before rolling back into the channel.

---

[5] Fisher, *Future Exiles*, p. 49

[6] C.H. Waddington, *Tools for Thought* (London: Cape, 1977), pp. 106-7

[7] James Gleick, *Chaos* (London: Heinemann, 1988), p. 47

As a process develops over time its parameters may change and, as Gleick comments, this results in changes to the topological landscape. This can be visualised as the valley branching in two. Whether the system travels down one chreod or the other is the critical point, the point of catastrophe.

In René Thom's catastrophe theory, this corresponds to a 'cusp' catastrophe: the change in the system's parameters results in a fold in the topological surface, an S shape with one part of the surface above the other.[8]

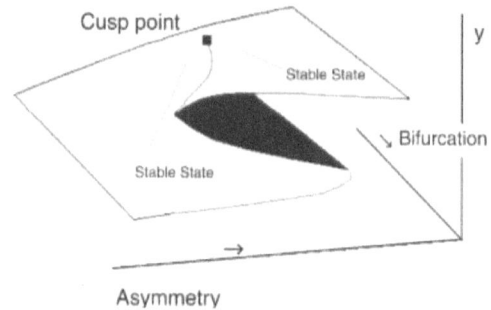

Figure 2: The cusp catastrophe model
Source: http://www.sciencedirect.com/science/article/pii/S1048984307000719

If the system is pushed to the edge of the fold it will drop into the lower chreod (travel down one valley channel rather than the other), resulting in the sudden discontinuous change known as a catastrophe. The cusp represents the critical point; to return to our earlier example, it is the threshold between one form and another.

In catastrophe theory, a catastrophe is a sudden, unexpected event, such as an earthquake or a heart attack, but can include any seemingly random phenomena, such as the fall of a leaf or the shape of a cloud. The theory defines it as a sudden change in a system, which occurs when external variables reach a certain point. One very simple example is water turning to ice; here the single external variable or parameter is the temperature, slowly and continuously decreased until a change in the system occurs and the water turns to ice. Catastrophe theory offers a set of mathematical models for the possible outcomes of such moments

---

[8] René Thom, *Structural Stability*, trans. D.H. Fowler (California; Wokingham: Addison-Wesley, Advanced Book Program, 1989), pp. 62-3

of instability.[9]

The connection between catastrophe theory and art and poetry is demonstrated by Thom's comment on surrealist painting:

> We can distinguish two major classes of unstable forms, each at an end of a continuous spectrum: first, forms that are nonforms by means of their very complicated internal structure – chaotic and not amenable to analysis; and, second, those that consist of a number of identifiable objects but whose composition seems contradictory or unusual, for example, the chimera and other monsters. Unstable forms of this second type are … the bifurcation forms whose representative point lies on a threshold between two or more basins of attraction, and their appearance continually oscillates between the adjacent attractors. The effect is to upset or disquiet the observer – this is the technique known to and exploited by surrealist painters.[10]

Analogy, or metaphor, brings together two or more different things through comparison or juxtaposition; there are two or more ways of interpreting the metaphor, the image is double- or many-sided. In catastrophe theory this is referred to as a 'bifurcation form', a situation with two or more basins of attraction, or two or more possible outcomes. A stable and consistent form has been brought to a point where it is about to become something else; it is between forms. The catastrophe in this sense is interpretation and the surrealist image is situated on the critical point before the situation goes one way or the other. It oscillates between interpretations: an optical illusion with two outcomes could be a vase or two faces; a damp stain on a wall with many outcomes could be mountains, trees, a figure or an animal. It shows the imagination at work.

One relatively stable region of the poem is the material fact of the text, the print on the page, which, no matter how inventively the reader views it, does not change. 'Invention cannot isolate itself from what is already present,' writes Fisher. 'This situating, this consistency, offered by the text's contours each time it is read, is the refusal of infinite licence to what the text means.'[11] The reader is limited, then, and the reading

---

[9] Thom, *Structural Stability*, p. 9

[10] Thom, *Structural Stability*, p. 14

[11] Fisher, *Necessary Business*, p. 213

contained within finite parameters. Within this consistency, however, there is a multiplicity of interpretations – and this is one of the features that might lead to the poems being described as 'fractal'.

Fractal shapes like the Koch snowflake and the Mandelbrot set demonstrate infinite length in a finite area. This is due to the self-similarity across scale, recursions of pattern within pattern, the same transformation repeated at smaller and smaller scales.

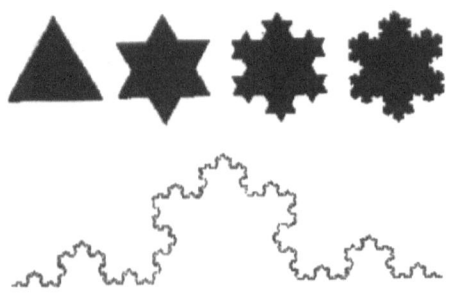

Figure 3: Koch snowflake
Source: http://www.stsci.edu/~lbradley/seminar/fractals.html

The Koch snowflake consists of a triangle with a smaller triangle, one third the size, on each of its sides, so that as you look closer, you see triangles on triangles, smaller and smaller. A more complex example is the Mandelbrot Set fractal, zooming into which reveals each curling tentacle bristled with further seahorse-like tails; the image never simplifies: it is endless, densely entangled; branches on branches, hairs on hairs. Fractal shapes have infinite length, yet finite area. Draw a circle around the original triangle of the Koch snowflake and no matter how many triangles are added to its sides it will never extend beyond it.

Fractals offer a visual analogy for complex, chaotic processes. Weather, for example, contains an infinite amount of variation within a finite space, never repeating itself yet contained within limited parameters. Clouds, coastlines, trees, blood vessels and bronchi: all are fractals. The branching of chreods can be described as fractal in that each chreod branches into further chreods. Within the process, sub-processes develop.

The phase space of the poem: applying the catastrophe set to poetry

Fisher draws on catastrophe theory as an attempt to provide a mathematical model for process: morphogenesis, the evolution of form, how an organism or a system gets its shape.

Thom's use of topology to parameterise the local states of the system might be applied to a poetic sequence or process: as long as the representative point of the system (its current state at any point in time) does not meet the catastrophe set (the set of models for catastrophic events, e.g. the 'cusp' catastrophe), the local nature of the system does not change. Whenever it does, there will be a discontinuity in the nature of the system, a change to the previous form.[12]

It might be possible to apply this to the poem as a process that continues with the reader. The system is not limited to the printed text of the poem but includes our reading of it. When we read the poem, what is the nature of the system and where does it change? Where are the discontinuities in the process of reading?

In the topological phase space of the poem, we can consider the space as divided into basins of attraction.[13] These might be visualised as the dips in the surface of a pinball machine, which attract and guide the ball-bearing as it moves around it. As the system changes over time, it can be similarly visualised as a point moving about a surface, whose shape represents the parameters of all its possible states. Basins of attraction (or attractors) lock the system into a particular pattern of behaviour as the ball-bearing traces the contours of its well. As the system changes, however, its parameters might also change, leading to alterations to the shape of the surface. This might lead to the representative point of the system becoming drawn towards another basin of attraction. A shift from one basin to another represents a catastrophe, a change in the form or behaviour of the system.

In the context of poetry, basins of attraction can be seen to correspond to how we perceive and recognise a form. A word may have more than one meaning, for example, and each of these is a potential attractor in the phase space of our reading. The division into basins is not rigid, however, and can vary for any given person according to psychological state and conscious or unconscious desires – as with Rorschach inkblots, for example.

---

[12] Thom, *Structural Stability*, p. 7
[13] Ibid., p. 39

Leonardo da Vinci recommended painters to look at patches of dirt on an old wall for inspiration: in these amorphous shapes, they would find shapes of figures and landscapes that could be used in their paintings.[14] This practice was later developed by the Surrealists, particularly by Max Ernst who devised the technique known as 'frottage', which involves placing a sheet of paper over a textured surface and rubbing it with pencil.[15] He found that the mind would discern fantastical forms within the textures. Oscar Domínguez's technique of 'decalcomania' proceeds according to similar principles: paint pressed between two sheets of paper, when pealed apart would reveal provocative textures.[16] These forms and shapes are the basins of attraction in our interpretative faculties, perhaps habitual patterns that the mind searches for in order to make sense of chaotic shapes.

To apply this back to reading, it could be said that we come to understand a word through past usage: reading activates memory, the word bringing an idea or image (as well as a host of other associated words) to mind. These are the basins of attraction for a word. Sentences follow patterns we come to expect, how one word interacts with another within a clause, and a context develops making the pull of one basin of attraction more powerful than others.

With Fisher's poems, however, the patterns of grammar and context are broken. A phrase might be left grammatically incomplete and may be juxtaposed with many different contexts in its neighbouring lines. This means that more than one basin of attraction might be active for any one word or sentence, as if the topological surface of the poem has become flatter, the basins shallower. A shift from one basin to another can now occur at any point: a word or phrase can be read one way, then suddenly seem to take on a different meaning. Such discontinuities can be encountered at any point in the process of reading. The system of the poem is thus an unstable form whose representative point at any given time lies on a threshold between two or more basins of attraction. It continually oscillates between adjacent attractors.

Thom uses the term homeomorphism to refer to topological spaces that have the same form.[17] A text might be said to be structurally stable

---

[14] Leonardo da Vinci, *Treatise on Painting*

[15] Matthew Gale, *Dada and Surrealism* (London: Phaidon, 1997), p. 240

[16] Ibid., p. 333

[17] Thom, *Structural Stability*, p. 12

if there is a homeomorphism of one reading process onto another, if one reading of the text is the same as another, throwing the trajectories of one onto the other. While it is questionable whether any reading process can be identical to another within such an ambiguous medium as language, it is the aim of certain texts, informational literature as an extreme example, to attempt to reduce the possibilities for interpretation as much as possible.

The paratactic method of Fisher's poetry, on the other hand, seems to want to open the language out to its greatest possible interpretive potential: 'their cultivation of plurivocity again brings back to language all its capacity of meaningfulness', 'it preserves the width, because the rotten danger in present-day living is a kind of reduction of language to communication to manipulate things ... to prevent going in many directions.'[18]

In *Necessary Business*, Fisher observes, in reading the poetry of Mottram, Prynne and Cheek:

> There's no way to predict the effect of the actions of any participant engaging with these poets' presentations. Predictability is thankfully lost at the thresholds between what is conserved and invented; stable and unstable...[19]

One reading of the text will likely differ from another; they may also resemble each other in places. They may start out from similar premises and end up going in different directions, or begin from contrasting assumptions and reach similar conclusions. In this way the trajectories of any two readings of Fisher's text may intersect, overlap and diverge at various points. The form of the poem, which is to say the shape of its process (which includes the reading), will be more or less unstable.

As more readings are made, however, it is possible that, as with most poems, the possible interpretations will begin to gravitate around a few well-worn basins of attraction, where a reader coming to the poem will already have a set of readings and contexts. It seems that this is the sort of situation Fisher is attempting to resist with the indeterminacy that results from the paratactic juxtapositions of collage.

Yet I keep trying to make sense of it, to provide an account that

---

[18] Fisher, 'The Preface to Brixton Fractals, 1985', *Gravity*, p. xi

[19] Fisher, *Necessary Business*, pp. 173-4

might go some way in attempting to understand what is going on in this work – to offer some sort of stability for other potential readers. I cannot help my interpretative faculties being incited to find meaning in its chaotic textures. And surely this is part of Fisher's aim in facturing these literary frottages. It is not enough to say of a Rorschach inkblot, 'It's an inkblot.'

It is far more limiting to arrive at a situation where a discourse of instability becomes a stable form for the poem. As Fisher comments in *Necessary Business*:

> In certain circumstances a homogenous disorder becomes stable, as catastrophe theory shows, becomes, so to speak, affirmative rather than radical, a difficulty many improvising artists in public fail to see. A new order or organised functioning is established…[20]

This is a danger for Fisher as writer, that the use of procedural or improvisatory methods and the production of chaotic forms do not become homogenous. It is also a difficulty for the reader: as it becomes easier to explain the work in terms of its instability, the less we actually engage with it; and the less we try to understand it and find meaning in it, the less we feel that instability as a genuinely disturbing and stimulating force.

The main thing to remember, perhaps, in trying to give the poem some stability of form which might allow its complexity to be appreciated, is that we do not remove the instability that is part of the poem's generosity.

Reading Brixton Fractals: 'African Boog' and 'Banda'

Brixton Fractals as a process developed and continues to develop over time. As Fisher mentions in the acknowledgments, 'All of the poems in *Brixton Fractals* appeared before those publications, sometimes in earlier drafts.'[21] 'African Boog' was published in 1983 by Ta'wil Books and 'Banda' in 1983 by Spanner/Open Field. *Brixton Fractals* itself was published by Aloes Books in 1985 and then by Tsunami, Vancouver

---

[20] Fisher, *Necessary Business*, pp. 230-1
[21] Fisher, *Gravity*, p. ix

in 1999, and subsequently collected in *Gravity* published by Salt in 2004. The books collected in *Gravity* are only one third of the longer project *Gravity as a consequence of shape*. And this is itself only part of an ongoing process which continues with the work's readers. As the process of the poem develops its parameters are subject to change.

This is clearly felt in *Brixton Fractals* where there are two distinct styles of poem, offering different reading experiences. The poems with titles beginning with A – 'Around the World', 'African Twist', 'Atkins Stomp' and 'African Boog' – have a very fractured style, where the lines do not seem to lead on to each other at all, while the poems with titles beginning with B have a greater semblance of continuity from line to line. Fisher writes in the preface that 'The chronology of the poems is generally alphabetically indicated. I wrote African Boog first…'[22] The A poems, then, were written before the B poems. In *Brixton Fractals*, the poems are not arranged in this order: 'Banda' is the first poem in the book, suggesting its pivotal importance as a piece. A comparison between this poem, the first in the book, and 'African Boog', the first written, will elucidate the effects the changes in parameters have in the process.

> Went dicing on my bike
>   Disappearance
> Meaning given as timbre
>   Relational invariants from a flux
>   She lives in advance of her days
>   Speed[23]

> Took chances in London traffic
> where the culture breaks
> tone colours burn from exhaustion
> emphasised by wind,
> looking ahead for sudden tail lights
> a vehicle changes
> lanes into your path and birds,
> over the rail bridge, seem purple.[24]

---

[22] ibid., p. xii

[23] Fisher, 'African Boog', *Gravity*, p. 37

[24] Fisher, 'Banda', *Gravity*, p. 3

'African Boog' begins with what appears to be a relatively simple note of a lived experience. 'Went' is a condensed form of 'I went' – an autobiographical presence implied by 'my'. The main instability is 'dicing'. 'Riding' or 'cycling' might coincide more fully with the reader's expectations. The use of 'dicing' activates a number of possible chreods for the reading to follow. The verb 'dice' means to chop into chunks, so the motion of the bike can be envisaged as dicing in and out of cars or trees. There is also the sense of 'dicing with death': an idea emphasised by the first line of 'Banda', 'Took chances in London traffic'. The dice is an emblem of chance. The bike ride represents the random journey, a Situationist *dérive* perhaps, which resonates with the chance procedures that seem to have played a part in the selection process of the poem's composition.

'Disappearance' comes as a surprise. It does not seem to follow from 'Went dicing on my bike'. A cusp catastrophe occurs, the system making a sudden leap to a new chreod. Yet there is a sound linkage to 'dicing'. The echo of 'dice' in 'dis' is made explicit later in the poem when the line reappears as 'Dissing on my skate board'.[25] Such transformations occur throughout the A-title poems in *Brixton Fractals*, enacting the combinatory action of the inventive memory, as exemplified in dream distortion. Words and phrases go through transformations, modelling the process of mutation language undergoes in the imagination. Such sound linkages between otherwise apparently unconnected lines invite the inventive reader to make connections between the independent substrates.

The sans serif font refers the reader to the resources where it is stated that the word is taken from the *German issue of semiotext(e)* edited by Sylvere Lotringer in 1982 and including work from Paul Virilio, Heiner Müller, Jean Baudrillard, Helke Sander, Martin Heidegger, Joseph Beuys and Michel Foucault. The word is a marker, acting like a wormhole, referring the reader to another text. At a later date, readings of 'African Boog' may be altered by further research into this text, but even without further investigation at this stage, surface recognition of a few of the writers' names can suggest the postmodernist, poststructuralist nature of the text and this colours the word in a slightly different hue to its usual sense.

'Went dicing on my bike / Disappearance / Meaning given by timbre'. There is no syntactic continuity between these three phrases and

---

[25] Fisher, *Gravity*, p. 37

any semantic continuity is not readily apparent. The lines break, change context. Like the first, the third line is condensed and notational in form. 'Meaning given by timbre' suggests a musical language, perhaps a tonal language like the Chinese languages, where the meaning of a sound is altered by the pitch at which it is pronounced. In music, timbre refers to the texture of sounds: the same pitch can be sounded in different timbres, on different instruments, for example. 'Meaning given by timbre' suggests that musical sounds have meaning: music considered as language.

Although the continuity between lines is fractured, structural stability can be arrived at to some extent with each line as a unit. 'Relational invariants from a flux' uses complex vocabulary, suggesting things which are similar and stay the same, certain constants emerging from chaos and change. 'She lives in advance of her days' introduces a female pronoun. The reader does not know who she is, or whether or not she is a personification of one of the previous abstract nouns 'Disappearance' or 'Meaning'. The first line can now be read retrospectively as '*She* went dicing on my bike'. Living 'in advance of her days' suggests living in the future rather than the present, using the imagination, the inventive memory. 'Speed', a second word from the *German issue of semiotext(e)*, may be related to the bike in the first line and denotes the rate of motion, but also of change.

Thus the first six lines of 'African Boog' form a complex of ideas relating to chance, motion and change. There are disappearances: something that was there that is no longer present, like the connectives elided through notational condensation, forming syntactic gaps. Things merge in, lose definition. And things emerge, relational invariants from the flux, like the meaning given by timbre from the flux of sound and noise, as the inventive reader begins to interpret the phrases as separate units and then to make possible connections between them. The poem is a Rorschach ink blot inciting the reader's inventive memory to oscillate between basins of attraction, a frottage of disconnected phrases from which forms emerge as perception is captured by these attractors.

The main difference in 'Banda' is the greater sense of continuity from line to line. The first letters of each line are not capitalised, inviting the reader's eye to enjamb the sentences. The opening lines can thus be read as a single voice. Although it is possible to allow the apparent stability of the lines to carry the reading, it is difficult to get a handle on a single, coherent overall meaning. This causes the reader to pay more attention to the individual lines and discontinuities begin to become apparent.

'Took chances in London traffic' seems structurally stable as a statement. But who took chances? As with the first line of 'African Boog', the pronoun is cut at the start of the sentence, leaving the subject of the verb ambiguous. The authorial 'I' renounces ownership of the text. Whether the sentence is read as first person or third person, plural or singular, is left open, a set of options for the reader.

'Took chances in London traffic / where the culture breaks' is syntactically stable, but on closer examination it is difficult to sustain semantic continuity between the two lines. It is possible to gain some stability with 'the culture breaks' as a concept, if the reader draws parallels with the fragmentation of cultural sources in the poem. But why should the culture break in London traffic? Although the two statements are glided into an apparent continuity, there is a fracture, a discontinuity between the lines. Yet there is a linkage in the pun on 'brakes', and this allows the chreod of 'traffic' imagery to remain stable. So following a slight perturbation, the reading is able to return to this basin of attraction.

The second line is not punctuated and so it is possible to read on into the third, extending the sentence to 'where the culture breaks tone colours…' But the next verb, 'burn', forces the reader to reorient and modify the syntax: 'where the culture breaks tone', 'colours burn from exhaustion', 'tone colours burn from exhaustion'. There are various points in 'Banda' and other B-title poems in *Brixton Fractals* where the text becomes like a Necker cube, the syntax swivelling as the reader reformulates the sentence between two or more equally valid constructions.

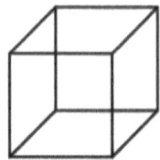

Figure 4: Necker cube
Source: http://www.evsc.net/research/necker

Bibliography

Fisher, Allen, *Gravity* (Cambridge: Salt, 2004)
────── *Necessary Business* (London: Spanner, 1985)
────── 'The Mathematic of Rimbaud', in *Future Exiles* (London: Paladin, 1992)
Gale, Matthew, *Dada and Surrealism* (London: Phaidon, 1997)
Ghyka, Matila, *The Geometry of Art and Life* (New York: Dover Publications, 1977)
Gleick, James, *Chaos* (London: Heinemann, 1988)
Mandelbrot, Benoit, *Fractals: form, chance and dimension* (San Francisco: Freeman, 1977)
────── *The Fractal Geometry of Nature* (New York: W. H. Freeman, 1982)
Thom, Rene, *Structural Stability and Morphogenesis* (1973), trans. D.H. Fowler (Reading, Ma: W. A. Benjamin Inc, 1975). References are to the 1989 edition published by Westview Press, Boulder, CO.
Waddington, C.H., *Tools for Thought* (London: Cape, 1977)

Fractalising the Front Line: Brixton in the poetry of Allen Fisher and Linton Kwesi Johnson[1]

WILL MONTGOMERY

endless destruction/ makes Brixton (*Brixton Fractals*, 81)[2]

In the late 1970s and early 1980s the London district of Brixton was the forcing ground for the emergence of a revised and expanded version of English cultural identity. From our own perspective it is hard, perhaps, to conceive of an Englishness that does not reflect the influx of migrants from former colonies during the post-war years. In our time, popular xenophobia has tended to focus on the 'asylum' issue, the influx of workers from new EU states and, in the wake of 9/11, the Muslim population. It is easy to forget that three decades ago it was the African Caribbean population and their culture that were routinely demonised. In this essay I will discuss the presence of these issues in poetry by considering the early 1980s work of Allen Fisher alongside that of an African Caribbean contemporary and fellow Lambeth dweller, Linton Kwesi Johnson – a poet whose radicalism is of a very different kind. My purpose is not to set an oral, populist mode against the oblique formal strategies of the avant-garde. Rather, I wish to suggest that continuities in the depiction of sound, violence and place can allow us to draw connections between two poets who, while living and writing in close proximity to one another, arrived at entirely distinct ways of registering and responding to political and racial oppression.

In the years after the riot of April 1981, the so-called 'Front Line' took on a totemic role in popular representations of second-generation black Britons. This was a small triangle of streets near the centre of Brixton, comprising Railton Road, Leeson Road and Mayall Road. The military metaphor suggested a nation divided antagonistically along racial lines. In those cities where there was a high non-white population this was certainly the case, as the riots in Liverpool and Manchester

---

[1] This essay first appeared in the *Journal of British and Irish innovative Poetry*. We are grateful to the editors for permission to reprint it.

[2] Allen Fisher, *Brixton Fractals* (1985), collected in *Gravity*. Further page references to this edition are given as *BF*.

later in 1981 suggest. Brixton in the early 1980s was a place of high unemployment, particularly among the black population. The housing was poor, there was a high incidence of homelessness and black people were poorly served by local schools. There was continual friction with the police, who were enthusiastic in the use of the so-called 'sus' law. This was a disreputable piece of 19th-century anti-vagrancy legislation that provided for the arrest of individuals considered by a police constable to be merely *likely* to steal from persons unknown.

In April 1981 the police had begun an intense stop-and-search campaign. In the week before the riot, 943 people were stopped, 188 arrested and 75 people charged. With either disastrous insensitivity or simple bloody-mindedness the operation was tagged 'Swamp 81' by the police, echoing Margaret Thatcher's famous remark in a 1978 television interview: "People are really rather afraid that this country might be rather swamped by people with a different culture." So the 'swamped' were swamping back: the intensive police campaign that, in the view of most commentators, precipitated the 1981 riot, was, metaphorically at least, a counter-swamping exercise, an attempt to reclaim territory from the interloper.

The Front Line was the site of resolute cultural resistance on the part of the black community. It was a place of squats and community groups. A number of the houses were used by young black people for 'blues parties' – loud and late-night events at which the latest Jamaican reggae imports were played. The police and some local residents complained of drug-dealing, street robbery and illegal drinking establishments. The area also drew other marginal groupings: in 1974 the UK's first gay community centre opened in a squatted building on Railton Road, with an openly gay nightclub in the basement.[3] There were also a number of revolutionary left groupings in the area.[4] The radical *Race Today* journal, edited by Darcus Howe and sometimes co-edited with Linton Kwesi Johnson, was based in the Front Line area, as were several grass-roots black campaigning groups. In short, several of the cultural tendencies most deplored by the Conservative press, rampant in the early years of Thatcherism, were present in undiluted form in just a few south London streets.

---

[3] Information sourced from miscellaneous documents at Lambeth Archives.

[4] The Revolutionary Communist Group, the Workers Revolutionary Party, Revolutionary Communist Tendency (which became the RCP). After the riots the SWP and Militant were prominent in local campaigns. See Shipley.

Allen Fisher was born in Streatham, just south of Brixton, in 1944 and he lived in Lambeth for much of the 1970s and 1980s. Fisher's first major poetic undertaking was his five-part *Place* project, an ambitious exploration of the hidden cultural topography of south London that occupied him between 1974 and 1981. I want to consider *Brixton Fractals*, the first part of his next major sequence *Gravity as a Consequence of Shape*.[5] The first section of it, the book *Brixton Fractals*, was written between 1982 and 1984 and published in 1985.

Fisher is highly regarded among readers of avant-garde poetry but his work has been ignored by the cultural mainstream. The other poet I will discuss is much better known, Linton Kwesi Johnson – one of very few living poets to be published in the Penguin Modern Classics imprint. Johnson was born in 1952 in rural Jamaica. He came to London in 1963 and went to Tulse Hill secondary school, where he joined the Black Panthers. He helped to organise a poetry workshop within the movement and worked with a group of poets and drummers. In the 1970s and 1980s he was part of the radical collective producing the journal *Race Today* and, as well as working as a radio and TV journalist, was involved in numerous political campaigns around black community issues. He found the poetic voice he has used since – a distinctive sifting of black British experience in Jamaican patois – with the book *Dread Beat & Blood*, published in 1975. An album of recordings of the same name was released by Island Records in 1977. Johnson's decision to recite over reggae backing tracks brought him a huge international audience. Disseminating his poetry as music, rather than via bookstores, has made him the most heard, if not the most read, of living British poets.

Linton Kwesi Johnson: the weight of the present

Johnson writes what he calls 'reggae poetry' and what many others call 'dub poetry' (see Johnson and Morris, 256).[6] Taking a cue from Jamaican toasters such as Big Youth, I Roy and U Roy, he usually reads over a musical backing. This was, in his account, almost forced upon him: music, he has said, 'kept intruding' when he began writing poetry

---

[5] The sequence comprises *Gravity* (2004), *Entanglement* (2004) and *Leans* (2007). Each contains several shorter sequences, many of which have seen separate publication as pamphlets or chapbooks.

[6] Johnson coined the term 'dub poetry' in 1974 to talk about the work of Jamaican DJs.

in patois (Johnson and Caesar, 66; see also Morris interview, 253). His poetry is of an explicitly political nature: 'I'm a one-theme writer,' he has said (Johnson and Morris, 259). And, of his 1970s work: 'quite a few of my recordings and verses in those days were simply serving a propaganda function' (Johnson and Caesar, 70). Johnson's 1970s writing was prophetic of the social disorder that would erupt in Brixton in the 1980s. In its filtering of social concerns through colloquial speech it could hardly be further from Fisher's *Brixton Fractals*, which is dense with citation from a large set of textual resources and which skips from one mode of discourse to another as line follows line (sometimes skipping within lines too). In his 1985 text *Necessary Business*, Fisher makes his position on the uses of poetry clear: 'Poetry's dominant function is aesthetic, is without concrete aim and does not tend towards fulfilment of a practical task' (Fisher, 1999, 52).[7]

I wish to explore the importance of Brixton as a *sounded* space to both poets. The aftershocks of colonial violence are perceptible in the work of each: as an explicit arena of conflict in Johnson's work, and as a refracted cognitive jolt in that of Fisher. Reggae is the backdrop to Johnson's early writing, with Jamaican-style sound system events providing a social setting for some poems and the music determining its rhythms.[8] However, reggae also introduced a distinct aesthetic of warping alterity to Fisher's already highly fractured poetry. The violent disjunctions of dub, and the association between sound systems and actual violence are discernible in the glancing references to sound, black culture and the police in *Brixton Fractals*. Another history, then, makes itself available in Fisher's text.

Johnson's work, long before the 1981 riot, took violence as its subject matter. In this, Johnson was taking a cue from the work of Frantz Fanon, particularly the confrontational Fanon of *The Wretched of the Earth* (see Fanon, 1967, 45).[9] Johnson has talked of his poetry's 'ambivalent relationship to violence', remarking:

> I was trying to relate the Fanonist ideas about the process of

---

[7] The four essays collected in *The Topographical Shovel* are intended to complement *Gravity as a consequence of shape*.

[8] This rhythmic template is something Johnson would later describe as 'very limiting' (Johnson and Morris, 259).

[9] Fanon's *A Dying Colonialism* (1965) is among the texts cited by Fisher in his bibliography for *Brixton Fractals*.

de-colonisation to my particular situation here, seeing a lot of internecine warfare going on between the youths of my generation. A lot of it do with sound systems, a lot of it to do with neighbourhoods. And, of course, that was happening on the one hand and at the same time we were being brutalised by the police and framed and criminalised (Johnson and Caesar, 66).

Johnson links what is now called 'black-on-black' violence and violence involving the domestic equivalents of Fanon's colonial powers, the British police. He seems to be rehearsing Fanon's point about anti-colonial rage and physicality: 'The native's muscular tension finds outlet regularly in bloodthirsty explosions – in tribal warfare, in feuds between sects and in quarrels between individuals' (Fanon, 1967, 42). It is worth noting that Johnson emphasises the relationship between sound systems and violence – music provides the environment in which physical aggression is expressed.[10] Johnson refers to exactly this in his early poem 'Five Nights of Bleeding', which documents several violent incidents in London in the early 1970s.

> Night number two doun at SHEPERD'S
> right up RAILTON ROAD;
> it was a night named Friday
> when everyone was high on brew
> or drew a pound or two worth a kally
> soun coming doun NEVILLE KING'S music iron;
> the rhythm jus bubbling an back-firing,
> raging and rising, when suddenly the music cut:
> steel blade drinking blood in darkness.
> it's war amongst the rebels:
> madness... madness... war (Johnson, 1975, 16)

It is a documentary poem, communicating the conflict-saturated experience of young black men. The implication is that something, somewhere, has to give. And, in the next section of the poem it does – the refrain of the poem changes, from 'it's war amongst the rebels:/ madness... madness... war' to 'and two policemen wounded./ righteous

---

[10] See Franco Rossi's *vérité* film drama *Babylon* (1980), scored by Dennis Bovell, who arranges Johnson's music. See also Bradley for discussion of the emergence of the Jamaican sound system and its links to violence.

righteous war'. Another early poem, 'Doun de Road', follows a Fanonian sequence of categories of violence, moving from internal conflict among the oppressed group to violence directed against the coloniser: 'fratricide is only the first phase', writes Johnson, ending the poem with 'time for the second phase to show' (Johnson, 1975, 22, 23).[11]

There is a strong impression of physical crisis to Johnson's writing of this 1970s: 'the bile of oppression was vomited' is a phrase that occurs in 'Five Nights of Bleeding', for example; 'Rage' begins: 'Imprisoned in memory/ of the whip's sting,/ tear in the flesh// and the fire burning within,/ his eyes sing pain silently:/ twin daggers piercing flesh'; and his first book, *Voices of the Living and the Dead*, ends with the line, in capitals: 'BLOOD! BLOOD! BLOOD! BLOOD!' (Johnson, 1974).[12] Johnson's analysis of reggae, published in a 1976 article in the journal *Race & Class*, examines the violence around sound systems through a Fanonian lens. Citing Fanon's writing on dance under colonialism, and his description of the way that a 'hampered aggressivity' finds its way out in a 'volcanic eruption' of cathartic frenzy (Fanon, 1967, 45), Johnson moves to the postcolonial situation in Jamaica. Here Fanon's auto-destructive 'fraternal bloodbath' (Fanon, 1967, 42) of violence, a means of forgetting colonialism, is not sublimated in the self-loss of dance: it is enacted in the many feuds that occurred around the sound systems. Johnson writes:

> [...] the catharsis does not come through dance, for the violence that the music carries is turned inwards and personalised, so that for no apparent reason, the dance halls and yards often explode into fratricidal violence and general pandemonium (Johnson, 1976, 400).

Following the West Indian critic Gordon Rohlehr, Johnson locates the historical sedimentation of colonial violence in the 'bass, the basic rhythm, the inner pulse' of reggae (Rohlehr, cited in Johnson, 1976, 401).[13] Johnson writes, '[...] for the oppressed Jamaican, history is not

---

[11] In Fanon's slightly different scheme, the first phase of the 'insurrectional period' (Fanon, 1967, 69) represents anti-colonial violence and the second phase the 'building-up of the nation' (Fanon, 1967, 73).

[12] Johnson's early writing often carries echoes of the apocalyptic physicalism of Aimé Césaire – a poet greatly admired by both Johnson and Fanon.

[13] Johnson has spoken of how he sometimes used to use a bass guitar while writing his

a fleeting memory of a distant past, but the unbearable weight of the present' (ibid, 402). Slavery, in this view, exerts a *continuing* pressure on the postcolonial Jamaican that is both psychological and, through music, physical. While there were clearly numerous highly specific cultural, political and religious factors contributing to the emergence of the music of 1970s Jamaica, the distinctive atmosphere of 'dread', as it was called, might be attributed to a musical somatisation of past violence within the culture. Singers and toasters – what Johnson calls 'dub-lyricists' – give this impulse verbal expression, often combining a social documentary function with historical themes.

In Johnson's work, then, we can find these Jamaican concerns transplanted to the doubly deracinated situation of the British African Caribbean population. His writing identifies similar conditions of violence within the community and anticipates the turning outward of that violence that occurred in April 1981. The poetry, in rhythm and content, acts as a kind of sounding board for the situation of young black Britons – immersed in Jamaican music, with its inheritance of re-coded trauma, but attempting to negotiate a liveable life in the demoralised and often hostile inner cities of 1970s Britain.

Allen Fisher: endless destruction

With its overlapping of distinct discursive terrains, *Brixton Fractals* does something analogous to the blurring of temporal sequence in dub.[14] Fisher's development of an allusive and fragmentary poetics looks back to Charles Olson's documentary techniques, on one hand; on the other, it absorbs the disjunctive musical methods that were, quite literarily, in the air of Lambeth as he was writing.

The book's glancing allusions to African Caribbean culture and to social unrest in Lambeth insinuate the impacted memory of another culture into an unfamiliar aesthetic terrain. My contention is that reggae and dub form part of the aural unconscious of *Brixton Fractals*.[15] This is

---

poems (Morris, 252).

[14] i.e. the manipulation of recordings in the studio, often with disorienting use of faders and such effects as echo, phaser and reverb.

[15] This form of music is heard in the work of other British poets: see, for example, John James's *Toasting* (1979), Barry MacSweeney's *Far Cliff Babylon* (1978) or *Colonel B* (1980), or Ken Edwards's *Drumming & Poems* (1982).

only one current in a complex work, but I think it is important to note that the confluence of sound and violence that Johnson identifies on the Railton Road finds a refracted – or fractalised – presence in Fisher's book.[16]

Early in the *Place* project, Fisher's speaker is 'mesmerised by natty dread' (see *Becoming*, in Fisher (2005), 236).[17] and there are several such glancing references in *Brixton Fractals*. The book bears the formal stamp of the modernist avant garde, of Olson's notions of place and experiments with page space, of Fluxus and of Fisher's admiration for the syncretic lexical reach of JH Prynne's poetry.[18] Yet, alongside the various uses the avant garde has for the fragment, *Brixton Fractals* also admits into its framework a musical sensibility that has a distinct vocabulary of rupture and distress.

An analogy can be drawn between the artificial temporality made available by music studio techniques and the way the *Gravity* and *Place* sequences use compositional procedures. On facing pages of one *Brixton Fractals* poem, 'Ballin' the Jack', for example, the last line of the right-hand page is a variant of the first on the left; the second last of the second line on the left-hand page, and so on. 'African Boog', also in *Brixton Fractals*, ripples with mirrorings and variations. A later poem in *Gravity*, 'Cha Cha', works variations line by line on the preceding poem, 'Camel Walk' (see Fisher and Thurston, 16, for discussion of these techniques).

In 1995, Fisher summarised his mode of working thus:

> …the poetic strategy is one of slow discomposition, disruption of autobiographical voice through the use of many voices, aspiration to multiple and collage form through the pasting of many sources, many spacetimes, and a subversion of collage form through a use of re-narration, a simulation device evident elsewhere in this poet's work (Fisher, 1995, 111).

---

[16] A confluence that was commonly observed in popular depictions of Brixton. In one local-press account of the 1981 riot, for example, there is the following overheated description of just such a meeting: '[…] for some the violence and disorder represented a certain kind of freedom. Reggae music blared from some windows above the wail of police, fire and ambulance sirens, shedding an incongruous if not grotesque light on how bitterness leads to callousness' (*South London Press*, 14 April 1981, 3).

[17] See also *Becoming*'s, "tapping plimsolls outside/ a reggae shop", ibid, 233.

[18] Discussed, along with the work of cris cheek and Eric Mottram, in Fisher, 1999.

This 're-narration', the repetition of elements of the poem, is essential to the patterns of repetition that unfold within individual poems, within *Brixton Fractals* the book, and within the *Gravity as a Consequence of Shape* sequence as a whole.

These experiments with 'spacetime' imply overlaps in cultural memory. The allusions in *Brixton Fractals* to African Caribbean experience and to social unrest in Lambeth insinuate the impacted historical memory of another culture into an unfamiliar aesthetic terrain. This is part of the formal design of the work. Fisher defines fractals in his preface as 'an extremely irregular action, broken design or fragmented object' (*BF*, xi). The book is, in consequence, a polyphonic clashing of discrete vocabularies, or, in Fisher's words again, a 'technique of memory and perception analysis' (*BF*, xi). While *Brixton Fractals* does not attempt to ventriloquise black Brixton, culturally distinct forms of memory and perception leak into his text. The result is a form of writing that projects a mobile cognitive landscape marked by both pattern and decoherence. Benoît Mandelbrot's notion of the fractal as an underlying 'self-similar' structure within apparent disorder provides an analogy for the organisation of fragments in Fisher's *Gravity* project. Geographical and textual conceptions of space intersect as Fisher's 'broken design' opens windows between actual locations and the diverse cultural forms that are embedded in them. Formal, semantic and sonic analogies cause conceptual and phenomenal environments to fold into one another.

Fisher's 'fragmented object' has an appended list of 'resources', which are cross-referenced to the 14 poems and linked to a compendious bibliography. The reader can follow Fisher's pointing finger and look up texts by Adorno, Beuys, Conrad, Diogenes Laertius or Einstein. He or she is referred to articles on such subjects as particle theory, geometry, fossil footprints in Tanzania and the ice moons of Jupiter and Saturn.[19] However, this bibliography is not meant as a coercive form of pedagogy, crumbs from the table of a scholar-poet. Quite the reverse: what Fisher

---

[19] Fisher has described what he calls the 'Complexity Manifold': 'The proposal is that the Complexity Manifold gathers the aesthetics at all levels and all functions of a poet's production, both consciousness and product, and is responsible for what is gathered and held, ordered, disrupted, retained and lost. Poetics, in this sense, spins across the epistemological boundaries of scale and energy. A poet's attitude to and understanding of quantum field theory will affect that poet's experience of gravity, drawing and reading, just as a painter's comprehension of the annual Cup Final affects that painter's interest in television as well as the local ball game' (Fisher, 1999b, 115).

calls a 'cultivation of plurivocity' (*BF*, ix) encourages the synthesis of diverse materials at the same time as implicitly querying any claims to singular authority in the discourses it draws on. Andrew Lawson indicates the implications of the poetry's multiple vocabularies when he suggests that the poems 'operate in a kind of continuous present where sensuous bodily experience merges with an eclectic, theoretical stance whose values are polyphony, mobility dissonance, alternative topologies, ways not so much of seeing (advertising has out-Dada'd Dada in that department) but of *experiencing* space' (Lawson, 418).

The vast experiential matrix that Fisher mobilises is conceived with an interest in the points at which elements from different discursive domains interfere with each other and produce new tangents of meaning. One locus of such productive frictions is a meshing of vocabularies in Brixton – bookshelf and boombox converge in the writerly consciousness that informs Fisher's polyphony. In the words of Tim Woods, writing of the *Place* project: 'Two sorts of space emerge: one is the empirical, rational space perceived as a void to be filled up. The other is what might be termed "affective space", a space charged with emotional meanings, community symbolism and historical significance' (Woods, 42). The 'affective space' of *Brixton Fractals* contains both the ambient presence of Jamaican music and the police as markers of a social unrest grounded in historical injustice.

Most of the poems' titles are derived from the names of jazz and blues dances – 'African Twist', 'Atkins Stomp', 'Black Bottom', 'Boogie Stomp', and so on (see Fisher, 1982, where these terms were first outlined). But, rather than American jazz or blues, reggae is the black music that is most important to *Brixton Fractals*. Jamaican music enters a text that is extremely alert to the aural in brief, slanted references. In 'Ballin' the Jack', for example, Fisher writes:

> In a Brixton queue stopped for lack of identification
> harangues slowed through a tannoy
> Hands worn hard with broom handling,
> scrub pavement, paint railings, polish steps,
> dread fingers dub in laundromat. (*BF*, 23)

In 'Atkins Stomp', he writes 'Listen to the baste of the reggae' (*BF*, 34), twisting the letters of 'beats' and 'bass' into 'baste'.[20] The same poem

---

[20] The word 'baste' is in sans serif font to indicate its derivation from a particular text

references the front line, with 'Dicing down Mayall Road/ Research into primeval echoed polyphony' (*BF*, 33). 'African Boog' has 'Brixton market frequent, Brixton market full music' (*BF*, 40) and 'In a maximal echo-chamber' (*BF*, 40) – a citation from Baudrillard that spills over into the vocabulary of dub.[21] Loudspeakers, too, are a recurring motif in the sequence: '[…] two sets of loudspeakers/ face each other […]' (*BF*, 6); 'Carried the system down Coldharbour/ on the right shoulder/ two circular speakers/ plate the inner ear […]/ moving with a deliberation/ seldom found in poetry' (*BF*, 9);[22] 'Citizens break into loudspeaker/ space fills/ with a yellow/ glow from the walkway/ bricks…' (*BF*, 53). And sound, crucially, is linked to violent social unrest:

> On one side a ley line buckles
> into the wall of 'The George',
> in the machine a solenoid blows
> a rush of green vans and police weapons
> send the needles into peak
> and damage the Dolby. (*BF*, 3)

The George pub had a notoriously racist and homophobic landlord, and it was torched during the riots. Here that moment of violence is depicted as a kind of warping, or 'buckling' of 'affective space' as the ley line becomes dangerously material. The solenoid is a component found in microphones and loudspeakers. The needles and Dolby suggest a recording device, implying perhaps that the fusion of sound and violence imposes an intolerable stress on the poet-as-witness. Fisher's characteristic method of combining registers allows him to transpose what for Johnson is an account of the physical and emotional distress encrypted in music into a more generalised crisis of poetic representation. Lines such as '"Volume Control"/ as a measure of decay patterns' (*BF*, 9) suggest a sonic monitoring of social entropy. Does he have the tools to record or transmit this tear in the social fabric? Or will it all blow?

Numerous references to social disorder and its policing occur within the book. Images of burning cars and police cordons are accompanied

---

among the poem's many 'resources'. The same applies to 'primeval' in the following quotation.

[21] The phrase comes from Baudrillard's early-1980s essay on terrorism and the media, 'The Theater of Cruelty', 114.

[22] Coldharbour Lane is a road in central Brixton.

by aural images – rising and falling police sirens; helicopters hovering malignantly over Brixton. In 'Accretion' the lines 'Encircled by a ribbon of officers./ The air was made open/ Helicopters over paradise/ Are you kidding?' again evoke a riot situation (*BF,* 34). A light, implying surveillance, shines 'from a helicopter onto a tulip' (*BF,* 41) in 'African Boog', and, on the penultimate page of *Brixton Fractals*, a helicopter contemplates a social intransigence that is figured as a form of linguistic resistance:

>   Beneath helicopters
>   Brixton abandoned
>   Challenges the closure of meaning. (*BF,* 82)

Here Fisher, seems to be exploring the productive capacities of social decay – the notion that 'endless destruction/ makes Brixton' (*BF,* 81). The severe economic doctrines that were in the ascendant at the time are met with a sprawling and uncontainable discursive mesh that thrives on undoing as much as doing. At the end of *Brixton Fractals* the sound of the police siren acts in the manner of a rocket-like weapon:

>   a new siren on a police weapon
>   fills the walkway
>   It leaves a burnt fizz overhead
>   grooves the mud plane on the roof (*BF,* 74)

The insubstantial becomes threateningly substantial as the siren sound flies overhead and into the roof. Fisher's leap from sound to violence suggests a meeting point between the two – a trauma, perhaps, that passes from affective to physical states. It recalls '…the force/ felt in the chest/ as speaker loudness increases' of earlier in *Brixton Fractals* (*BF,* 5-6) and is comparable to Johnson's understanding of the colonial counterhistory memorialised in the musical performance of reggae. Social authority becomes weaponised in an instant, as the gap between symbolic and actual violence is suddenly removed.

In *Brixton Fractals*, then, the text's rapid transformations perform a realisation of latent and actual violence in Brixton. It is a book in which sound, the body, technology and social unrest are bound together. By adapting some motifs from the presence of sound system culture in Brixton, the book allows another index of suffering to make its presence felt. The aural evidence of 'dread' opens a non-European fissure in the text's expansive collage work.

Brixton Fractals and the early work of Johnson perform entirely different analyses of 'place'. Nonetheless, the coincidence in these poems of a somatised disturbance that finds aural expression suggests a hidden vector of affiliation – much like the subterranean waterways that run through Fisher's *Place*. *Brixton Fractals*, to use another aural metaphor, is a stethoscope applied to a wounded body, an aesthetic instrument attuned to the crackle and hum of cultural dissolution. In that very process of decay, it finds the possibility of renewed linguistic possibility.

Law-breaking law-enforcement in the service of a corrupt notion of national identity brings with it the violent denial of cultural difference. Fisher's incorporation of 'many voices… many sources, many spacetimes' is clearly meant as an endorsement of a poetry in the tradition of the modernist avant-garde: polyphonic, informed by collage and procedural approaches and with a broad cultural and historical reach. It is also a poetry that is an implicit repudiation of the monocultural Britain that elements of the Right in Britain were hankering after. Brixton was a thorn in the side of such tendencies, as Fisher recognises when, in *Necessary Business*, he cites 'Brixton 1981' – the riot – as an index of a wider aesthetic crisis (Fisher, 1999, 22).

In one of several allusions to the poet in *Brixton Fractals*, Fisher has William Blake sitting on Kennington Common 'over the Effra-Washway' (*BF*, 26). This links Blake by underground river to Brixton a few miles further south. Kennington Common (now Kennington Park) has a history of radicalism: Jacobite rebels were hanged there in 1746 and it was the site of the huge Chartist rally of 1848. Fisher's Lambeth becomes a figure of visionary dissent, much as Brixton itself was an emblem of radical nonconformism for the British right. Using extensive citation to create an effect of estranging otherness, *Brixton Fractals* acts as a listening device that picks up a powerful undertow of political and racial conflict, actual and historical. Sirens, loudspeakers and the sheer discursive viscosity of the text combine to create an ambience of incipient overload as the cultural energies it records "send the needles into peak/ and damage the Dolby" (*BF*, 5).

References

Baudrillard, Jean (1983). 'The Theater of Cruelty,' in *In the Shadow of the Silent Majorities*. New York: Semiotext(e).

Bradley, Lloyd (2000). *Bass Culture: When Reggae was King*. London: Viking.

Fanon, Frantz (1967), *The Wretched of the Earth*, trs Constance Farrington, London: Penguin, 1983 [1967].

Fisher, Allen (1982). 'Ideas on the Culture Dreamed Of.' London: Spanner.

Fisher, Allen (1985). *Brixton Fractals*, collected in *Gravity*. Cambridge: Salt, 2004 [first edn Aloes Books, London 1985]).

_____ (1995) 'Writers' Notes: Allen Fisher'. *West Coast Line*, 29: 2, 1995, 109-111.

_____ 'Necessary Business' in *The Topographical Shovel* (Willowdale, Ontario: Gig Editions, 1999 [originally published by Spanner Editions in 1985; revised 1990]).

_____ (1999b) 'The Poetics of the Complexity Manifold.' *Boundary 2*, 26:1 (1999), 115-118.

_____ (2004). *Entanglement*. Ontario: Gig Editions.

_____ (2005). *Becoming. In Place*. London: Reality Street Editions [first edn, as *Becoming, being most of Place book IIII and much of book V*, London: Aloes Books, 1978].

_____ (2007). *Leans*. Cambridge: Salt.

Johnson, Linton Kwesi (1974). *Voices of the Living and the Dead*. London: Race Today, 1983 [1974].

_____ (1975). *Dread Beat & Blood*. London: Bogle-L'Ouverture Publications.

_____ (1976). 'Jamaican Rebel Music', *Race & Class* 17:4 (1976), 397-412.

_____ and Mervyn Morris (1989). Interview. Markham, E.A. (ed.) *Hinterland-Caribbean Poetry from the West Indies and Britain*. Newcastle upon Tyne: Bloodaxe Books, 1989), 250-261.

_____ and Burt Caesar (1996). 'Linton Kwesi Johnson Talks to Burt Caesar at Parkside Studios, Brixton, London, June 1996.' *Critical Quarterly* 38 (4), Winter 1996, 64-77.

_____ and Scott Thurston, 'Method and Technique in the work of Allen Fisher', *Poetry Salzburg Review* 3, autumn 2002, 10-27.

Lawson, Andrew (1989). 'Life after Larkin: Postmodern British Poetry,' *Textual Practice*, 3:3, winter 1989, 413-425.

Rossi, Franco (1980). *Babylon* (film).

Shipley, Peter (1981). 'The Riots and the Far Left', *New Community* IX: 2, Autumn 1981, 195-197.

South London Press (1981). News story on Brixton Riot, 14 April 1981, 3.

Woods, Tim (1996). 'Allen Fisher's *Place* project and the "Spatial Turn"'. *Parataxis* 8/9, 1996, 39-46.

Allen Fisher's Apocalypse Then:
Between *Place* and *Gravity*: Technique and Technology

ROBERT SHEPPARD

It is tempting to suggest that Allen Fisher's *The Apocalyptic Sonnets*, published in 1978, forms the pineal link between his two major projects *Place* (1971-1980) and *Gravity as a consequence of shape* (1982-2005), and I would proceed without hesitation to this argument were it not for three qualifications.

Firstly, although the texts were published towards the end of Fisher's period of work on *Place*, near the uncertain era (1980-84) that Fisher has referred to as one of 'entrenchment and awe' (Fisher 1985b: 163), an artistically blocked 'situation of punctuated flux where technique lost most of its predictive value', *The Apocalyptic Sonnets* were actually written in 1976-77, coterminous with the first project. (Fisher 1985b: 163) *The Apocalyptic Sonnets* show anything but a lack of direction; they exhibit a faith in their techniques, and I hope to show that, even if Fisher did not reflect on the achievements of this admittedly minor project, it was nevertheless predictive of the techniques of *Gravity as a Consequence of Shape*, as well as being a significant work in its own right. It is possible that the 'retrenchment' was a reaction to the damage to self-confidence and the loss of *collective* energy caused by the events at the Poetry Society, but the writing of the sonnets themselves, with their exuberant and contentious experimentalism, belongs to the period of the greatest upheavals at the Poetry Society.

Secondly, in his volume of early selected writings, *Scram or The Transformation of the concept of Cities* (1994), which expressly concerns itself with providing examples of conceptual work, such as *defamiliarising*----------*, or excerpts from the *Blood-Bone-Brain* conceptual-performance works, along with samples of 'dramatic and other monologues' (Fisher 1994: 7), as well as selections from topological-lyrical passages of *Place* itself, *The Apocalyptic Sonnets* are neither featured nor mentioned (Fisher 1994: 8). However, with a writer such as Fisher, who explicitly offers a volume such as *Scram* (and also the 1975 inventory of works in progress *Prosyncel*) to contextualize his own work, it is sometimes necessary to read his work *against* the conceptual and generative schema he sets up. If the intention of Fisher's poetics is to activate the reader or audience – though I am getting ahead of my argument here – then part of that activity might involve resistance to all authorial and authoritative pronouncements.[1]

Thirdly, mention of poetics introduces a document which probably has more claim to be the link between the two major projects, one from which Fisher's comments above regarding 'entrenchment' and his failing sense of 'technique', were drawn. This is the poetics essay *Necessary Business*, which was written between 1980-84, provided with a 'Foreword' in June 1985, and published the following month by Fisher's own Spanner press. Deriving from critical but eccentric readings of works by Eric Mottram, J.H. Prynne and cris cheek, it develops a poetics of the 'new pertinence', which is largely that of *Gravity as a Consequence of Shape*, upon which Fisher had begun work in 1982, but, of course, this poetics – like most poetics – does not predict practice (as I hope may be shown of *The Apocalyptic Sonnets*), but establishes the conditions for what will be attempted.

Place exemplified, formally speaking, a method of connecting and juxtaposing materials that became one of the privileged styles of the British Poetry Revival of the 1970s: the field of patterned energies, with nodes, or notes, of facts disposed upon the page in a primarily spatial disposition (the resultant white space being often performed as silence), a mode loosely derived from the work of Charles Olson and from a face-value reading of his poetics essay 'Projective Verse' (1950), as well as nodding towards the ideogrammic method of juxtaposition of Ezra Pound's *Cantos*. Iain Sinclair's *Lud Heat* (1975) and Lee Harwood's *The Long Black Veil* (1970-2) and *Notes of a Post Office Clerk* (1975) which have the added heteroglossic dimension of prose passages, fit the bill. Barry MacSweeney's suppressed volume *Black Torch* (1977) and Eric Mottram's *Elegies* (1981) are also exemplars. The Olsonian proselytising of Mottram himself, a crucially important figure for Fisher, and an obvious candidate for the tripartite speculations of *Necessary Business*, is essential here. Mottram's densely allusive exposition, 'Open Field Poetry', published in the magazine *Poetry Information*, probably influ-

---

[1] *Poetics* I define quite strictly as the products of the process of reflection upon writings, and upon the act of writing, gathering from the past and from others, speculatively casting into the future. Poetics is a discipline, though a flexible one, a discourse, though an intermittent mercurial one. Poetics is a writer-centred self-organising activity, a way of letting writers question what they think they know. Poetics exist for poets and the poetic community generally, to produce (to quote Rachel Blau du Plessis) 'a permission to continue' (DuPlessis, R, 156). See also my *The Necessity of Poetics* (Liverpool: Ship of Fools, 2002) and Sheppard 1999.

enced many writers to adopt this style, approach, or assimilative improvisational activity – 'the poem could now use whatever material in whatever form that comes into the process of composition' – but also to follow Olson, in exploring the *petites histoires* of geography (as Fisher did) (Mottram 1977a: 6). For example, Mottram's keynote paper for the Polytechnic of Central London conference, 'Inheritance Landscape Location: Data for British Poetry 1977' was premised upon the primacy of the otherwise obvious statement that 'a poet works at the intersection of his time and his place', and a plethora of British Poetry Revival poets are read in this light (Mottram 1977b: 85). The dominance of a poetic mode placing itself at the centre of a supposed Pound-Olson tradition, and the privileging of the investigation of 'place' (for example, a whole edition of the magazine, *Joe DiMaggio* (no. 11, 1975), was dedicated to poetry of place), led Adrian Clarke and myself, writing in 1991, to question 'a concern with alternative "traditions" and "bodies of knowledge" – the most deadening being a 70s' obsession with "place"' (Clarke and Sheppard 1991: 122). The oracular dramatic monologues of *Unpolished Mirrors*, which were published monthly as a serial from Spanner, suggest that Fisher, too, was trying to find a new way to articulate his interest in the matter of London in this last part of *Place*, separate from the presentation of factual quotations and lyrical caveats in paratactic utterances on the spatialised page. When one of his characters, Christopher Wren, remarks, 'I have been the historian too long/ immersed in wreckage hurled at my feet', he might also be speaking for Fisher (Fisher 1985c: 57).

The final Spanner instalment of *Unpolished Mirrors*, serial H, not collected in the 1985 Reality Studios volume of the same title, nor in the Reality Street complete *Place*, published in 2005, presents a number of 'map(s) of approaches' to the project, along with a prospective diagram of it, dated 1971 and clearly indicating 1980 as the year of its abandonment/completion (Fisher 1981: 92-4; 99-101). The proffered reading strategies demonstrate that the role of the reader, facing the resistance and interference of various 'cut-ins', and of a variety of 'mirroring' texts that demand to be read against one another, favours a non-linear passage through the one-hundred-page parts of the project's five main books. (Only one 'approach' is 'considered void': a chronological reading of these published books, although that is exactly what the reader is led to do in the 2005 volume [Fisher 1981: 99].) This global structural complexity does much to offset the accusations of inertness and spatial flatness in *Place* at a localized reading level; we are being instructed not to dwell on any single part. Fisher's contention that in the act of reading any passage one is positioned as 'the loci of a point on a moving sphere' with relation to the entire project is found handwritten onto the 1971 diagram (Fisher 1981: 101; the phrase is also found in the text itself, in Fisher 1976: n.p.; Fisher 1979: 23; Fisher 2005: 251). This is almost an affirmative answer to the self-doubt he reveals in 'a map of approaches: six': 'readers have asked ... whether an arbitrary page selection would offer sufficient readability' (Fisher 1981: 100). Readers need to navigate and keep moving across the territory of the text, armed with these 'maps', wherever they begin. The problem for the reader is that the extrinsic motivators to move through the text are not matched well by intrinsic motivators to move across the page. The eye is in danger of slipping from word cluster to word cluster. If the page is spatialised, and particularly if grammar is relaxed too much, it arguably lessens the temporal aspects of syntactic or rhythmic flow in favour of white space silences. Derek Attridge writes that the 'distinctiveness of poetry' demands that 'the verbal singularity that is performed by the reader includes *a sense of its real-time unfolding*' (Attridge 2004: 71).[2]

However, the problem with open field poetics is not rhythmic, since there exist vital non-linear and visual poetries, but the paucity of content as poems trail off into 'notes', or its obfuscation in a field clogged with factual data. Fisher often avoids both extremes. Indeed, the most profitable way to conceive of the *Place* work, and one which introduces a readerly dimension into the process (a dimension that will prove crucial to *Gravity as a Consequence of Shape*) is to follow Peter Barry and rationalise *Place* as a 'content-specific' work. He argues, with some conviction, that readers

> need to reactivate a body of reading in order to enter the poem. It is important to realise, though, that doing this isn't just a preliminary to the reading of the poem: a reciprocal process takes place in which we read the sources in the light of the poem and the poem in the light of the sources.... So the text is ... readerly in two senses:

---

[2] Attridge is open to the possibility that some poets 'use spatial arrangement to create effects in part by resisting the expectation that poems occur in time,' but he is thinking of a narrow range of concrete poetry (Attridge 2004, 72). Nevertheless, this may be used as a defence of 'open field' writing and of non-linear poetry.

firstly, it is *about* reading, and secondly, it demands the reader's sustained participatory engagement with its materials as well as with 'the words on the page'. The kind of reading required is thus an active ... process like study. (Barry 1993: 199-200)

This reminds us that *Place* was itself a conceptual response to *readings* about place, rather than improvised field-notes or site-specific spontaneous jottings, and some of the most effective passages of the project are where the past and present are juxtaposed, as in the amusing and instructive contrast of '1583 When we went our perambulation at Vicar's Oke in Rogation Week £0.2.6d' with: '1973 Bus fare back from search for Vicar's Oak £0.60p' (Fisher 1976: n.p.; Fisher 2005: 37). Developed in the poetry, fiction, and later documentary, of Fisher's acknowledged contemporary, Iain Sinclair, and filtered through the novels of Peter Ackroyd, narrative modes of this ironic temporal juxtaposition would define a literary sub-genre in the 1980s and later. Where Fisher is at his most original is where he intuits the psychosomatic condition of the present city-dweller in terms of pollution and influences that are geographical, historical, economic and political. Even though Alfred Watkins, the 'discoverer' of ley lines, is listed in the resources to the 1976 *Place*, there are no Sinclair-like forces at play, no malign lines of influence between (arbitrarily selected) sites. Fisher prefers to divine, the lost (but real) rivers of London, vanished tributaries that he uses both as 'a metaphor for thought' and as the presentation of the physical causes of present-day impediment and ill-health (Barry 1993: 201). One page reads entire:

> our health is failing
>
> already the potions of Epsom & sea salts
>   at Balham Hill and Brixton Causeway wells
>   through a bed of oysters
>   is stagnant
>
> feeding our bodies with the stench of its yawn
>
> from the beds of sexless oysters
>   our fingers retract
>   smelling of cigar smoke (Fisher 1976: n.p.; Fisher 2005: 23)

The sudden lyrical outburst about the 'yawn' of fatigue gripping 'us' – the text is emphatically civic in its concerns – and the image of both polluted fingers and contaminated oyster beds (sexless beds suggest an associated human infertility) are neatly poised against a history of Epsom's famously restorative salts, yet it does not require contextualising 'information' as recommended by Mottram and partly validated by Barry, although it may be possible to read afresh the 'sources' in the light of the poem, as the latter suggests.

By the time of Fisher's *Necessary Business*, the terms of engagement have significantly altered, and this document may be read as the first developed poetics of linguistically innovative poetry. Its poetics of 'the new pertinence' is defined as one

> that undertakes its aesthetic function from the ground – from its activity… Poetry does not collaborate with society, but with life; its field of collaboration is predominantly aesthetic, that is its main function. Whatever else I may get from a work of art, because its dominant function is aesthetic it requires my engagement to create it, to produce it. The significance I most warmly value derives from this production, its affirmation of life. (Fisher 1985b: 164-5)

I have written of *Necessary Business* elsewhere, firstly, because it seems to me to isolate some of the characteristics of poetics as a semi-autonomous discourse for writerly and communal development; it exemplifies poetics' often incomplete and speculative nature, as well as its often hybrid formal properties, miming the procedures and processes of the poetic work it assists bringing into being. Secondly, *Necessary Business* delineates a particular poetics developed in *Gravity as a Consequence of Shape*, emphasising as it does the dimension of the aesthetic (rather than the conceptual) as the essential one for art. Fisher's use of Mukařovský's concept of the 'aesthetic function' as a primary operative feature for the reader, allowing him or her to enlarge his or her creative faculties in readerly engagement with the art object's incompleteness, *is* the 'necessary business' of Fisher's title. (See Sheppard 1999; and 2005: 195-9.)

Fisher launched the first 'showing' of *Gravity as a Consequence of Shape,* in October 1983 at Mottram's King's Readings at the University of London. *Banda*, later to be the opening poem of *Brixton Fractals*, was originally published jointly by Fisher's own Spanner and Mottram's characteristically named Open Field (a misnomer for this new work, of course). What impressed me at the reading and beyond was the sheer impaction of the materials, as I found myself positioned as an active reader of the text, performing my 'engagement' of the 'aesthetic function' through its very artifice and technique, creating as they do the sense of being in the thick of things, in an unfinished, half-formalised world, that presents itself as fields of conflicting energies: 'Took chances in London traffic/ where the culture breaks' (Fisher 1985a:1; Fisher 2004a: 3). The resistance Adrian Clarke and I registered towards 'open field' work, coupled with delight at the texts in *Brixton Fractals*, explains the pride of place we gave to this work in our anthology of late 1980s London linguistically innovative writing, *Floating Capital*. (1991) We wrote:

> Its appearance both confirmed and accelerated a shift away from ideals prevalent in the 60s and 70s in favour of approaches that attend more closely to the paving slabs than to 'open field' poetics and more closely to their language than to either.... (Clarke and Sheppard 1991: 122)

The opening lines of 'Bel Air' suggest the insistent jamming of materials against one another, from the surprise of 'octobers' functioning as a verb, to the 'obo' (a nail, but for a moment one thinks of the reed instrument) hitting a tooth. Intrusions of the new, a series of actions and reaction, are stabilized by apparent cause and effect, from the smallest element (the punning 'fluff') to an entire continent. The poem becomes a paradoxical record of events that may never happen, but that happen, imaginatively, as the reader assembles what I call their *creative linkage*, as collage enacts a syntactic miming of the effects of spacetime, the sense of multiple realities recorded near-simultaneously.[3] The thrusting

---

[3] See my chapter 'Creative Linkage in the Work of Allen Fisher, Adrian Clarke and Ulli Freer in the 1980s and 1990s' in *The Poetry of Saying*. Liverpool: Liverpool University Press, 2005: 194-213. I use the same coinage much more personally in 'Linking the Unlinkable' in my 1999 *Far Language*. Exeter: Stride Publications, and elsewhere (of my own poetry) as 'a general and technical term for the aesthetic and ethical enterprise of linking the unlinkable. Such links can be articulated on a surface which is like the skin of delirium, with simultaneously more disruption than would be connoted by the term 'juxtaposition' – and also less. The links, melted into the materials, disappear. Discontinuity work(s) to make continuities'. (Sheppard 1995, 112)

rhythm, the loose connectives of what I feel compelled to call a pseudo-syntax, engages the reader in the collaborative construction of meaning, line-by-line, not page-by-page, as in *Place*. Tom Raworth, of course, with his extended sequences of works from *Writing* (written 1975-7), through to *West Wind* (written 1983), had prefigured this rapid-fire tickertape of constant juxtaposition, and may have directly influenced both Fisher's writing and performance. However, the pseudo-syntax combines the certainties of closure with textual openness. The rudiments of narrative present a jump-cut consciousness that connects, almost prophetically, criminality, the State and capitalism, but which is controlled by a decentred but present narrator (or at least a ghostly narrational function created by the recurrent use of the first person).

> At last it octobers, a tremendous
> mist descends on my head
> trip a cat
> an obo hits my incisor
> I fall back
> 'Good Morning, this is the News'
> Is this naiveté or integrity –
> this simpleness or confidence to gaze
> with intelligent vitality with
> numerosity a
> splendid buzz from a razor that,
> spaced out on a slowed down recording,
> reveals a fluff in the magnetic arrangement.
> This is Europe
> it's not even a terminal.
> Forget arrangement. Stop.
> 'Thankyou, but this gets us nowhere.'
> A Burglar near the end of the century
> looks out over his balcony
> and reinterprets the State,
> Everything now appears to take place outside
> Work's quantum determines the permanence of violent conditions.
> Of course he's sick of it!
>   (Fisher 1985a: 39; Fisher 2004a: 44)

This is no longer a content-specific poetry. Fisher is not making references for readers to 'study'; he is making art for readers to engage with. Whatever sources are brought into the text – and they are emphatically multiple, in a desperately assimilative gesture, partly recorded by Fisher's 'resource' lists at the end of his volumes – the readerly activity is less 'like study', but still demands, by its very juxtapositions, that the reader engages with it, though he or she has to operate its imperfect fit. 'Everything now appears to take place outside,' seems exactly right, but even this statement is positioned between the Burglar's political hermeneutics and the line's possible, but imperfect, cohesion with the line that follows, which emphasises the rhythms and energy of labour.

Whereas Attridge correctly demands that a reader experiences the unfolding of poetry in a temporal virtuality, in Fisher's multiple world, it unfolds in an approximation of the impossible experience of spacetime. At their best, the poems of *Gravity as a Consequence of Shape* offer this partial experience of multiplicity in one indeterminate discourse, as in the opening of 'Bel Air', what Fisher calls elsewhere an 'aspiration of multiple and collage form through the pasting of many sources, many spacetimes' (Fisher 1995a: 110). Where the poems do not 'work' is precisely where there is neither the creative linkage of 'Banda' or 'Bel Air', nor even the laying bare of the device, as found in 'African Boog', where separate sources are presented in varying typefaces and lineation, but – to keep to examples from *Brixton Fractals* – the kind of non-dramatised cut-up of source material found in 'Boogie Stomp', which at one point seems almost to describe its own inert compaction (in its least inert phrase): 'an intellect steeped in empiric lockjaw' (Fisher 1985a: 58; Fisher 2004a: 64).

The end of serial H of *Unpolished Mirrors* offers a checklist of 'related publications' to the *Place* project and also 'other books by Allen Fisher' (Fisher 1980: 104). *The Apocalyptic Sonnets* is one of these 'others' and is therefore explicitly situated as not related to *Place*. Another work, *William Rufus*, is announced as 'still in progress with the work *Faust Undamned*', which is an (unfinished) project of which *The Apocalyptic Sonnets* were also advertised as being a 'part' (Fisher 1980: 104). This meandering creative tributary seems to have dried up during the delicate years of the early 1980s, but, if we follow Fisher's metaphor of subterranean rivers being like thought, then perhaps these mostly hidden channels will also reveal something of his creative practice prior to his progression to *Gravity as a consequence of shape*.

The Apocalyptic Sonnets – the only part of the project to appear – was published in 1978 by Ric and Ann Caddel's important small press, Pig Press, and has never been reprinted whole (though it is anthologised in part in Jeff Hilson's *The Reality Street Book of Sonnets* (2008): 109-114). The plain white cover of this unusually half-lithographed and half mimeographed pamphlet displays the name of the artist Robert Clark above the title and Fisher's name. The litho pages are indeed a series of seven untitled etchings by Clark which, while dark and brooding, and suggestive of apocalyptic disintegration, do not seem particularly related to the poems (which are, in fact, related to other etchings). The mimeo pages contain the 16 'sonnets', which are described as 'scores' rather than as finished texts. They had appeared in cris cheek's magazine *Rawz* and in Eric Mottram's *Poetry Review* (Vol 67, Number 1 and 2, 1977), but as I have no direct experience of how, as 'scores', they became the bases of subsequent live or textual performances, I will treat the texts as final, and read them against Fisher's schema. A note before the scores indicate that they 'follow Dürer's THE APOCALYPSE woodcuts 1497-8 issued in 1511 and two etchings from the same period: THE FOUR WITCHES (and) THE DOCTOR'S DREAM' (Fisher 1978: n.p.). The word 'follow' is an ambiguous one, suggesting less than 'modelled upon' or 'structured upon'. The most obvious evidence of this 'following' is the presence of the titles of the Dürer works (in a different typeface, here represented by italics) in nearly all of the texts, but occasionally they are developed in the narrative. Further paratextual patterning is provided by the titles of the poems themselves, each relating to an art work – none of them by Dürer or Robert Clark – from Duchamp to the Damned, from Franz Kafka to Fritz Lang (I will examine a poem called 'The Tired Death' below). The sources for each title are listed at the end of the pamphlet. The curious concept 'follows' is introduced again, when Fisher describes poem nine, 'The Wedding March', as being 'Eric Von Stroheim's film title', (Fisher 1978: 17) but adds, 'The score follows a performance given by COUM at the I.C.A. in 1976', which suggests the text may be a rough attempt to structure itself on a performance, but it is not clear how, and may be irrecoverable or irrelevant to this reading (Fisher 1978: 17).

Each of these 'titles' is really a 'name' for its text (to use a distinction of John Ashbery's) since they are all borrowed; only occasionally does one discern a thematic connection between them and the texts they 'introduce'. Equally perplexing are the poems' dedications. Each is dedicated to a member of the Labour government of the day (1976), for example: 'To Anthony Wedgwood Benn, M.P./ Secretary of State for Energy' (Fisher 1978: 10). This reads particularly strangely now, given that Tony Benn as he is now, is an octogenarian veteran of left-wing struggles, long since relieved of his first and only brush with collective ministerial responsibility. Between the writing and the contemporary reading of the work falls the shadow of the Thatcher administration (1979-1991). It is difficult to see (or remember) how the rather ineffectual administration of Jim Callaghan, which Thatcher would oust in 1979, could have been demonised in this apocalyptic context, although its policies in Northern Ireland were controversial and probably counter-productive (and this leaves its trace on *The Apocalyptic Sonnets*). There is little discernible connection between the ministers and the poems, although the first poem is dedicated to Peter Shore, the then Secretary of State for the Environment, and this emphasises Fisher's typical focus on the psychosomatics of the environment that is treated in several of the poems that follow.

These paratextual devices, and the presence of Dürer's titles in the texts, combine with a number of other structural repetitions to provide significant patterning. While the 'Apocalyptic' of the title points us towards the Dürer woodcuts, the formal description of the 'scores' as 'sonnets' suggests a literary genre that is ghosted here. Surprisingly, given Fisher's 'open field' credentials of the time, the lines are mostly ten syllables in length, occasionally in iambic feet, particularly in the poems' opening lines, but otherwise are best read as syllabic. There is even a sprinkling of internal rhyme in the sequence. Each poem is a sort of double sonnet of 28 lines, in quatrains. But the last four lines are indented like the couplet of a Shakespearean sonnet and function as a conclusion; each one mentions 'Technology'. Formally speaking, these poems approach the use of custom-built 'constraints' rather than inherited literary 'conventions', to borrow the Oulipo movement's apt distinction, and like the French experimentalists Jacques Roubaud or Jacques Bens, Fisher is here drawn to the pseudo-sonnet (as Thomas A. Clark and Tom Raworth were in Britain; Jeff Hilson's anthology *The Reality Street Book of Sonnets* is a recent survey of this sub-genre). Fisher mercurially escapes from the pedagogy of open field by refusing it as a singular technique.

The third poem – which I quote below in full – demonstrates how these structurings are disposed upon the page, and can be used to exemplify other recurrences across the sonnets. The figure of Faust – whether the 'Unbound' of Fisher's abandoned project or not - often appears in the first or second stanzas. In the fourth stanzas a place is named, usually in London, whether the central Westminster where the MPs meet, or Tooting, a location familiar from *Place*. In poem 14 the location, moved to stanza three, is Belfast, perhaps a sardonic remark upon direct rule from Westminster; Ulster is figured as one of the provinces of London.

'THE TIRED DEATH'

To Mrs. Shirley Williams, M. P.
Secretary of State for Science and
Education, and Paymaster General.

A Boys' Brigade bugle the church outside;
a wise Faust arched into shade, overhead
aircraft seems to disappear leaving its
signature, a drone on his skin, vibrates

in nerves' connections locking clut cluster
of entertainment, white noise and little
into his reactions. He enters the
building headache that does not dissipate.
          (Fisher 1978: 3; Hilson 2008: 110)

This poem projects a very particularised world through its loose phrasing and looser syntax; it is not yet the pseudo-syntax of *Brixton Fractals* but one in which commas chop across phrases, leaving disjointed grammatical units. Rather like a contemporary canvas by Gerhard Richter, the impressions gets blurred the closer one approaches the detail. The opening line, for example, combines a not unusual series of lexical items in discordant union. The Boy's Brigade familiarly uses bugles, and meets in church halls, but the actual syntactic action amounts to something more mysterious. The semi-colon that leads the reader to Faust, the poem's central character, is distracting. Faust's wisdom is to withdraw from this scene, although he is unable to, since he is figured as someone who registers the world corporeally and neurally. A droning signature on the skin is mildly Kafkaesque, but the nerves' and the poem's connections (or lack of them) seem to generate the familiar Fisher psychosomatic response to the built environment, a white-noise migraine. Everything is a 'clut cluster' – perhaps best read as a verbal stutter, for there is no word 'clut', although it also connotes claustrophobic *clut*ter – focussed upon 'Piccadilly corridors', in that up-market part of London.

> Piccadilly corridors process their
> pre-conscious conditioning, calculate
> behind closed pores and bolted cells, skins that
> polish collective thrones, clean suicides.

The thick artifice of alliteration suggests that the 'description' we read has been constructed, at least in part, by this laying bare of the device, so we cannot completely trust its apparent mimesis. The puns on 'pores' (for doors) and 'cells' suggest that the skin again reacts, this time to named interiors of buildings. The menace of 'clean suicides' registers the insufferable order of corridors, this text written some years before 'sick building syndrome' entered (and subsequently left) popular discourse concerning the psychosomatics of architecture. The epileptic menace of fluorescent lights is a final shot at the theme, before the title from Dürer intrudes, although the 'leeches thriving on exhaust fumes' and the 'burnt/ out nerves' ('Nerves' is the title of a subsequent sonnet, see below) returns the reader to the body, a return announced also by the word 'sacra' (actually a plural form) which, despite a trace of the sacred in its etymology, is a bone of the pelvic arch.

> Fluorescent whirr stoning. Their sacra is
> re-emphasised, sanctity conjures
> *John Before God and the Elders*, reciting
> repetitions around a table, they
>
> petition to lift scalpels together,
> break notches in holsters, humming Air
> Force charity songs, audience ratings
> indicate speech phones and choices, the height
>
> of their voices' groans, a Irative act,
> generates a breed of invisible
> leeches thriving on exhaust fumes and burnt
> out nerves of craftsmen cracking jokes for bread.

Conjuring for a moment superimposes the apocalyptic judgement depicted by Dürer onto the Piccadilly backdrop, or upon the stranger world of potential surgery, gang-show entertainments, or anger ('Irative' is a neologism, but operates as an adjectival form of 'ire' in my blind reading). Deskilled craftsmen are forced to turn into entertainers in this world, prey to the parasites of the city-scape.

> Where Technology is misunderstood,
> kept behind Velvette curtains, it becomes
> proper to sanction the art that does not
> interfere, does not allow breath to clear.

After the sonnet turns, quasi-traditionally on its *volta*, represented also by indentation, and offers its 'conclusion' with a rhyme that hints at the Shakespearean couplet, this particular meditation on 'Technology' contrasts with the activities of the redundant craftsmen. Whether the misunderstood Technology is kept behind the synthetic Velvette curtains – perhaps it will be unveiled suddenly like a new car at the Motor Show, or perhaps it is camouflaged by this cheap plush – it is connected with, and opposed by, art (always lower-case). It is clear that it is society in general, and its proprieties, which 'sanction' – the word carries an echo of earlier 'sanctity' - an 'art that does not interfere'. Fisher's own art – as exemplified by this very poem – is an art of patterned interferences. False Technology privileges a non-interventionist artifice that suits its own aggrandisement. This interpretation is confirmed by the poem's final phrase, its unusually precise syntax and parallel repetitions of 'does not'. An art in complicity with this form of Technology 'does not allow breath to clear'. Throughout the 16 poems there are repeated references to breathing and throats, to a lack of free and fresh air, and particularly to Faust's own 'suffocation'. (Fisher 1978: 2)

This reference outwards from the single poem both confirms and undermines my semantically centrifugal reading of 'The Tired Death'. The recognition of repetitions of many lexical items across the sequence – references to chests, lungs, nerves, and Warmth, for example – undermine my attempt to read a single poem in isolation. A paradigmatic arrangement and substitution within classes of very many lexical terms – for example, 'sacra', 'thyroid', 'gambrel', 'fances', all anatomical features – are spread across the poems, not unlike the structural repetitions already noted, but both providing structure through repetition (one of the most ancient elements of poetic artifice) and decentring the stability of the discourse through restless variation and apparent foregrounded substitution. It is not unlike the effect of realising that the 'description' of Piccadilly is determined by words that alliterate with its name. Once this mode of foregrounded artifice is responded to by a reader, everything falls into place, and everything falls to pieces. Its aesthetic function forces the reader to take a binocular view of artifice and reality, and to assemble the possible world offered as he or she can. It is a precursor to the spacetime modalities of *Gravity as a Consequence of a Shape*.

While *The Apocalyptic Sonnets* once belonged to a project called *Faust Undamned*, the Faust featured in these sonnets is not the shadowy historical original (who incidentally was a contemporary of Dürer in fourteenth century Germany), or his subsequent transubstantiation into Pan-European legend, as the scholar who sold his soul to the devil for eternal life and an omniscient perspective upon history, the legend picked up by Marlowe and others, but the creation of another titanic German, Goethe, whose verse drama *Faust* is a comparatively late addition to the corpus. It is also one in which Faust – trading in language and knowledge for a life of action and rich sensual experience – is already effectively undamned; if at the end of Part One, he is implored by Mephistopheles to 'Come to me', (Goethe 1987: 148), it is not to eternal damnation, since in the lesser-read Part Two he is redeemed. Marguerite, whom he had seduced and reduced to committing a mortal sin, is already redeemed in Part One, and she too appears in a number of Fisher's sonnets; there is one comic vision of Mephistopheles, as a drunken vagrant, in sonnet four, an ecological trickster with 'finger-lickin' oiled skin', contaminated by, but existing on, fast food refuse (Fisher 1978: 4).

Fisher's Faust is subject in a number of poems to the psychosomatics of urban life, often figured as choking, and therefore leaving him unable to speak, but occasionally he becomes communicatively affective as well as literally infectious: 'Coughs defecate pain from Faust's chest into/ his throat causing his speech to moisten eyes'. (Fisher 1978: 13) In the first sonnet, where another body-part is invoked, and picked up in sonic wordplay, in the pun on 'gamble':

> Talk from tightened throat springs from his gambrel,
> with Faust gambols into future's risk.
> Of himself this Faust demands collective
> consciousness without discrimination;

> without condemning those who would machine
> gun the crowd in their urban erotic
> hate. (Fisher 1978: 1)

This aptly demonstrates the repetitive variations, since, in contrast to 'this' Faust as a ruthless revolutionary terrorist, he is elsewhere depicted as a victim, although the sly pun on the word 'committed' alerts the reader to Faust's complicity in his own, and others', mortality, in the erotics of the random gunman's targeted crowd.

> Faust is committed to death without
> knowledge of the day for execution
> and no assurance it will be that simple. (Fisher 1978: 8)

Marguerite, when she appears, is often associated with Warmth (repeatedly with capitals), an undefined quality that is further related to orgasm, which is described as her 'volition, expectant pleasure breaking/ cask's code: Eros Energoumenos' (Fisher 1978: 14). She is thus possessed by the devils of erotic love, but is also associated with Marcel Duchamp's fragile 'bride' – one poem is entitled 'Large Glass' – which casts Faust as a seducing bachelor, but this can appear, in the different context of poem ten, as liberating: 'in room where the cosmic ceiling opens/ she fucks with her man this understanding'; part of this understanding is her transformative assimilation of Dürer's Hell (Fisher 1978: 14). She

> Refuses to
> die, fights the Cold who kill Warmth Becomes
> *The Apocalyptic Woman*, glowing
> constellation burning perception's doubt. (Fisher 1978: 10)

She expresses utopian 'joy of rifting landscapes her/ shifting body boundaries', in opposition to Faust's psychosomatic oppression (Fisher 1978: 10). No wonder, therefore, in poem ten's final quatrain, that 'Her Technology belongs to Being/ folding unfolding the land the language' in un-alienated interaction and interpenetration of place, body, and utterance (Fisher 1978: 10). Clearly the life-enhancing Technology evoked here is different from the one endorsed by Faust in poem three. Since each poem ends with some reflection on Technology, this demands further investigation.

Eric Mottram, in 1977, identified Fisher as belonging to the Anglo-American tradition of poets – famously for William Carlos Williams, the poem itself was theorised as machinic – for whom technology and mechanisation were potentially liberational:

> As Allen Fisher's *Paxton's Beacon* and 'Reigate' (a section in *The Art of Flight* 1975, which includes the experience of driving a car) show, a poet can at least make a gesture of mediation between individual life and machine without futile either/or choices, (Mottram 1977b: 101)

And part of what we see in *The Apocalyptic Sonnets* is a refusal to cut off technology from art. Even Heidegger, whose resistance to the technologicalisation of the post-War West is well-known, and who certainly did not see Technology as belonging to the realm of Being (as Fisher suggests), nevertheless sought to recover the etymological origin of the word for aesthetics, in a way that supports Fisher's definitions:

> The word stems from the Greek. *Technikon* means that which belongs to *technē*. We must observe two things with respect to the meaning of this word. One is that *technē* is the name not only for the activities and skills of the craftsman but also for the arts of the mind and the fine arts. *Technē* belongs to bringing-forth, to *poiēsis*; it is something poetic. (Heidegger 1993: 318)

That Heidegger saw this truth, or unveiling, denied by modern technology, need not detract from Fisher's long-term refusal of this split between scientism and aesthetics, since both emphasise the rôle of the poetic in the technical. One suspects that Fisher, whose debt to Raoul Vaneigem's *The Revolution of Everyday Life* is indicated by its providing of an epigraph to *Place* (book one), would agree with a commentator on the work of Henri Lefebvre, author of the similarly titled *Critique of Everyday Life*, that the spaces of that life are shot through with technologies that we would be wise to discriminate between:

> A bad understanding and use of technology results in a catastrophic spatial and temporal antagonism between man and nature, establishing a certain inescapable alienation in everyday

life. But a good understanding of technology has infinite potential for life as a work of creation. For technology mediates the production of space. (Aitken 2004: 47)

These extremes – and various positions between them – are exemplified by *The Apocalyptic Sonnets*, ranging from Faust's 'misunderstood' or 'bad understanding' of Technology to Marguerite's unalienated *technē* as *poiēsis*. In a vision that is inflected through Dürer's woodcut of the seven apocalyptic trumpets, poem eight confirms the Heideggerean fear of technology as a 'setting-upon that challenges the energies of nature' (Heidegger 1993: 321):

> Today's Technology's dragon-control
> labelled evil, burning not producing,
> where art is seen as unproductive for
> getting its generational act. (Fisher 1978: 8)

But Faust, in another poem, in another guise, exemplifies the 'bad use' of Technology. There he

> misuses Technology's control
> lulls Marguerite to obedience an
> ache mimicked in groin beat repeats sound, key
> to his religion, perpetuates creed. (Fisher 1978: 12)

Seduction, control and religious dogmatism are equated in a wilful evil that goes beyond the 'misunderstood', or Technology that 'is of its own … volition', (Fisher 1978: 13), or even one that allows for 'government … control of human genes', to use two other examples (and in the latter case, one where the scientific and ethical jury is still out, since government control of the genome today may prove preferable to its patented ownership by integrated world capitalism) (Fisher 1978: 9). Mediated through Dürer's 'The Beast with Two Horns', this Technology is simply oppressive. But when 'Michael's Fighting of the Dragon' provides the backdrop to Faust's 'free energy', 'Then his Technology, his science, his art/ with sharper, clearer breath his blows are raw'; Technology becomes finally poetic, and, characteristically, Faust's suffocation is lifted to enable his effective resistance to false Technology's 'dragon-control' (Fisher 1978: 11). In Fisher's spacetime world-view, it is not a sin to thirst for knowledge with Faustian comprehensiveness, but heroic.

The final sonnet allows Faust his breathing-space. Uniquely addressed by a narrator in an ecstatic, utopian tone to Faust himself, once again free of the bronchial constrictions that elsewhere negate his capacity for speech, he is transformed into a revolutionary energy that he counterpoints, finally, with Marguerite's own. He is thus like one of Blake's (male) spectres in the act of being re-united with his (female) emanation, as he sees her beauty in his mirror (which is, in fact, a scene borrowed from Goethe). This concluding sonnet transcends the location of London – the universal sun and earth literally take its place in stanza three – and its 'Bride' may well (again) be the technologically-produced entity of Duchamp's 'Large Glass', an exemplary modern work of sexual union and separation, rather than Dürer's retinally crowded representations of *The Book of Revelations* with its late medieval morality. The text, complete with paratexts, reads:

'NERVES'

To James Callaghan, M.P.
Prime Minister and First Lord of the Treasury.

Doctor Faust's chest deep breathes. Oh that it may
continue this Spring shocked morning without
rupture. Down a hill she gallops, golden,
of course, unfashionable, the throng's routine

holds its own balls. Marguerite unclasps it
the flow, it rains from her eyes the perfume
consumes setting nostrils she appears
to rise lightens shadows, Faust's storm that

wells a strength unleashed inhaling deep in
to the solar plexus as these two scents
merge sun and earth opening the crocus
the ten senses of their ascending form.

Not always Faust, will your gates be open,
your cask's keep dances as it forms this tree –
fifteen full chains – its own obsolescence
this four legg'd seat's power devours this book.

Know this now Doctor your fists are blossoms
opening their joints to receive the light.
The glass dice are scattered as they once caused
to scatter the image in your mirror

becomes clear water boiled into air. Moves
now the horizon your dream unrests and
condenses clouds until separating
Bride-winch reaches tension's electric storm.

The actual Technologies renew their
spirals. The change they resurrect carries
still unknown charge. These skills guide this
pregnant encumberance (*sic*), to allow the birth, respect.
                    (Fisher 1978: 16; Hilson 2008: 114)

Technologies – note the plural here – are renewed, reborn, guided by a skilled technician, to authorise a vision of a utopian future in which 'technology has infinite potential for life as a work of creation', and in which respect plays its part. 'Respect' can be read either as a noun or a verb, and could have the force of an imperative (as does much of the poem). The dedication to the figurehead of a fading fag-end of the once reforming social-democratic Labour government of the 1960s (with its Wilsonian faith in 'the white heat of technology' for the country's advance much cooled) is, in this instance, openly ironical.

The Apocalyptic Sonnets, with their use of constraints and insistent patternings, emphasise the non-open field, indeed procedural and processual, poetics of Allen Fisher, and operate at the conceptual end of his project range. However, the lyrical and narrative materials develop a loose argument concerning technology (good and bad) and place. Although the texts are described as 'scores', my reading, working against some of Fisher's self-presentations of his work, treats them autonomously as finished pieces. In their use of a loose syntax that approaches a pseudo-syntax, and in their establishment of narrative modes, however indeterminate, they predict the forms of creative linkage of the best poems of *Gravity as a Consequence of Shape*. Their use of other art-works – particularly Dürer's – as titles, as structuring devices, as patterns that are 'followed', pre-figures the use of the alphabetic dance titles and the structural homologies of Blake's Notebook which order and guide the later project. Such followings both structure and interfere. The use of repetitions and correspondences, even of individual words selected paradigmatically across poems, such as 'drone' or 'Warmth', and word association – the systematic use of alliteration and such obvious surface features as 'Belfast' echoed by 'Heldfast' – prefigures the serious use of what Fisher dubs 'rime' in the later work to both structure and disrupt a reader's active aesthetic engagement, although this kind of 'mirroring' was well developed and exemplified in *Place*. Indeed, there are a number of ways in which the 'scores' relate to the co-terminus *Place*. The thematics of a psychosomatic reaction to London is a dominant element. However, the use of shadowy archetypical characters, here borrowed from Goethe, both suggests the oracular monologues he wrote later as *Unpolished Mirrors*, but also suggests the generic characterisations, such as that of the Burglar, that web together the narrative threads of *Gravity as a Consequence of Shape*. One of these characters, the Engineer, is particularly indebted to the liberational technologies explored in the sonnets. In 'Birdland', the most successfully complex of the *Brixton Fractals* poems, he constructs a machine for flight that is 'named jouissance', echoing Marguerite's positive identification with orgasm (Fisher 1985a: 72; Fisher 2004a: 80). In the 1995 poem 'Mummer's Strut', a 'Technologist' actually appears, as a more ambivalent figure, emphasising the options we have between technolog*ies*. The statement, 'In civilised societies technicians are rich' evokes the ironic Blakean response that the corollary must be that somebody else must be kept impoverished (Fisher 1995b: 715; Fisher 2004b: 73). On the other hand, the poem ends with an echo of Dante's ultimate ascent to Paradiso, as the Technician mimes the constructions of Leonardo, the ultimate artist-scientist (the second line is a quotation from his *Notebook*):

> Tomorrow the Technician will
> make the strap and the attempt
>
> to see the stars. (Fisher 1995b: 719; Fisher 2004b: 79)

If, as a technician of the word himself, Fisher was temporarily to lose faith in the predictive function of poetic technique in the early 1980s, it is clear that his recovery from 'punctuated flux' can be retrospectively seen to have been predicted itself by these 16 outstanding poems (Fisher 1985b: 163).

Works Cited

Aitken, A., 'Spotless', *Radical Philosophy*, 126, July/August, 2004: 46-48.
Attridge, Derek. *The Singularity of Literature*. London and New York: Routledge, 2004.
Barry, Peter. 'Allen Fisher and "content-specific" poetry', in Hampson, R. and Barry, Peter, eds. *The New British Poetries: The Scope of the Possible*. Manchester: Manchester University Press, 1993.
Clarke, Adrian. and Sheppard, Robert. 'Afterword' to *Floating Capital: new poets from London*. Elmwood, Connecticut: Potes & Poets Press, 1991.
DuPlessis, Rachel Blau. *The Pink Guitar*. London and New York: Routledge, 1990.
Fisher, Allen. *Apocalyptic Sonnets*. Durham: Pig Press, 1978.
―――― *Place I-XXXVII*. Carrboro: Truck Press, 1976.
―――― *Becoming*. London: Aloes Books, 1979.
―――― *Unpolished Mirrors Serial H*. London: Spanner, 1980.
―――― *Brixton Fractals*. London: Spanner, 1985a.
―――― *Necessary Business*. London: Spanner, 1985b.
―――― *Unpolished Mirrors*. London: Reality Studios, 1985c.
―――― *Scram or The Transformation of the concept of Cities*. Peterborough: Spectacular Diseases, 1994.
―――― 'A statement of poetics...', *West Coast Line*, Number Seventeen (29/2), fall 1995a: 109-10.
―――― 1995b. 'Mummer's Strut', in Tuma, K, ed. *Anthology of Twentieth Century British and Irish Poetry*. Oxford and New York, Oxford University Press, 2001: 712-20.
―――― *Gravity*. Cambridge: Salt, 2004a.
―――― *Entanglement*. Toronto: The Gig, 2004b.
―――― *Place*. Hastings: Reality Street, 2005.
Goethe, J.W. von *Faust Book One*. Oxford: Oxford University Press, 1987.
Heidegger, Martin. 'The Question Concerning Technology', in *Basic Writings (revised and expanded edition)*. London: Routledge, 1993.
Hilson. Jeff. ed. *The Reality Street Book of Sonnets*. Hastings: Reality Street, 2008.
Mottram, Eric. 'Open Field Poetry', *Poetry Information* 17, 1977a.
―――― 'Inheritance Landscape Location: Data for British Poetry 1977', Polytechnic of Central London, 1977b.
Sheppard, Robert. 'A Thumbnail', *West Coast Line*, Number Seventeen (29/2), fall 1995: 112.
―――― 'The Poetics of Poetics: Charles Bernstein, Allen Fisher and 'the poetic thinking that results', *Symbiosis*, Volume 3.1, April 1999.
―――― *The Poetry of Saying*. Liverpool: Liverpool University Press, 2005.

Reading 'Mummers' Strut'

SCOTT THURSTON

In 1995, Allen Fisher published a poem entitled 'Mummers' Strut' in an issue of the magazine *West Coast Line*,[1] accompanied by a statement of poetics. The poem is organised into twenty-seven short numbered sections, mostly in couplets, ranging from two to twenty lines in length. The predominant impression is of a fragmented discourse that is hard to read as constructing a consistent speaking voice of a narrator on a single theme, and yet the poem offers numerous, more subtle, continuities throughout. The division into sections emphasises the fragmented nature of the text but also suggests areas of local coherency that can be compared across the whole. The principle technique that Fisher employs in this and other works is a form of collage; combining materials taken from other texts, often altering them in the process (a technique Fisher calls *re-narration*). This altering of the quotations from other texts amounts to what Fisher calls a 'subversion of collage form' (*WN*, p. 110). These elements are in turn juxtaposed with Fisher's own self-generated material. Throughout his long poetic sequence *Gravity as a consequence of shape*, of which 'Mummers' Strut' is a part, Fisher provides lists of resources he has used in the construction of his poems, usually located at the end of a book, like a bibliography. What is particularly notable about 'Mummers' Strut' is that, unlike most of Fisher's output, it includes endnotes which precisely indicate the origins of each part of the poem's fabric. This provides a rare opportunity for an exact comparison of the materials Fisher has drawn on and their final appearance in the text of the poem. It is hoped that such a comparison will suggest ways in which Fisher's hypercomplex work can be understood and appreciated as literary art.

In the *West Coast Line* statement, Fisher offers a description of a compositional procedure that is divided into three stages: research, selection and presentation. Fisher's description of the research stage divides his sources for 'Mummers' Strut' into six sources of discussion on 'the human condition' and works concerned with 'aesthetics and architectural order' (*WN*, p. 109). The former category contains the work of rock-

---

[1] Allen Fisher, 'Writer's Notes: Allen Fisher' and 'Mummers' Strut', *West Coast Line*, no. 2 vol. 29 (1995), 109-10 and 28-37. Further references are given after quotations in the text as *WN* ('Writer's Notes') and *MS* ('Mummers' Strut').

musician Kurt Cobain, the 'pseudo-clinical and case study' research of Helmuth Plessner, William Blake's notebooks, William Cowper's 'Ode to Peace' and Peter Kropotkin's political writings (*WN*, p. 109). The latter category includes Cicero on oratory and aesthetics, Pliny on painting, M. Quatremère de Quincy on aesthetics, and works on architecture by Vitruvius, Hegel, Eugene-Emmanuel Viollet-Le-Duc, Gottfried Semper and Heinrich Tessenow. Fisher subsumes the remainder of his sources as 'culminating' in one of Leonardo da Vinci's notebooks and Dante's *The Divine Comedy*, although references are also made to Anthony Kenny's work on Wittgenstein and the work of Hugo von Hoffmannsthal on aesthetics.

The selection stage of Fisher's procedure involves choosing from this range of research data, and the presentation stage involves deciding how the words generated during the research and selection stages are actually laid out on the page with 'stanzas broken into fragments indicated by line-breaks' (*WN*, p. 110). Fisher actually offers his own reading of the first section of the poem in order to illustrate the stage of selection. The section of the poem is quoted here for comparison:

1
A technician turns the radio to
drown screams from neighbours

When the hungry come for food
the dog barks until they go

The connection fraught
with stray wires

Before this begins and now
it is bleeding and now the barking

drowns the screams and the
hungry have gone.
(*MS*, p. 28)

Fisher's commentary on this extract is as follows:

> The reader is immediately referred to 'a technician' and a description of an activity 'turns the radio...' The second part of the stanza abruptly adds an observation that may or may not apply to the same space and/or time – the ambiguity of this abrupt addition is both rhymed and commented upon in the third two-line couple of stanza one, 'The connection fraught / with stray wires'. That is, the connection between the first couple and second couple is fraught, and the radio rhymes with stray wires rhymes back again onto screams. The connection is then confirmed in the fourth, 'Before this begins and now', which apparently immediately connects by narrative sentence with the fifth part, 'drowns the screams' – referring back to part one and 'the / hungry have gone' referring to part two. Thus the selective procedure is first a choice generated by the wish to rhyme, such as in stanza two where 'rock / it' matches 'rocket', but is also a matter of using the research to simulate an incident-set, which is then re-narrated by an 'as if this were happening' voice. (*WN*, p. 110)

This rather clinical account is interesting because it focuses only on the patterns of connection and disconnection in the text without attempting to say what effect this might have on the reader's experience of the text. Fisher does not appear to want to anticipate a reader's interpretation of the significance of this patterning nor describe his own as a reader of his own work and therefore does little more than state technical particulars. The poem itself offers a condensed figure for this poetics, 'The connection fraught | with stray wires', which Fisher describes as both 'rhyming'[2] with and commenting upon the previous lines. Thus what is on one level a metatextual 'response' to an abrupt juxtaposition, is, on another level, another juxtaposition *and* another connection: a fraught connection is still a connection.

Fisher's notion of 'simulat[ing] an incident-set' has one foot in the writings of Jean Baudrillard and the other in the work of the Situationist

---

[2] It should be noted that Fisher's use of the term 'rhyme' is not restricted to the repetition of sounds but can include the repetition of ideas which may not be expressed in the same linguistic form. In the above example 'radio' is rhymed with 'stray wires' because of the old-fashioned term for radio as 'wireless'. Less clearly Fisher suggests a further rhyme of wires with screams, perhaps purely because they are both plural nouns.

International.³ In Baudrillard's essay, 'Simulacra and Simulations',⁴ simulation replaces the notion of representation in the light of a view of contemporary life as having lost any distinction between the real and the imaginary. Fisher does not appear to be emphasising such a view of contemporary life but rather uses simulation to emphasise a means of representation that is not simply directed at an object in the world, but which itself is an object in the world, implying a complex orientation towards form that Fisher's use of collage indicates. Situationism, in the works of writers such as Debord and Vaneigem, offers the terms *situation* and *détournement* as most useful for understanding Fisher's poetics of the incident-set. In 'Toward a Situationist International' Debord writes:

> Our central idea is that of the construction of situations, that is to say, the concrete construction of momentary ambiances of life and their transformation into a superior passional quality.⁵

The idea of constructing situations, or transforming the situations of everyday life into something more radically engaging, represents an aim the Situationists attempted to achieve through the technique of *détournement*. Debord describes détournement as 'the reuse of pre-existing artistic elements in a new ensemble'⁶ and adds:

> The two fundamental laws of détournement are the loss of importance of each détourned autonomous element – which may go as far as to lose its original sense completely – and at the same time the organization of another meaningful ensemble that confers on each element its new scope and effect.⁷

---

³ A link made by Fisher in an interview I conducted with him, published as 'Method and Technique in the work of Allen Fisher', *Poetry Salzburg Review* 3 (2002) 10-27, p.15.

⁴ Jean Baudrillard, 'Simulacra and Simulations', in *Selected Writings*, ed. by Mark Poster (Cambridge: Polity Press; Oxford: Basil Blackwell, 1988), pp. 166-84.

⁵ Guy Debord, from 'Toward a Situationist International: Excerpt from a report on the construction of Situations and on the International Situationist tendency's conditions of organisation and action', in *An endless adventure… an endless passion…an endless banquet: A Situationist Scrapbook*, ed. by Iwona Blazwick (London and New York: Verso/ICA Publications, 1989), pp. 26-28 (pp. 27-28).

⁶ Guy Debord, 'Détournement as negation and prelude', in ibid., p. 29.

⁷ Ibid., p. 29.

Such a definition exactly describes the poetics of collage and re-narration active in Fisher's work. In an interview I conducted with Fisher, his explanation of the concept of the incident-set implicated both the construction of situations and the idea of détournement. Fisher said:

> Rather than confront the burden that you're experiencing as a daily social-political norm internally, instead of internalising it, the Situationist view would be to just turn it back on itself and make the situation for yourself. That's a very crude summary, but effectively what that leads to saying is that, if I'm researching in lots of little areas, many of which might be to do with troubled ecologies or something of that kind – let's take that as an example – it's quite possible to arrive at a position where you can say the way to deal with this complexity of problems is to situate it here, to actually make an incident out of these understandings, even though the incident hasn't necessarily occurred, but it has now, here it is. So it's like making the poem itself an incident in a sense.[8]

The connection with Situationism lies in Fisher's notion of 'making the situation for yourself' by turning (or détourning) it 'back on itself'. The incident-set is a way for Fisher of dealing with a 'complexity of problems' by situating it and making 'an incident out of these understandings'. The idea of the poem itself as an incident echoes the notion of simulation, since the poem, rather than attempting to *represent* this complexity of problems, in fact attempts to *enact* the complexity by means of techniques such as collage and détournement, thus emphasising its objective status in the world against a subordinated, representational relationship to the world. The re-narration of an incident-set by an 'as if this were happening' voice indicates the role of a constructed voice in creating various effects of continuity within the text, which is, in fact, the product of a number of different discourses. This voice is, however, by no means straightforwardly identifiable.

To return to the opening section of the poem with some of these notions in mind, two situations are described; one in which a technician appears to ignore his or her screaming neighbours and another in which, when hungry people approach somewhere – possibly the technician's

---

[8] Allen Fisher/Scott Thurston, 'Method and Technique in the work of Allen Fisher', *Poetry Salzburg Review* 3 (2002) 10-27, p.15-16.

house – for food, a dog barks at them until they go. The phrase 'it is bleeding' in the fourth stanza suggests that the dog is bleeding, which might explain why it is now the barking which drowns the screams even though the hungry have gone. The section seems to be concerned with human suffering – from violence or hunger – as dependent on the responsibility of others, and also leading to the suffering of animals. The incident-set, or situation in a Situationist sense, that is simulated here has the feel of a self-contained moral allegory which is rearticulated towards the end of the poem as section 25:

25
Technician turns the radio to
drown screams from neighbours

when the hungry come for food
    (*MS*, p. 36)

Here the technician appears not as a technician but as 'Technician', another of the many appearances of technicians in the poem which will be considered later. In this situation the appearance of the hungry could now be the cause of the neighbours' screams, suggesting a possible development of the situation in section 1.

    Whilst such paraphrase is important in determining the themes of the poem, it should be read against the poem's détourned or collaged form. Although the first section is not annotated, and therefore cannot be read off against its sources, the fact that the third couplet informs the reader that the connection between the first two stanzas is problematic ('fraught | with stray wires') suggests a poetics of collage and juxtaposition in constructing this section. Much of the poem as a whole presents resistances to an easily paraphrasable content, whilst also conveying themes to the reader. The main means of this resistance is the use of collage/ détournement.

    The collage form of the poem is made dramatically obvious in section 2 of the poem which uses fragments of the lyric for the song 'Negative Creep' written by Kurt Cobain, the singer-songwriter of Seattle rock band *Nirvana*, from the 1989 *Bleach* L.P.:

2
This is out of our range
This is out of our range

This is out of our range
.....

This is getting to be
This is getting to be

This is getting to be
.....

I'm a Negative Creep
I'm a Negative Creep

I'm a Negative Creep
and I'm stoned
    (*MS*, p. 28)

This is re-narration, wherein Cobain's lyrics are collaged and détourned into a new context, his use of the first-pronoun becoming that of an undetermined voice in the poem. Although organised into couplets the lines strongly suggest the structure and rhythm of a rock song. Whilst the repetitions of the lines exactly follow the second verse of the original song, at two points Fisher has elided two phrases: 'and it's crude' and 'like drone'[9] respectively. This demonstrates how re-narration subverts collage form by altering the source that has been collaged. This allows one to speculate on why Fisher elided these phrases, although it is possible that, if Fisher simply heard the song, perhaps on the radio, he was only using his memory of the lyrics in the poem. The first line, as a complete sentence, appears as a collective voice recognising a state of limitation. Whereas the printed lyrics denote repetition by adding a 'x3' at the end of the line, Fisher repeats each line in total and orders them into couplet fashion, with the ellipses standing in for one line. This has the effect of generating a striking pattern on the page and, within the

---

[9] Kurt Cobain, 'Negative Creep', from Nirvana, *Bleach* (Sub Pop records: ASIN: B0000035E7, 1989). Lyrics can be found at http://hjem.get2net.dk/nirvclub/lyrics/bleachl.htm#creep.

section's figure of sound, the elisions also anticipate the full-line that is supplied after the third repetition of 'I'm a Negative Creep'; that is 'and I'm stoned'. Whilst the repetition plays up the musical insistency of the lines, it also creates a tone of reiterative despair.

There are also subtle plays here in the indeterminacy of what the word 'this' refers to. It seems paradoxical to suggest that 'this' – which implies the proximity of something – is 'out of our range'. The opening line of the original song also uses the word 'this' in the line 'This is out of our reach',[10] suggesting 'this' might be referring to the song itself. In the first section of the poem, in the line 'Before this begins and now', 'this' might similarly be read as referring to the poem. To suggest that the song is out of one's range suggests that it might be hard for one to sing it in key, whilst that it is 'out of our reach' suggests that something is beyond our ability to achieve or comprehend. The elided phrase 'and it's crude' as a further comment on the limitation, might have been considered by Fisher to overstate the point here, although the elided line itself in a way enacts limitation.

Turning to the next set of repeated lines in the poem ('This is getting to be'), the lack of a qualifying adjective gives a different role to the ellipses. Again, the original lyric suggests a limitation in that the lack of range is beginning to sound monotonous ('like drone'). Without this phrase in the poem, the lines hang uncompleted, or as somehow simply emphasising their own ostensive existence: they are getting to be, in order *to be*. This creates a greater variety of tone than if the elided phrases were included. The final lines introduce a first-person pronoun, which balances the initial assertion of a collective situation with an individual situation.

The assertion of an identity as a 'Negative Creep' (emphasised by capitalisation) who is 'stoned' is another abrupt change in tone, although the limitation suggested in the opening lines and the ambiguous assertion in the middle of the section contributes to a theme of difficulty, or the facing of problems, which gains its most direct expression in the assertion of an I who calls itself a 'Negative Creep'. Of course, the pathos of these lines could be read as descending into bathos with the frankness of the assertion 'I'm stoned', and yet the exclusion of the phrases 'and it's crude' and 'like drone' actually creates a more serious tone than the original song, which, after registering its sense of limitation, switches to a more

---

[10] ibid.

celebratory and nihilistic 'Fuck! Yeah! Drone! Stoned!'.[11] Therefore, Fisher's re-narration of these lines appears to be emphasising their sense of difficulty and limitation. As Fisher suggested in the above-mentioned interview, Cobain is standing for a 'complexity of problems',[12] alluding to the singer's suicide in 1994. Thus the inclusion of fragments of his lyric becomes another incident-set of the human condition: Cobain's suffering and/or the suffering of the alienated voice re-narrated in the poem is metonymically connected to the suffering of others.

Section 7 contains the lines:

> This is getting to me
> This is getting to me
>
> This is getting to me
> .....
>
> I just wanna take off
> I just wanna take off
>
> I just wanna take off
> .....
>
> (*MS*, p. 30-31)

Here re-narration has developed a stage further, the ambiguous line now transformed to form a complete sentence by the exchanging of 'be' for 'me', which nevertheless remains within the theme of difficult problems which are 'getting to', i.e. becoming unbearable for, the voice. The lines 'I just wanna take off' however appear nowhere in the original song, and yet they are presented in the same format and follow the same rhythm and diction as the other lines. This is perhaps the extremity of re-narration where it has become a kind of ventriloquism, the collage process giving way to an actual miming of the source in a similar style. The effect of these lines is to declare a need for escape, as if the situation has now become completely intolerable.

To return to the second section, the lines from Cobain's lyric are then followed by a sequence of lines that link with aspects of the voice

---

[11] Ibid.

[12] Fisher/Thurston, 'Method and Technique in the work of Allen Fisher', p.19.

of the first section. The lines are as follows:

> Sometimes it works
> and sometimes it doesn't
>
> rock
> it
>
> begin another grasp
> from the inside
>
> rocket
>
> (*MS*, p. 29)

The voice here seems again to comment on the poem under way, and the risks involved in, for example, quoting rock lyrics, that is, sometimes this technique works, sometimes it doesn't – reminding the reader of 'The connection fraught | with stray wires'. The phrase 'rock | it' can be read as referring to the rock lyrics quoted but also suggests a possible imperative 'to rock' the poem underway, that is, to give it some of the reckless abandonment and strong rhythms associated with rock music. Consequently, there is a possibility of renewal and development in the suggestion 'begin another grasp | from the inside': to approach the writing of the poem from another angle, perhaps this time from the inside of the poet's consciousness and experience rather than from those sources he or she finds outside him or herself. This also makes a link with the 'Before this begins and now' in section 1. The word 'rocket' as it rhymes on 'rock | it' seems a potential figure for this new beginning, perhaps one with qualities of speed and power, although it might also have destructive capabilities as well as explorative ones. It also goes back to the Cobain line 'This is out of our range' and links forward to 'I just wanna take off', giving both another sense. These reflections seem taken up again immediately in the following section which opens: 'So much so difficult to take in' (*MS*, p. 29). This is perhaps a reflection on the number of discourses which the voice feels implicated in, and obliged to face, suggesting the strategy of beginning again 'from the inside'.

As Fisher explained in the interview, the notebook of William Blake is part of the 'schema' of *Gravity as a consequence of shape*.[13] According to

---

[13] Ibid., p. 18.

Fisher, although he does not specify this exactly, there is an annotated way of relating each notebook page to each page of the *Gravity* project so that Fisher knows which notebook page he is to consider when writing a particular poem. In some cases the notebook is actually quoted from and in others it doesn't appear at all. In 'Mummers' Strut', sections 6 and 7 include re-narrated lines from Blake's notebook of 1808-11, in section 7 leading to the further re-narration of the Cobain lyrics. The original entry in Blake is itself a bizarre re-narration of Aesop's fable about a dog, who, whilst swimming across a river (or looking into a river) with a bone in his mouth, notices his reflection in the water, and, taking the reflection to be another dog, with another, even juicier, bone, snaps at the image and in so doing loses his one and only bone to the bottom of the river. The moral is thus something along the lines of 'be thankful for what you've got' or a warning against coveting one's neighbours' possessions. Blake's version is as follows:

pp.60-61   To Venetian Artists

    That God is colouring Newton does shew,
    And the devil is a Black outline, all of us know.
    Perhaps this little Fable &c.
[on next page:]
    Perhaps this little Fable may make us merry:
    A dog went over the water without a wherry;
    A bone which he had stolen he had in his mouth;
    He cared not whether the wind was north or south.
    As he swam he saw the reflection of the bone.
    'This is quite Perfection, [here's two for one! what a brilliant tone! *del.*] one Generalizing Tone!
    'Outline! There's no outline! There's no such thing!
    'All is Chiaro Scuro, Poco Pen, [& *del.*] it's all colouring.'
    [Then he snap'd & *del.*]
    Snap, Snap! he has lost shadow and substance too.
    He had them both before: now how do ye do?
    'A great deal better than I was before.
    '[I've tasted shadow & *del.*]
    'Those who taste colouring love it more and more.'[14]

---

[14] William Blake, *Complete Writings*, ed. by Geoffrey Keynes (Oxford and New York: Oxford University Press, 1992), p. 554.

Blake's argument here needs some contextualising as it continues a long debate, in his notebooks and in his annotations to Sir Joshua Reynolds' *Discourses*, about contemporary painting and science, including his attacks on the Venetian school of artists. In Blake's argument, the quality of outline in painting is privileged over the diffuse and homogenised colouration he sees in painters like Rubens and Rembrandt. He links such artists to a 'generalizing' tendency (see the above quotation 'Generalizing Tone') which he also criticises heavily. Furthermore, his annotations to Reynolds also include attacks on the new science of Newton, Bacon and Locke, whose experimental empiricism he sees as inimical to the innate capacity for vision and inspiration that he believes is the true source of art.

To read Blake's fable in the context of these arguments is to become aware of the irony of his comments that 'God is colouring Newton does shew, | And the devil is a Black outline'. Blake links the general culture's privileging of colouration with Newton's (absolutist) view of the universe and God, whilst casting his own privileged outline in the role of the Devil – a characteristic Blakean reversal akin to those enacted in 'The Marriage of Heaven and Hell'. Indeed, elsewhere in the notebook, Blake links the perception of outline to madness, although the tone is also ironic and quite possibly self-referential: 'Madmen see outlines and therefore they draw them'.[15] At any rate, it is quite clear that the fable is used to critique the privileging of colouration: in the reflection, the mirror of art, the dog sees and admires 'one Generalizing Tone!' that links the two bones together, in spite of their crucial dissimilarity. The dog further perceives that there is 'no outline! There's no such thing! | All is Chiaro Scuro, Poco Pen, it's all colouring'. *Chiaro-scuro* ('half-revealed') is a term in painting referring to the treatment of light and shade – the use of which by the Venetian painters was severely criticized by Blake in the annotations. Blake's use of the term 'Poco pen' is no less critical and is glossed by Geoffrey Keynes's note on another passage from the notebook entitled 'Public Address', where the term appears as 'Poco-Pui'd'. Keynes links this spelling to the use under consideration 'formerly read as *Poco-pen'd*' (explaining Fisher's variant quotation of it, from Erdman's edition of the notebook), arguing that a correction of *Piu* for *Pen* is acceptable and that *Poco-Piu'd* is a conjunction of two Italian words meaning *a Little More*, or, in this context, 'overdone'.[16]

---

[15] Ibid., p. 549.
[16] Ibid., p. 928.

As the fable dictates, the dog's enrapture with the reflected bone, standing in for a coloured vision of the world in art, leads to his loss of both 'shadow and substance'. The final irony, however, is that, instead of bemoaning his loss and folly, the dog is actually so smitten with his deluded tasting of colour that he loves it 'more and more'. Thus Blake suggests that a similar taste for colour and shadow in artists is a delusion at the expense of a knowledge of particular outline and substance.

This debate over conflicting modes of representation and the philosophical implications of commitment to one over the other is reduced in Fisher's text to the following excerpts:

6
Outline.
There's no outline

There's no such thing
All is Chiaro Scuro Poco Pend and Colouring

7
A dog went over
the water without a wherry

A bone which he had stolen
he had in his mouth

As he swam
he saw the reflection
(MS, p. 30)

Reading this re-narration of Blake in the poem in section 6, the assertion of 'Outline' followed by 'There's no outline | There's no such thing' may be an argument about the usefulness of the concept of outline to the poetics of the poem. Thus, it may be a critique of the poem's succession of juxtapositions as leading to a diffuse, homogenous texture; suggesting that all that is possible in such a complex negotiation with discourses in transition is to achieve a kind of chiaro-scuro, a half-revealed, partially-penned situation – there are no hard outlines to be seen or copied. Such a reading would link to the passages already identified which consider the short-comings and difficulties of the poem; the fraught connections, the 'Sometimes it works | and sometimes it doesn't' and 'So much so difficult to take in'.

In section 7 the re-narration continues by retelling the story of the dog (Fisher now re-narrating Blake re-narrating Aesop) setting out on the river without a 'wherry'; a 'wherry' being a light shallow rowing-boat or a large light barge (OED), although possibly this puns on 'worry' also. The dog also reminds us of the one that appeared in section 1. The story breaks off at the point that the dog sees its reflection, at almost the point where section 6's text begins in Blake's text. Instead of the negotiation with the nature of the reflection and whether it is something that should be ignored or engaged with – such possibilities are juxtaposed with the development of the alienated (and ironically reflective) voice of section 2, which here articulates: 'This is getting to me' and 'I just wanna take off'. At this point, the juxtaposition of voices and jump from one narrative to another suggests that the weight and importance of these arguments raised by the re-narrated Blake are just too difficult for the next voice to cope with, because the arguments function as a major critique of the whole discourse under way. This amounts to yet another subversion of the collage form: the fragments taken from such diverse sources, separated by nearly two hundred years, are re-narrated and then juxtaposed in such a way as to suggest an argument between different positions, or a reaction to an argument – thereby creating an incident-set.

Section 10 contains the densest set of re-narrated quotations from various authors in the poem and brings into focus the research cluster of aesthetics and architectural order. The first three lines are:

10
Climate no longer an obstacle
In civilised societies technicians are rich

A long story of robbery
(*MS*, p. 31.)

The lines derive from the opening pages of the first chapter of Peter Kropotkin's *The Conquest of Bread*,[17] which begins with a description of

---

[17] Peter Kropotkin, *The Conquest of Bread and Other Writings*, ed. by Marshall Shatz (Cambridge and New York: Cambridge University Press, 1995).

the power of the contemporary means of production before developing an analysis of it based on anarchist principles. Kropotkin describes with a certain awe the fact that

> on the wide prairies of America each hundred men, with the aid of powerful machinery, can produce in a few months enough wheat to maintain ten thousand people for a whole year. [...] Climate is no longer an obstacle. When the sun fails, man replaces it by artificial heat. [...] In our civilised societies we are rich.[18]

Whilst the first quotation from Kropotkin is quoted as the original, 'Climate no longer an obstacle', the second quotation is re-narrated to identify 'technicians' rather than 'us' as the rich in 'civilised societies', which has also changed from '*our* civilised societies' (my emphasis) as Kropotkin has it. This is the second, but not the last, appearance of the word technician, or of some variant of it, in the poem. The re-narration of Kropotkin here provides a harsher analysis of the situation. Kropotkin himself goes on to ask 'Why then are the many poor?'[19] and answers:

> It is because all that is necessary for production – the land, the mines, the highways, machinery, food, shelter, education, knowledge – have been seized by the few in the course of that long story of robbery.[20]

In his re-narration, Fisher makes a direct link between the technicians and the technology which has been seized, going right to the heart of Kropotkin's argument. The reappearance of the technician, who in the first section of the poem appeared socially irresponsible, now appears implicated as responsible for a 'long story of robbery'. Nevertheless, the fact that the term *technician* is one that is more readily equated with the position of a worker implies an ambiguity about this situation. It might be that it is the technicians as workers, particularly in a (truly) 'civilised' society, who are the wealthy, and they have been robbed. Alternatively, it is also possible that it is the technicians who are ironically robbing their own class of its productions. This critique of the position of the

---

[18] Ibid., pp. 11-12.

[19] Ibid., p. 12.

[20] Ibid., p. 13.

technician is echoed in the work of Michel de Certeau.[21] At any rate, the re-narration of these lines in the poem continues to generate an incident-set that is concerned with the causes of human suffering. The next five lines are:

Wisdom taken from eloquence

Wisdom without eloquence
Without exception

perfection and finish
are unnatural
(*MS*, p. 31)

These lines are taken from two passages in Cicero's *De Inventione*,[22] the first of which is:

> For my own part, after long thought, I have been held by reason itself to hold this opinion first and foremost, that wisdom without eloquence does too little for the good of states, but that eloquence without wisdom is generally highly disadvantageous and is never helpful.[23]

Cicero's book on rhetoric is concerned with the implications of oratory for civic life and therefore a connection with Kropotkin's analysis of

---

[21] Michel de Certeau explores this theme in *The Practice of Everyday Life*, through the notion of the 'third man', a kind of mediator between theory and practice who is an engineer. De Certeau argues that: 'the "third man" haunted enlightened discourse (whether philosophical or scientific) and continues to do so today, but he has not turned out with the personality which had been hoped. The place he has been accorded (currently being slowly overtaken by that of the technocrat) is a function of the process that all through the nineteenth century on the one hand isolated artistic techniques from art itself and on the other hand "geometrised" and mathematicized these techniques'. Michel de Certeau, *The Practice of Everyday Life* (Berkeley and London: University of California Press, 1984), p. 69. The suggestion that the ideal third-engineer's place is being taken by the technocrat, and that this arises from the separation of art from its techniques and the objectification of those techniques, suggests a connection with Fisher's technicians.

[22] Marcus Tullius Cicero, *De Inventione, De Optima Genere Oratorum, Topica*, trans. by H.M. Hubbell (Cambridge, MA: Harvard University Press; London: Heinemann, 1976).

[23] Ibid., p. 3.

civilised society is readable in this leap between discourses, as well as the relevance of the poetics of rhetoric for the practising writer. Cicero expresses the view that in public-speaking, wisdom which is not eloquently expressed does little good and eloquent expression without wisdom is never helpful. Fisher re-figures this distinction in the poem. By asserting 'Wisdom taken from eloquence' Fisher echoes the sense of robbery in the previous line but ambiguously expresses the first and/or second part of Cicero's argument, given that wisdom 'taken from' eloquence may leave either quality by itself. 'Taken from' is also able to suggest that wisdom can be gained from eloquence. The following line 'Wisdom without eloquence' is a less ambiguous statement but would seem to bear an unstable relation to the previous, in that it may or may not be read as reiterating or contrasting with either sense of the previous statement, or contrasting with the suggestion of deriving wisdom from eloquence. The effect of this is to throw into question whether wisdom and eloquence can actually be separated as straightforwardly as Cicero seems to suggest, implying that the means of expression may not be so easily distinguished from its contents. To put this in terms which may be relevant to Fisher's poetics, it is clear in the collage and re-narration technique that forms and contents are always implicated by each other and one without the other is impossible.

The parallelism set up in these lines prepares for the next phrase 'Without exception', which both qualifies the previous statement (suggesting wisdom without eloquence is unexceptional) and leads into the next; 'perfection and finish | are unnatural'. These lines derive from a much later passage in Cicero which comes toward the end of Cicero's description of the story of the painter Zeuxis. Zeuxis was such a renowned artist that the citizens of Croton wished him to paint their temple of Juno. Zeuxis decided that he would produce a painting of Helen and asked the citizens to find the most beautiful women of the city to act as models. The women were assembled and selected, and Zeuxis chose five of them. His reason for this was, as Cicero describes:

He did not think all the qualities which he sought to combine in a portrayal of beauty could be found in one person, because in no single case has Nature made anything perfect and finished in every part.[24]

The last part of this passage is re-narrated in the poem as 'Without exception | perfection and finish | are unnatural'. To return to the Kropotkin, if there has been a long story of robbery, this may be

---
[24] Ibid., pp. 167-68.

attributable to situations in which leaders' eloquence without wisdom and wisdom without eloquence have had dire implications for the State. Nevertheless, the juxtaposition with the idea that nature is never capable of perfection is perhaps a way of rescuing the situation – although wisdom may persist without eloquence and vice-versa, perhaps this is the natural state of things, or at least one which may not be so disastrous. Alternatively, the lines may suggest that the perfection and finish of eloquence in public speaking is unnatural and therefore one should seek, or at least not attempt to hide from, an account of events that may be imperfect and less polished. Thus the previous lines may be advocating wisdom without eloquence, or wisdom 'taken from' eloquence for this reason – to avoid the 'finish' of an eloquent account of events. This may also play with the notion of completeness, suggesting that completion is unattainable. This can be connected with Fisher's own quite deliberate avoidance of finish or perfection in the myriad jumps and gaps of his collage. The re-narration processes of the poem also resist any sense of a decorous rhetorical style, as they are the construction of many voices pasted together and written on, over and through, rather than being readable as the voice of a single speaking subject.

The next four lines are:

Three lines on a panel
an exchange between two Technicians

competes sequester'd derision
completes aesthetic decision

(*MS*, p. 32)

In the chapter from Pliny's *Natural History*[25] to which the first two lines refer, Pliny also tells the story of Zeuxis told by Cicero above and describes the famous painting competition between Zeuxis and Parrhasius. Pliny then goes onto describe Parrhasius' achievements, which included winning the palm in the drawing of outlines – an interesting connection back to Blake. Fisher's 'Three lines on a panel | an exchange between two Technicians' refers to Pliny's telling of the story

---

[25] Pliny, *Natural History*, trans. by H. Rackham (Cambridge, MA: Harvard University Press; London: Heinemann, 1952).

of the painters Protogenes and Apelles. Apelles went to visit Protogenes and, on finding him absent, drew a very fine line on a blank canvas in Protogenes's studio to show he had been there. When Protogenes returned, he recognised Apelles's work and drew a still finer line on top of Apelles's line. Apelles returned and added a third line which was so fine as to leave no more room for any further line. Protogenes decided to keep the panel to be admired as it was. As Pliny writes, the canvas 'looked like a blank space, and by that very fact attracted attention and was more esteemed than every masterpiece':[26] a case of how an 'unfinished' work can be admired.

In Fisher's re-narration of this story, Protogenes and Apelles have become technicians – adding another layer to the identity of the technicians in general in the poem as well as alluding to the Greek word for art (*techné*), from which *technician* is derived. In his *Natural History*, Pliny tells us that the great painters of the time were often very wealthy – possibly the rich technicians of the second line of the section. The next two rhyming lines ('competes sequester'd derision | completes aesthetic decision') although not identifiable as a re-narration of Pliny seem to refer in the first instance to the competition between the two painters. The phrase 'sequester'd derision' links to a quotation from William Cowper's poem 'Ode to Peace' in section 9: 'dewy mead and sequester'd shed' (*MS*, p. 31), although it might also suggest the way in which the competition or exchange proceeds in isolation: each painter making their mark separately, and, although the competition seems good-natured, with a certain amount of derision for the other's skill. Fisher rhymes this statement, however, with 'completes aesthetic decision'. This might refer to the competition creating an occasion for the construction of lines as an aesthetic performance in itself or to the panel becoming regarded as a 'completed' aesthetic object although the lines on its largely blank surface are barely visible. The lines of course might also be read as the lines of a poem, so that the idea of an exchange of technicians on a panel might also become a figure for the processes of collage and re-narration, incorporating multiple voices into the work.

The competition between technicians appears as a theme of the rest of the poem, too, which describes the actions of a 'competing Technician' (*MS*, p. 33) who becomes 'This second Technician' (*MS*, p. 33) contrasted with 'The first Technician' (*MS*, p. 33), although, unsurprisingly, the difference between the two is not clearly defined,

---

[26] Ibid., p. 321.

encouraging the reader to perceive this duality as two sets of qualities of the persona, held in relation but not necessarily opposing, although 'competing'. It is at this point in the poem that another persona, The Burglar, appears as the sender of a postcard which quotes terms from Vitruvius's *On Architecture*:[27]

> The Burglar's postcard reads:
> *taxis, diathesis, economia*
> (*MS*, p. 32)

These terms derive from Vitruvius's exposition of his basic principles of architecture:

> Now architecture consists of Order, which in Greek is called *taxis*, and of Arrangement, which the Greeks name *diathesis*, and of Proportion and Symmetry and Decor and Distribution which in Greek is called *oeconomia*.[28]

As another reference to classical aesthetics, alongside Cicero and Pliny, these terms seem to contrast with the earlier notions of perfection and finish being unnatural. However, the fact that this information arrives on a postcard from The Burglar, who surely seems implicated in the long story of robbery, might suggest that this information is to be treated with caution. As the poem continues, it suggests, in fact, how the postcard is read:

> It is read as combining form into order
> with a comprehension of flavours
>
> in the best place
> understand sub-atomic and cosmic time-space
> For the Technician this will provide
> strength, utility and grace
> (*MS*, p. 32)

That the postcard is read as 'combining form into order' suggests that

---

[27] Vitruvius, *On Architecture*, trans. by Frank Granger (London and New York: Heinemann and G.P. Putnam's Sons, 1931).

[28] Ibid., p. 25.

taxis (order) and form are being distinguished. Therefore, if form can be disorderly, in the way that the poem itself seems to have proceeded so far, then order is perhaps now being considered as an aesthetic option, although qualified by a 'comprehension of flavours', which might suggest that order must allow for the individual qualities or flavours of the materials to be appreciated, as is possible in a poetics of juxtaposition.

The next couplet contains a statement that can be related to Fisher's concerns in an essay entitled 'The Poetics of the Complexity Manifold', where he states that an artist's understanding of quantum-field theory will affect their experience of gravity, drawing and reading.[29] The line 'in the best place' however, might also be referring to Vitruvius's criteria for the optimum positioning of a building.[30] Fisher updates Vitruvius's concerns about the local availability of building materials and the avoidance of certain other kinds of conditions such as marshy ground by bringing in a consideration of the fabric of space-time, both on the quantum and cosmic scale. This suggests that the positioning of buildings can be considered within much larger, and much smaller, contexts than Vitruvius may have been interested in. The reversal of the more usual 'space-time' to 'time-space' sets up an end-rhyme with both 'place' and 'grace' neatly linking two terms for spatiality with the very different quality of grace. The idea of the cosmic is also taken up in later lines that feature the 'cosmic torus' (*MS*, p. 32), a 'cosmos | expressed by a knot' (*MS*, p. 33) and references to 'the stars' (*MS*, p. 37). The final couplet of the section directly quotes from Vitruvius's general propositions about the siting of public buildings:

> The assignment of public buildings [...] should be so carried out that account is taken of strength, utility, grace. Account will be taken of *strength* when the foundations are carried down to the solid ground [...] of *utility*, when the sites are arranged without mistake [...] of *grace*, when the appearance of the work shall be pleasing and elegant, and the scale of the constituent parts is justly calculated for symmetry.[31]

---

[29] Allen Fisher, 'The Poetics of the Complexity Manifold', *boundary 2*, no. 1 vol. 26 (1999), 115-18, p. 115.

[30] Vitruvius, p. 31.

[31] Ibid., p.35.

At this point in the poem it is difficult to determine exactly what 'this' in the line 'for the Technician this will provide' refers to. It may be the three terms on the postcard, which may have been sent by the Burglar to the Technician, or the understanding of quantum and cosmic space-time, or both. At any rate, 'this' will provide the technician with another triad of strength, utility and grace. The civic concerns of Vitruvius's writings also provide a possible connection back to the political considerations offered by Kropotkin and Cicero. It is unsure whether the technician will be provided with these three qualities as a person, or whether these qualities will be at the technician's disposal for whatever work they may have under way. Vitruvius's use of these terms to denote solid foundations and plentiful materials, efficiency of use and a pleasing appearance again might seem irresistible qualities to attribute to a poetics, although not a poetics of collage and re-narration in which perfection and finish are called into question. In spite of this the Vitruvian triad of *taxis*, *diathesis* and *economia* reminds one of Fisher's three stages of research, selection and presentation. If research can be likened to collage and selection to montage,[32] then this is well reflected in the close relation between *taxis*, 'the balanced *adjustment* of details',[33] and *diathesis*, 'the fit *assemblage* of details'.[34] *Economia* would then also seem an appropriate equivalent for presentation.

Vitruvius's terms are taken up in a different form in the next two couplets of section 11:

11
Where house is the first idea in building
a first matter of importance becomes load-bearing

this means wall, which leads to column
and a grace known as functional beauty
(MS, p. 32)

---

[32] Gregory L. Ulmer distinguishes collage/montage in the following way: '"Collage" is the transfer of materials from one context to another, and "montage" is the "dissemination" of these borrowings through the new setting.' Gregory L. Ulmer, 'The Object of Post-Criticism', in *Postmodern Culture*, ed. by Hal Foster (London and Sydney: Pluto Press, 1985), pp. 83-110, p. 84.

[33] Vitruvius, p. 25.

[34] Ibid., p. 25.

These lines are derived from G.W.F Hegel's *Aesthetics: Lectures on Fine Art*[35] where Hegel is considering classical architecture. The elements in Hegel's account which are re-narrated by Fisher are as follows:

> If we look more closely at a house and examine its mechanical proportions [...] the first thing of importance in this connection affects load-bearing. As soon as load-bearing masses are mentioned, we generally think first [...] of a wall as the firmest and safest support [...] Greek architecture [...] employs the column as the fundamental element in the purposiveness of architecture and its beauty.[36]

One of Hegel's main sources is Vitruvius, and the re-narration of Hegel's writing by Fisher re-iterates the Vitruvian principles of strength, utility and grace that close section 10. The discussion has therefore continued along the lines of ordered, rational ideas about architecture, far from the poetics of the poem itself. The next three couplets however constitute the most direct statement of poetics in the poem:

> In every poem of truth
> The Technician demands fiction
>
>
> In every resemblance to the real
> technique demands incompleteness
>
> Fiction and incompletion constitute the art
> that she imitates
> (MS, p. 32)

These lines re-narrate passages from M. Quatremère de Quincy's *An Essay on the Nature, the End and the Means of Imitation in the Fine Arts*[37] in which De Quincy argues that:

---

[35] G.W.F. Hegel, *Aesthetics: Lectures in Fine Art*, trans. by T.M. Knox, 2 vols (Oxford: Clarendon Press, 1975), II.

[36] Ibid., pp. 665-66.

[37] M. Quatremère de Quincy, *An Essay on the Nature, the End and the Means of Imitation in the Fine Arts*, trans. by J.C. Kent (London: Smith, Elder and Co., 1837).

> We have already, in analysing the constituent elements of every art, laid it down that all resemblance must necessarily be *incomplete*, and we shall presently, when reverting to the subject, further show that all imitative resemblance is of necessity *fictious*.[38]

De Quincy's book is described by the translator as an exposition of Aristotle's *Poetics*. De Quincy outlines his argument as follows:

> Whatever qualities and properties are dependent on the especial nature of the model, material or instruments of any art, will be wanting to another whose model, material, and instruments are different. And this is what constitutes the *incompleteness* of every art in as far as resemblance is concerned. What constitutes the *fictious* character of an art is its inability to produce any other than an apparent and feigned impression of the imitable object, one which is opposed to that of the thing itself or of the absolute truth.[39]

At this point, the arguments concerning an alternative aesthetics, which originated with the re-narrated Cicero in section 10, return with full force. The valorisation of fiction and incompleteness seems an extension of the consideration of perfection and finish as unnatural. In their reversals of the prior terms (although not reversing the argument), incompleteness reads as a rhyme on finish, and fiction as a rhyme on perfection; as in De Quincy's argument, fiction is considered a quality short of the absolute truth. The parallelism in these lines adds to the forcefulness of this re-narration, and the fact that the demands are made, in turn, by the Technician and technique itself reflect the fact that, in De Quincy's argument, incompleteness appears to derive from the limits of the specific art form (technique), whilst fiction derives from a failure to approach absolute truth, which may also be considered a general human failing. The identification here between the Technician and technique is reiterated and transformed when the elements of fiction and incompletion are said to 'constitute the art | that she imitates'. Although the verb 'imitates' here might be slightly problematic, in that

---

[38] Ibid., p. 82.
[39] Ibid., pp. 113-14.

to imitate an art might be different to practising an art whose main aim is imitation, also notable is the sudden appearance of the pronoun 'she', where one might have expected the technician. In reading this passage as one of the most direct statements of a poetics that celebrates simulation and collage, the switch to 'she' appears to suddenly situate the artist outside the established context for the discussion.

In conclusion, this reading of 'Mummers' Strut' has adopted Fisher's challenge in the *West Coast Line* statement to consider it as 'exemplary of Allen Fisher's poetics in action' (*WN*, p. 110). The reading has sought to demonstrate how techniques such as collage and re-narration have been used to simulate incident-sets – where détourned elements are juxtaposed – where themes as general as 'the human condition' and as specific as 'aesthetics and architectural order' have been articulated and developed.

To read Fisher's work is to experience a complex tension between rapid juxtapositions of different materials and patterns of continuity generated through repetition and rhyme: between discontinuity and continuity. A reader must actively negotiate the jumps and continuities in order to build his or her own reading of the poem. The above reading of 'Mummers' Strut' has delineated a few of these jumps and continuities in examining the description and expression of human suffering, the self-awareness of a voice who appears to be writing the poem and a complex argument about aesthetics, politics, oratory, art and architecture which does not develop logically but develops by means of juxtaposition and re-narration. The poem attempts to relate a large number of discourses without homogenising their terms into one argument from one point of view. Instead the differences are left to resonate across the gaps in the collage, and this is what allows the reader space for their own engagement.

One of the most important statements of Fisher's poetics is contained in his long poetics essay *Necessary Business*, where he uses the idea of the 'chreod'[40] to talk about consistencies, and the disruption of them, in the poetry of cris cheek, J.H. Prynne and Eric Mottram. Fisher describes how reading the work of these poets builds up an awareness of consistencies, for example of rhythm and sound patterning, which he identifies with the concept of the chreod, adapted from C.H. Waddington's biological terminology meaning 'necessary path', which

---

[40] Allen Fisher, *Necessary Business* (London: Spanner, 1985), p. 196. Further references to this publication are given after quotations in the text as *NB*.

describes how 'change is canalised once started in a certain direction' (*NB*, p. 196). Fisher argues however that these poets 'deliberately break or fracture' (*NB*, p. 196) this path, thus deconstructing their own 'consistent and chreodic memory' (*NB*, p. 211) and that which the reader builds up during his or her reading. This fracturing 'intuitively invents new memories' which 'revitalise the reader's historical desire in production' (*NB*, p. 211).

This fracturing is central to the techniques that interest Fisher in these poets, but is also evident in Fisher's own poetics. It can be linked to the notion of defamiliarisation, as the breaks or leaps, between, for example, a notebook entry of William Blake followed by the lyrics of Kurt Cobain, are intended to disrupt normal habits of reading and therefore to engage the reader in new ways. Fisher, however, does acknowledge the extent to which his engagement as a reader depends both on the patterns of connectedness as well as their fracturing, otherwise the fractures would not be perceived (*NB*, p. 213). Fisher politicises his view of reading by seeing it as historically-contextualised production – rather than consumption.

The methodology of Fisher's use of many sources in his work, and the techniques he uses to juxtapose them to engage the reader, is ultimately made possible by his view of the aesthetic function of poetry, which derives, as Robert Sheppard has discussed,[41] from his reading of Jan Mukařovský's essay *Aesthetic Function, Norm and Value as Social Facts*.[42] As Fisher argues, many activities contain an aesthetic function, and 'non-art activities transform into art when their aesthetic function is given prominence' (*NB*, pp. 180-81). However, the converse of this is true in that art activities similarly cease to be art if another function predominates over the aesthetic, for example the political or informational. Therefore, where 'poetry predominately makes political engagement possible derives from its aesthetics', not its political function (*NB*, p. 181). The implications of this for Fisher's use of resources in his work is that he manages to create poems, which although full of information about scientific theory, or history etc,

---

[41] Robert Sheppard, 'The Poetics of Poetics: Charles Bernstein, Allen Fisher and "the poetic thinking that results"', in *Symbiosis*, no. 1 vol. 3 (1999), 77-92 (pp. 86-87).

[42] Jan Mukařovský, *Aesthetic Function, Norm and Value As Social Facts* (Ann Arbor. MI: University of Michigan, 1970). In the acknowledgements to *Necessary Business* Fisher notes: 'Particular mention should be made of the [...] ideas from Jan Mukařovský' (p. 167).

are not involved in, to paraphrase Wittgenstein, the language-game of giving information about scientific theory, history etc.[43] Robert Sheppard has noted how Mukařovský's essay 'unwittingly confirms the [...] answers to Wittgenstein's question, when Mukařovský states: '"The aesthetic function, by dominating over the informational function, has changed the very nature of the information"'.[44] As Sheppard argues, the importance of Fisher's reading of this essay is that Mukařovský's work preserves the 'arena of the aesthetic as the centre of literary life'.[45] It therefore functions for Sheppard as 'a bulwark against theories that tend to collapse the distinction between art and life'.[46] This is the ground therefore on which Fisher makes a key assertion in the foreword to *Necessary Business*:

> Poetry does not collaborate with society, but with life; its field of collaboration is predominately aesthetic, that is its main function. Whatever else I may get from a work of art, because its dominant function is aesthetic it requires my engagement to create it, to produce it. The significance I most warmly value derives from this production, its affirmation of life. (*NB*, pp. 164-65)

By determining the dominant function of poetry to be aesthetic, Fisher is able to emphasise that it therefore affirms life through its need to be produced by a reader: it requires 'participators to consider their activities [the functions of an artwork] as Art' (*NB*, p. 181).

In a related passage from a later essay entitled 'Breaks Margin', on the work of Ulli Freer and the painter Harry Thubron, Fisher argues that:

> The predominant function in art, the aesthetic, is concomitantly one of the functions of consciousness. Consciousness and aesthetics share the summary of their activity as patterns of

---

[43] Wittgenstein wrote: 'Do not forget [...] that a poem, even though it is composed in the language of information is not used in the language game of giving information'. Quoted in Veronica Forrest-Thomson, *Poetic Artifice: a Theory of Twentieth-Century Poetry* (Manchester: Manchester University Press, 1978), p. x.

[44] Robert Sheppard, 'The Poetics of Poetics', p. 87.

[45] Ibid., p. 87.

[46] Ibid., p. 87.

connectedness, which are patterns necessary for life. They are patterns that provide the structures for ethical, moral, and social understanding and efficacy, and they change, can be changed. Loss of the renewing and changing capacity of this patterning ... amounts to a loss of significant life.[47]

This statement links aesthetic practices to the functions of consciousness. 'Patterns of connectedness' have a moral and social, therefore a political, role. Fisher emphasises how these patterns change and, indeed, how lack of change amounts to 'loss of significant life'. The means of change and renewal, as we have seen, include the breaking of patterns through Fisher's techniques of collage and re-narration.

Works Cited

Baudrillard, Jean, 'Simulacra and Simulations', in *Selected Writings*, ed. by Mark Poster (Cambridge: Polity Press; Oxford: Basil Blackwell, 1988), pp. 166-84
Blake, William, *Complete Writings*, ed. by Geoffrey Keynes (Oxford and New York: Oxford University Press, 1992)
Cicero, Marcus Tullius, *De Inventione, De Optima Genere Oratorum, Topica*, trans. by H.M. Hubbell (Cambridge, MA: Harvard University Press; London: Heinemann, 1976)
Cobain, Kurt, 'Negative Creep', Nirvana, *Bleach* (Sub Pop records: ASIN: B0000035E7, 1989)
Cobain, Kurt, 'Negative Creep', lyrics consulted online at http://hjem.get2net.dk/nirvclub/lyrics/bleachl.htm#creep (23/8/00)
Cowper, William, 'Ode to Peace', in *The Poetical Works of Cowper*, ed. by H. S. Milford (London and New York: Oxford University Press, 1950)
Debord, Guy, 'Toward a Situationist International: Excerpt from a report on the construction of Situations and on the International Situationist tendency's conditions of organisation and action', in *An endless adventure...an endless passion...an endless banquet: A Situationist Scrapbook*, ed. by Iwona Blazwick (London and New York: Verso/ICA Publications, 1989), pp. 26-28
―――― 'Détournement as negation and prelude', in *An endless adventure... an endless passion... an endless banquet: A Situationist Scrapbook*, ed. by Iwona Blazwick (London and New York: Verso/ICA Publications, 1989), p. 29

---

[47] Allen Fisher, 'Breaks Margin', *First Offense*, no. 8 (1993), 54-63 (p. 56).

De Certeau, Michel, *The Practice of Everyday Life* (Berkeley and London: University of California Press, 1984)

De Quincy, M. Quatremère, *An Essay on the Nature, the End and the Means of Imitation in the Fine Arts*, trans. by J.C. Kent (London: Smith, Elder and Co., 1837)

Erdman, David V., ed., *The Notebook of William Blake: a photographic and typographic facsimile* (Oxford: Clarendon Press, 1973)

Fisher, Allen, *Becoming: Place Book Four and part of five* (London: Aloes Books, 1979)

———— *Necessary Business* (London: Spanner, 1985)

———— 'Breaks Margin', *First Offense*, no. 8 (1993), 54-63

———— 'Writer's Notes: Allen Fisher' and 'Mummers' Strut', *West Coast Line*, no. 2 vol. 29 (1995), 109-10 and 28-37.

———— 'The Poetics of the Complexity Manifold', *boundary 2*, no. 1 vol. 26 (1999), 115-18

Fisher, Allen and Thurston, Scott, 'Method and Technique in the work of Allen Fisher', *Poetry Salzburg Review* 3 (2002) 10-27, p.15-16

Forrest-Thomson, Veronica, *Poetic Artifice: a Theory of Twentieth-Century Poetry* (Manchester: Manchester University Press, 1978)

Hegel, G.W.F., *Aesthetics: Lectures in Fine Art*, trans. by T.M. Knox, 2 vols (Oxford: Clarendon Press, 1975), II

Kropotkin, Peter, *The Conquest of Bread and Other Writings*, ed. by Marshall Shatz (Cambridge and New York: Cambridge University Press, 1995)

Mukařovsky, Jan, *Aesthetic Function, Norm and Value As Social Facts* (Ann Arbor: University of Michigan, 1970)

Pliny, *Natural History*, trans. by H. Rackham (Cambridge, MA: Harvard University Press; London: Heinemann, 1952)

Sheppard, Robert, 'The Necessary Business of Allen Fisher', in *Future Exiles: 3 London Poets: Allen Fisher, Bill Griffiths, Brian Catling* (London: Paladin, 1992), pp. 11-17

———— 'The Poetics of Poetics: Charles Bernstein, Allen Fisher and "the poetic thinking that results"', in *Symbiosis*, no. 1 vol. 3 (1999), 77-92

Ulmer, Gregory L., 'The Object of Post-Criticism', in *Postmodern Culture*, ed. by Hal Foster (London and Sydney: Pluto Press, 1985), pp. 83-110

Vitruvius, *On Architecture*, trans. by Frank Granger (London and New York: Heinemann and G.P. Putnam's Sons, 1931)

Lines of flights:
Allen Fisher and the human comedy

CLIVE BUSH

This essay will mainly be concerned with the second extended collection of poems in the sequence *Gravity as a consequence of shape*, the first volume of which *Gravity* was published by Salt Publishing in 2004, the same year as *Entanglement* (the name given to this second volume) and published by The Gig, a Canadian press. The third volume of this project, which was begun after the completion of *PLACE* in the late 1980s is called *Leans* and has not yet been published or to use Fisher's terminology, assembled.[1] This essay will not scrutinise *Entanglement* in linear mode, nor will there be a separate summarizing of techniques and contents, rather it will read one among many pivotal poems (they are of course all pivotal) then briefly give a sense of the book as a whole and suggest some other directions.

All the poems negotiate, under various names and practices, Fisher's poetic world in which dance, physics, bioenergetics, quantum physics and ecology help construct both form and content. All Fisher's texts in some way link with each other, and the way he works shows that 'transformational' practices are not only part of his daily on-going process of multiple creative actions across different media and modes, but the activity itself is offered as a key thematic and a way of the self in the poetic world he presents. This means that one moment of the process should reveal endless lateral connections to everything else he does. I want to look at the sources of one major theory of assemblage in one poem that foregrounds that theory as part of the text.

On page 81 of *Entanglements* is a poem entitled 'Philly Dog: In Memory of Eric Mottram 16.1.95'.[2] The title alone, perhaps, is worth some pages of commentary: philosophically what has that word *memory* got to do with '16.1.95', for example. To be sure the charismatic, and influential professor-poet Eric Mottram was definitively stopped

---

[1] This essay was written in 2006. *Leans* was published by Salt in 2007. I am grateful to Frances Presley who helpfully commented on a draft of this essay.

[2] Allen Fisher, *Entanglement* (Toronto: The Gig, 2004), p. 81. Further page references are given in the text.

working on that date. But what of 'In memory of', a sign which indexes laterally to religion and official funerals, poetic elegy, as well as the past: *un disparu*, a signified double-disappeared?

The title itself, 'Philly Dog' is one among many ingeniously discovered dances that head or lead Fisher's poems or assemblages of recent years. *Google* will give you 4,050,000 hits on that phrase and the serious scholar is referred to them. Those of us who still personally remember Eric Mottram with affection, will revert to our private knowledge of his links with the University of Pennsylvania, his life-long study of American culture, his direct involvement with many American poets and artists, and his abiding love of dogs.

The poem begins with fragments from Mottram's book on William Burroughs of 1977.[3] In so doing it becomes part of the poem - that is, it moves into the text and out to its own detached world. Burroughs was a twentieth-century master of the cut-up, the rearranged text and chance procedures which he pioneered with Brion Gysin.[4] The world invoked was a Grosz-like world of twentieth-century sexual decadence, violence, terror and capitalist wastage.

The extracts selected from Mottram's text deal with the need of twentieth-century artists (we might recall a Passolini, Genet or Bataille) to confront the cynical operations of power with a reconfiguration of the obscene, to offer a way of creating large cross-disciplinary areas of knowledge and materials which involved 'a large spatial order', to explore ways of living and surviving that depend on 'dropping out of the current power structure' and to attempt to rediscover what 'forces, unexplored or to be recovered or renewed, the body may hold as the field of Psyche and Eros' (81).

The poem that follows celebrates and rehearses the tripartite subject matter extracted from Mottram. However, there is less of a concern with actual power (no Burroughsian expressionist figures here like Dr Benway, in *The Naked Lunch* a descendent of Dr Caligari) nor is there a Mottram-like combination of a past cultural and personal memory through a re-apprehension of directly-named cultural pasts

---

[3] Eric Mottram, *William Burroughs: the Algebra of Need* (London: Marion Boyars, 1977). This is the edition Fisher cites. The first edition was published by Intrepid Press (Buffalo, NY, 1971) in the Beau Fleuve Series #2 edited by Allen de Loach. An even earlier version had appeared in *Intrepid #14/15* (1970).

[4] See for example Sinclair Beiles, William Burroughs, Gregory Corso, Brion Gysin, *Minutes to Go* (San Francisco, CA: Beach Books, Texts and Documents, 1968).

and artists – whether it be an ancient Tunis, a Braque or a Neruda.[5] That sense of an actually peopled world and the possible coherence of a re-presentable past with a sense of its temporality is gone. Mottram's learned civility, his great love of the past in its construction of the very essence of the human soul, for all the insistent anguish, seems as if it belongs to another world – perhaps bearing the last traces of the privileged world of Cambridge at mid-century – a discriminating view from one of Leavis's 'talented tenth'.

It is important therefore to notice 16.1.95. The sense of power and the nightmare world is simply omnipresent in Fisher and what is emphasised now are just two of Mottram's concerns, the desperate question of alternative survival, including a new sense of the self's relation to the world, and a largely science-driven revision of a sense of the world in 'large spatial order.' *Multiplicity* becomes a key word and, in this poem and in many poems over the last decade, Fisher has been increasingly involved with the world proposed in the work of two French writers whose epiphanic moment was the events of 1968, but who dominated the academic world from the late 1970s and 1980s, through the 1990s and into our own time. In the middle of the poem to Mottram we find:

> Guy Debord and Félix Guattari continue as intersecting
> multiplicities – discursive and expansive versus
> involvement in multiplication of content
> The weight of any map, cortical or galacto-graphic.
> does not exceed the weight of any space-time it reproduces
> The map embeds itself into the projection the burglar makes
> As he walks the result factors in a blur
> homeomorphic to the boundary of the blur. (84)

One of Fisher's rhetorical procedures is to make a quasi-pedagogical statement, with the initial large abstractions inviting a discrimination which is then 'backed up' as an authorising gesture, by a quasi-scientific statement. Sometimes this leaks into a further statement with a narrative implication as here. What is questioned is the role of the subject in a world of complex, but fatalistic, scientifically-perceived natural operations. The tone in the placing of the agent is always tricky to determine. Does the burglar's walk set off the operations of the

---

[5] Eric Mottram, *Selected Poems* (London: North and South, 1989), pp. 48, 33, 65.

physical world, is he part of its larger scheme, and if so who is noting it? Whose is the voice behind the narrative mask? The relationship between the human being and the natural order is invited in both the alliteration and the descriptive adjective, 'homeomorphic'. The invitation is part of the process but it leaves an uneasy feeling because it indicates both the indifference of the bare fact and the chilly abstraction as the only possible indicator of a human world.

Debord is perhaps rather less important for Fisher in this later work than Guattari and his co-writer Deleuze. Debord was best known for his *Society of the Spectacle* (Paris, 1967), that dazzling denunciation of the modern to post-modern world that ransacked centuries of learning from Feuerbach to Trotsky, Marx to Mumford, Novalis to Mao, Herodotus to Jesus, and Shakespeare to Hegel, all in 221 post-Lutheran theses. In the spirit of forty years ago you can still find it un-copywrited on the web for all to download, borrow and steal.[6] After Debord we knew the world of representation was just lying and the life of the mind had been taken over by capitalist spectacle. Fragments of erstwhile realities had made a virtual world that could only be looked at. The spectacle was a social relation between people mediated by images and monopolizing time outside production. The real world was the set of images, inheriting 'the weakness of the Western philosophical project which attempted to understand activity by means of the categories of vision… and the relentless development of the particular technical rationality that grew out of that form of thought… the material reconstruction of the religious illusion' (thesis 19-20). Capital became images. Commodity itself was materialised illusion. Debord was quite clear: 'The dominion of the concentrated spectacle is a police state' (thesis 64).

It was to Debord's eternal credit that he commented on *actual history* in his work. Few modernist and post-modernist theorists from Sartre on (who always promised but never did it) have done so. It never entered the two main works of Deleuze and Guattari, for example. For Debord, the partial truths of Bakunin and Marx produced a fatally incomplete map for their political aims (thesis 91). Similarly, he reviewed soberly the claims of anarchists, early twentieth-century social-democratic revisionists like Edward Bernstein, and as for Lenin 'the representation of the working class has become the enemy of the

---

[6] Trans. Ken Knabb, Guy Debord, *The Society of the Spectacle* [Paris, 1967]. www.bopsecrets.org knabb@bopsecrets.org Further references follow by thesis number in the text.

working class' (thesis 100). The conclusion was startling, revolutionary theory had become the enemy of revolutionary ideology (thesis 124).

On another tack, he wrote that art, in the age of museums and mass communication, had equalised abstractly all art, which, now detached from local historical circumstance, disappeared into its own permanent vanguard. In the conclusion to the book were some reflections, very much in the spirit of the late 1960s, on schizophrenia:

> The spectacle obliterates the boundaries between self and world by crushing the self-besieged by the presence-absence of the world. It also obliterates the boundaries between true and false by repressing all directly lived truth beneath the real presence of the falsehood maintained by the organization of appearances. Individuals who passively accept their subject to an alien everyday reality are thus driven toward a madness that reacts to this fate by resorting to illusory magical techniques. (thesis 219)

It would be relatively easy to trace the effect of Debord on Fisher. The persona of the Burglar in the poem for Mottram: a post-Spenser-Bunyan, semi-allegorical figure is transfigured as the Debordean *situationist*, perhaps as one with a nostalgia for the Renaissance *time as festival* (Debord, thesis 139):

> On a folded sheet of nerve cells
> the Burglar plans his day
> uses signals from the thalamus
> among an array of reception areas
> *Situationist* between heredity and improvement after use
> He learns large through selection and
> Only partially via instruction
> Deriving shape from chemical voltage. (81, my italics)

Here the narrative voice offers a story *and* an interpretive commentary, and that commentary has the air of absolute factual enunciation. This is statement *tout pur*. The sense of 'authority' is intense, and it raises an uneasy feeling in the listener. It should also be clear we are in a very different world from the one Debord offers. There is no actual political or historical information here. It is intensely about the personal psychology of survival in ecological space. Debord's world, while attacking the whole trend of western philosophy was sufficiently engaged with it to take for granted an interpretation of the Cartesian split that guaranteed the reflective consciousness. Here, however, the Burglar rearranges his own biology. *Intention towards* and *being* biology become the same thing. The chemical voltage articulates both the being and the consciousness of the shape of identity itself. The external hence becomes a huge vitalist metaphysic, mathematically perceived.

The problem with this argument is that 'the external' is already a construct produced by the interiority of an imaginative process of mind, however unconsciously biologically prefigured, and depends on an antagonism to the concept of 'the internal' that leaves its transformed traces nonetheless. Further, this version of subject and world is as much subject to invasion or 'construction' as the old figure of the self and represented world.

The problem becomes one of agency in an autonomous planar world that in Fisher's work is of course always in satiric opposition to the kinds of reality condemned by Debord. Thus the key question becomes to what extent that planar world is defined by negative opposition to what exists (modes of thought, politics), and to what extent does it have a surplus of a helpful and genuine revisionary thinking.

The description of the Burglar, one of many figures that populate Fisher's world, is relatively straight-forward. He links with other figures in Fisher's earlier work like *Brixton Fractals*.[7] However, if the passage in which the philosophers are referred to is looked at again, one can see the poetic and linguistic moves with which Fisher defamiliarises the enunciation of the source and its implications. In apposition to the first three lines are a further three lines that are a mock-scientific statement in which 'gravity', that is 'weight' in old fashioned terms, itself coalesces the sign and signifier and breaks the opposition between 'mind' and object of mind. So the 'map' is at once 'cortical or galacto-graphic'. In short there is no intervention, agent or purpose. What we have is a correspondence theory that might even remind us of Coleridge and Wordsworth in which the 'or' suggests an isomorphism, through analogy, common to physical system and consciousness itself. The correspondence continues between the physiological term, cortex, and (the hyphen is inevitable) between galacto-graphic, itself a further compound of agent and perceived.

---

[7] See Clive Bush, *Out of Dissent: a study of five contemporary British Poets* (London: Talus Editions, 1997), pp. 183ff.

Where exactly *is* the implied 'graphographer'? In Fisher's world you can not catch him. He is a trickster, hoaxer or a deconstructionist in a state of permanent deconstruction. So is *pure movement driven by externality* itself an evasion or a reality we have not seen yet, or a world we want to get to, or a state of psychic preparation, or a poetic form of rhizomic flight? How does the poetry offer and refuse us the questions? Is Carnival the answer to the capitalist's permanent Lent. Certainly, the last two lines of the passage cited do not give us many clues. 'As he walks' is followed by syntactical incompletion. The phrase, the 'result factors' dips outside a temporal narrative by coalescing cause and effect. 'Factors', a neo-logistic verb, it suggests a management-style abstraction in which content is simply coalesced into methodological movement.

We do not know whether 'homeomorphic to the boundary of the spectrum' endorses the universal vitalist movement incorporating the body and the physics of light or whether it offers the point of view of a cynically objective scientist, or indeed the visionary poet. It is quite clear throughout Fisher's latest work that this is an open question. One could answer that the poetry oscillates between the two, but again that begs the question simply by asserting an ontological vehemence of pure binary movement. The benign and malign contraries are as close together as Blake's *Song's of Innocence and Experience,* where it is sometimes famously difficult to separate the two worlds. In choosing to use the language of the scientific world both with and against itself, Fisher has to negotiate the serious problem of the role of externality and distance. Much more than Debord, however, some, perhaps even most, of the answers to, and some of the sources of, the problems are to be found in the work of Deleuze and Guattari.

'*Je suis Marxiste, tendence Groucho,*' went the well-known graffito scrawled on a wall in Paris in 1968. A post-Dadaist gesture, it was a historical reply to Stalinist betrayals. In his introduction to Deleuze and Guattari's influential *Anti-Oedipus*, Michel Foucault wrote that, for twenty years after the Second World War, there had been a certain way of thinking: 'One had to be on familiar terms with Marx, not let one's dreams stray too far from Freud... And one had to treat the sign system with the greatest respect.' He then recalled:

> ...the five brief, impassioned, jubilant, enigmatic years. At the gates of our world, there was Vietnam, of course, and first

major blow to the powers that be. But here inside our walls, what exactly was taking place?[8]

Part of the argument, paraphrasing Foucault, goes something along the following lines. The war against the contemporary power masters is to be fought on two fronts, political and psychological. It was a revolution that had in fact begun with Reich and the Surrealists, and Foucault warned (in vain as it turned out) that, like the Surrealists at least, the work of Deleuze and Guatarri was in fact *an art not a theory.* The adversaries were clear: bureaucrats of the revolution and 'civil servants of truth'; technicians of desire who would reduce the multiplicity of the erotic to a capitalist exploitation of 'structure and lack'; and, finally, *fascism* – not simply that of the historical Hitler, Franco and Mussolini – but a condition of the entire post-modern world. This world was constructed psychically, because virtually, by right-wing media moguls. Technical manipulation drove a mass psychosis by converting desire into power drives conceived in and through our perception of our own and other people's bodies. It turned the political realm into the simplistic monologic of spectacle. 'Paying a modest tribute to St Francis de Sales,' Foucault added with Gallic insouciance, 'one might say that *Anti-Oedipus* is an *Introduction to the Non-Fascist Life.*'[9] In a parallel assertion one could argue that Fisher's poetry rehearses the possibilities of the non-fascist life.

Like a contemporary Saint, Foucault also spelt out the requirements for holy living. Free politics from paranoias; develop political strategies (in thought, action and desire) by 'proliferation, juxtaposition and disjunction' and not by 'subdivision and pyramidal hierarchization'; prefer what is positive and multiple: 'difference over uniformity, flows over unities, mobile arrangements over systems'; being productive means you are 'nomadic' not someone who sits in Pascalian stillness. Indeed, in the group the individual was obliged to constantly reinvent her or his individuality (a perpetual deconstruction of the self in the jargon), in order to destroy corrosive hierarchies and 'pyramidal' power.

Foucault, though, also spoke of the 'traps' of humour, and provocations which tempted him in relation to this work, at least occasionally,

---

[8] Michel Foucault, Preface to Deleuze and Guattari, *Anti-Oedipus; capitalism and schizophrenia*, trans. Robert Hurley, Mark Seem and Helen R. Lone (Minneapolis, MN: University of Minnesota Press, 1983), p. xi. Further references to this work follow in the text.

[9] Foucault, 'Preface', p. xiii.

to 'take one's leave of the text and slam the door shut': a moment perhaps not sufficiently noted.[10] Further, in satirising the monologic of the id, the exuberance of the schizophrenic's Versailles-like quasi-automaton-self paradoxically seemed to offer a rather aristocratic pleasure in the, well, er, where-exactly was it, body or mind of the Parisian dissenter. Like Genet's thief, the schizophrenic, taking on the sorrows of the world, says, look at me I am more 'umbly schizophrenic than anyone else, a super-mechanized mendicant hawking desire-machines around your territory.

Everything is a machine. Proust's great work is a literary machine of: asymmetrical sections, paths that suddenly come to an end, hermetically sealed boxes, noncommunicating vessels, watertight compartments in which there are gaps even between things that are contiguous, gaps that are affirmations, pieces of a puzzle belonging not to any one puzzle but to many, pieces assembled by forcing them into a certain place where they may or may not belong, their unmatched edges violently bent out of shape, forcibly made to fit together, to interlock with a number of pieces always left over. It is a schizoid work par excellence; it is almost as though the author's guilt, his confessions of guilt, are merely a sort of joke (42).

This is a classic post-modern commentary in which the text, by pure assertion, is realised in the *truth of* the implied world view of the critic's all-triumphant exposure of its '*revolutionary*' not to mention abstract, discontinuous flow-of-everything hypothesis. In a world of machines, it is clearly better to get a different machine, or see things in a new, machine-like way. The only possible reply is to borrow the Foucaultian right arm, and slam the door resolutely shut, with an appropriate 'bullshit', released gracefully from a moderately-organed and deterritorialised body.

The in-house intellectual exuberance of the neologisms had many merits, however, for it spawned a post-Surrealist storm of incongruent logics, grabbing bits from every discourse, scientific to literary, to make its own non-synthetic discourse. It rampaged through or floated from the micro-linguistic world of the destabilised sign to the macro-linguistic world of the sentence and semantics. It has kept the academy busy for years.

Fisher's poetry will embrace the world of *Anti-Oedipus* from the nomad to the non-organed body to the desiring-machines. Change

---

[10] Foucault, 'Preface', p. xiv.

the ideas and discourse and everything would change. Like all satire, however, it risked a Manichean world of binary oppositions in its multi-vocality which was, paradoxically, supposed to kill binarism for ever. The descriptive diction implied tended to the abstract. Sub-titles like 'The Conjunctive Synthesis of Consumption-Consummation' (the French word *consommation* can mean consummation as in marriage plus consumerism, as well as relating to food and eating) abound, and the language here signals a clue for the diction and fragmentary discourses, the runs of abstract words, that Fisher, too, has employed in his more recent 'post-collagist' texts.

At its best, however, *Anti-Oedipus* showed new ways of thinking about the multiple fields of human activity and traditional practices together with possible ways of understanding them. The intellectual collagist challenged the tired discourses of the self and other, nature and history, psyche and historical narrative. All this was refreshing. Distinctions between man and nature disappeared. Everything was *production.* Now there were organ-machines, desiring-machines, flow-producing machines, and energy-machines. Sartre's reflective consciousness was as dead as the dodo alongside the entire Hegelian tradition of critical philosophy, though paradoxically Marx was frequently invoked. Hegel may have been dumped, however, but Heraclitus was a star. Objects *flowed* and product was producing. By contrast Capitalist identity was an undifferentiated object frozen in its own nothingness: a body without organs, constructed by false consciousness, assuming there was any such a thing as consciousness. The body without organs had nothing to do with the body, it was without an image, but nonetheless catatonic (like a body in a hydrotherapy tub), perpetually reinserted into the process of production: 'it coupled production with antiproduction, with an element of antiproduction'(8). It was as if Ubu Roi and Azdak dancing in tandem had taken over the Philosophy Department at the Sorbonne.[11]

Their solution began with placing 'schizophrenation' against 'Oedipalisation' (68). The happy dancing schizophrenic replaced the couch-bound patient consumed in neurotic stasis, doubtless having read too much Hegel. It was very much in the spirit of the sixties where David Cooper and R.D. Laing, not to mention William Burroughs, in their respective cultures, had also explained that the paranoid was a man in full

---

[11] For Ubu Roi, see Alfred Jarry, *Ubu Roi*, 1896; for Azdak, see Bertoldt Brecht *The Caucasian Chalk Circle*, 1948.

possession of the facts. Norman O. Brown in America talked like Jesus about losing your life to save it.[12] Deleuze and Guattari talked about crossing the 'threshold'. Wilhelm Reich's influence lingered, not only in his brilliant attempts to think through sexual repression and fascism, but also in the ubiquity of his scientific discourse.[13] Forget *names and the idea of representation*, the theory of names is *just an effect* (86). Naturally the effects don't have any causes, they are just occupations of domains and 'the operation of a system of signs' (86).Quite how you describe the effects without naming something was left on hold.

The real issue now was *The Present*, history was pure collage served up in disembodied fragments, a naturalist's Cook's guide to disjointed but re-flowing temporalities, trapped as a surplus reality: the *booty* haunting a consciousness which didn't exist:

> To seize an intensive real as produced in the *coextension* of nature and history, to *ransack* the Roman Empire, the Mexican cities, the Greek gods, and the discovered continents so as to *extract* from them this always-surplus reality and to form the *treasure* of the paranoiac tortures and the celibate glories, all the pogroms of history, that's what I am, and all the triumphs too, as if a few simple *univocal events* could be extricated from this *extreme polyvocity*: such is the 'histrionism' of the schizophrenic, according to Klossowski's formula, the true program for a theatre of cruelty, the mise-en-scene of a machine to produce the real. (87 my italics)

In terms of the discredited philosophy, however, the problems in this post-structuralist view of the world with its primitive or non-existent theory of time, and historical narrative and memory, were precisely in the italicized words above. The neologisms papered over the cracks that traditional philosophy had insisted *were* cracks. *Histrionism*, for example, invoked hysteria and history: psychic state and narrative. But quite how any of these shifty paradoxes were either enabling to the subject or enlightening to the community were quite unclear. Quite

---

[12] Norman O. Brown, a Freudian (and superficially Marxist) revisionist, was the author of two very influential books in the mid-twentieth century: *Life against Death* (1959) and *Love's Body* (1966).

[13] Wilhelm Reich, a communist and student of Freud wrote both *The Mass Psychology of Fascism*(1933) and *The Function of the Orgasm* (1942).

how did nature and history *co-extend* themselves without raising the problem of consciousness? The violently colonialist words were un-ironically employed, *ransack, treasure, extricate* (let it not be said that mining was ever the key imperialist-colonialist goal).

Were the authors really so innocent that they did not realise there could be a 'fascism' of the polyvocal as well as the univocal, or that capitalism had not intensified the polyvocal so mercilessly that white noise was the result? Unable, like the forgotten Sartre, to make a distinction between the extra-temporal nature of ethics (Pascal) and the profound historicity of Marx, they coalesced the domains and gave it the name *machine*. While adopting the world view, Fisher's work will set out to rescue a sense of the person within the discourse promoted by the French savants.

It is, however, the second work by Deleuze and Guattari, *A Thousand Plateaus,* that dominates *Excavations*, and this in spite of the huge bibliography of many other 'resources' provided as usual at the end to let the reader into Fisher's textual world.[14] In this work, part of the whole philosophical project *Capitalism and Schizophrenia*, Deleuze and Guattari outlined their project for 'nomadic thought'. Conductivity replaced representation, gravity-less movement, gridded State space, and the 'tool-box', the concept. A certain impersonality characterized the *Soi* as against the Freudian *Moi* or ego. Images of roots and trees (Darwin, Chomsky) had fostered a binary division of world and book, nature and art, and were rejected. Instead multiplicity replaced unity at all levels of thought and experience. What replaced the root was the *rhizome* – the subterranean stem (7).

This botanical image dominates the whole work. It suggests endless non-hierarchical connective points, semiotic chains traversing coding, that is it can look at the arts, sciences, and social struggle as collective assemblages without typological distinction. Depth has gone. In this multiply-layered world multiplicities are *flat*. Its activity works by a whole-group movement. You can destroy an ant but not the general shape of ant activity: 'there is a rupture in the rhizome whenever segmentary lines explode into a line of flight, but the line of flight is part of the rhizome' (10). It is hence anti-genealogical. One of the rhizome's rhetorical uses in the book supports ethical homilies that occur often at the end of chapters to comfort with an end-of-sermon optimism, after describing the dark night of the monological capitalist soul. Here,

---

[14] Gilles Deleuze and Félix Guattari, *A Thousand Plateus*, trans. Brian Massumi (London, New York, NY: continuum books, 2004). Further page references follow in the text.

however, is one at the beginning:

> Always follow the rhizome by rupture; lengthen, prolong, and relay the line of flight, make it vary until you have produced the most abstract and tortuous of lines of *n* dimensions and broken directions. Conjugate deterritorialized flows. Follow the plants.... (12)[15]

Genetic axes, deep structures (they particularly had it in for Chomsky) were out. In spite of their horror of binary oppositions, binary *choices* are all over the work. The splendour of the *short-term idea* and memory, including forgetting, combines with the nervous temporal and collective rhizome. The *long-term memory* (family, race, society and civilization) acts in an *untimely* way. Better get rid of that.

Drift, a socialist target of right-wing fatalism before 1968, now becomes an anarchic biological possibility thrown against the capitalist's over-determined world. That world is to be undermined by supplements, surpluses and margins to use the favoured diction. The biological world is mined for analogy. The terror-haunted world of social-Darwinism, and the sense of terrifying original religious implications of the Darwinian revolution itself ('the stars she whispered blindly run'),[16] is replaced by a huge vitalistic (Spinozian) metaphysic of a nature that's on your side and whose movement is expressed in magnificently ornate, indeed baroque, Latinate abstractions (here italicized) of this less than ironic counter-reformation against God the father, the son and the Wolfman:

> Every voyage is *intensive* and *occurs in relation* to thresholds of *intensity* between which it *evolves* or that crosses. One travels by *intensity; displacements* and *spatial figures depend* on *intensive* thresholds of *nomadic deterritorializations* (and thus on *differential relations*) that *simultaneously define complementary sedentary reterritorializations.* (60)

---

[15] As Peter Orlovsky, Allen Ginsberg's partner, said to a group of Warwick University students in 1979: 'Plant nut trees'.

[16] Alfred Tennyson, 'In Memoriam' in *The Poems and Plays of Tennyson* (London: Oxford University Press, 1953), p. 231.

How will Fisher deal with this kind of language with its dogmatic enunciation of the relation between nature and consciousness? Heisenberg said that we have to remember that what we observe is not nature in itself but nature exposed to our method of questioning.[17] Is there anything in this work that suggests that Deleuze and Guattari's two-way perspective of the plateaus incorporating perception and nature itself might only be the result of a question, or historically relative or temporary? Unfortunately not. A new total generality *out there*, which my language articulates, delivers truth: 'In short the way an expression relates to a content is not by uncovering or representing it. Rather, forms of expression and forms of content communicate through a conjunction of their quanta of relative deterritorialization, each intervening, operating in the other' (97). The world of deterritorialised assemblages as such reigns as a permanently true physics and metaphysics unperceived by earthly assemblies. The machine-like language that represents it hardly offers the scientist's modesty, even with a good exteriority playing a major role in a decent strata!

So what of the old discourses on the junk heap of history and how does poetry relate to them? Can you really have an ethics, let alone a practical political ethics figured purely on a revised abstract ecological discourse about a world of assemblages? Never mind the language, whose abstractions are going to attract a mass movement rather less than even that of dialectical materialism? Perhaps, however, in the terrible world of the twentieth century their absolutism can be forgiven, and their saving carnivalesque spirit be used to challenge the psychology at least of the discourses of power. Yes, the class system is enforced by powers which operate from language to the gestures of a face-masked man enforcing death-like control on the helpless; yes, minority needs are constantly smashed by those who own and enforce centrist normality; yes, there is a complex sign system that enforces this and links laterally to other signs in powerful representational systems that must be undermined. But why invent this academic anti-university-driven theoretical abstractedness to authenticate an anger many of us share, so deterritorialisation risks becoming a nirvana of contentless posture, a deification of *attention* (in both opposing senses forming a seamless circle) needing permanent emergency? 'I will not reason and

---

[17] Werner Heisenberg, *Physics and Philosophy* (London: George Allen and Unwin, 1958), ch. 2.

compare,' said Blake, 'my business is to create'.[18]

In Fisher's poetic redeployment of the plateaus both the pleasures and dangers of these texts are fully present. How much does he finally create his own system within and outside the model of plateaus? To return to the Mottram poem, the thunder against the psycho-fascism of the mediating social machine of capitalism is clear in the diction and phrases: multiplicity and the self, the consumer and consumed, the open-ended world proposed ('interruptions inconclusions'), the doubt of identity and the rejection of circularity. Against the 'faciality' (one of the best and most engaging of the chapters of *A thousand plateaus*) of the oppressors Fisher invents an amusing tale of cats and human-headed lions, which here breaks the rather sententious enunciation of the Deleuze and Guattari world. In a Whitmanian mood ('I think I could turn and live awhile with the animals'),[19] Fisher updates the American poet's almost Nietzschean, satiric nineteenth-century diatribe against that self-obsessed and permanently guilty neurosis of the Victorian sinner, to embrace the French writers' neo-logistic world.

> I become animal with a fascination for the outside
>   related to a multiplicity that becomes dwelling within me
>   This book an assemblage unattainable and multiplicit
> in a structure growth offset by laws it self-invents
> by deterritorialization and connect with other multiplicities
> of combination rhizomatic determinations magnitudes
> and dimensions I become defined by an outside
> change as I become intruder and rumour. (81)

The adoption of the personal voice and the *confession* of method aligns itself here with the French philosophers' stance toward the world. Their revisionist project is delivered virtually without change: exteriority, multiplicity, assemblage, the vitalistic structural growth, deterritorialisation and the ubiquitous rhizomatic determinations, magnitudes and dimensions end in a flurry of Latinate abstractions. Except at the end there is a slight shift. For the 'I' suddenly delivers itself as the initially announced revised self, operating in acknowledgement of these fields,

---

[18] William Blake, 'Jerusalem' in William Blake, *The Complete Poems*, ed. Alice Ostriker (Harmondsworth: Penguin Books, 1977), p. 651.

[19] Walt Whitman,[Song of Myself] 'Leaves of Grass' [1855] in *Complete Poetry and Collected Prose* (New York, NY: The Library of America, 1982), p. 58.

constructed with the internal rhyming 'intruder and rumour'. That is very deft, for rumour is a threatening narrative from outside, working inwards and outwards. It also announces a fragmentary purposeful act, although that 'defined by' is still very paradoxical in relation to it, and ultimately evasive. The Burglar has already been reviewed, but he, too, is further 'defined' in a world of micro-chemical and atomic patterns which are represented in him and which he manipulates variously. The adoption of the rhizomic world both constructs him and gives him the consciousness to act purposefully and in recognition of what he is doing. There seems to be a rather fantastic correspondence theory implied here between mind and nature. In a recognition of nature validated by 'correct' scientific apprehension, the self perceives equally accurately interiority as a pure mirror of exteriority. Without the benefit or clarity of organizing syntax, the micro-patterns of the physical, chemical and biological world and the attributes of the self simply add on to a list. It is useful enough for the purposes of satire. The burglar, in fact, becomes a list or rather happily adds himself to *the* list as the animal itself had related to an organic multiplicity which is then flatly claimed as 'dwelling'.

The problem with 'dwelling', however, is that for Heidegger, its best theorist, it is not part of a list but a dream world marked by happiness. Poetry builds up the nature of dwelling in a saying of images.[20] I think that is what Fisher is attempting to do. There is, however, relatively little sense of that here, for the enumeration of the forms of nature and consciousness seem to be abstractly given in advance by the sanctioning theory, as if there were a nature of number. And there is a further problem with this exteriority declared simply to be inwardness because it only awkwardly gets round the notion of *distance* which is always a factor in exteriority. It was Heidegger also who clearly articulated the problem 'the thorough-going calculative conversion of all connections among all things into the calculable absence of distance'.[21] For Heidegger, this was a refusal of nearness and concealed the connection of nature to nearness. If the Burglar simply declares the scientific description of the world to be inside him, it is with difficulty converted into dwelling, because the world is already to a degree exiled in the monologic of the scientific discourse in which the question of nearness and distance is simply ignored.

---

[20] Martin Heidegger, *Poetry, Language, Thought*, trans. Albert Hofstadter (New York *et al*: Harper Colophon Books, 1975), p. 226ff.

[21] Martin Heidegger, *On the Way to Language*, trans. Peter D. Herz (San Francisco, CA: Harper and Row, 1971), p. 105.

Feyerabend said that science is *only one* discourse about the world.[22] If science is to claim all multivocality, is there not as great a danger as formerly there was in its exclusiveness of domain? In the attempt by the French writers to create an all-embracing discourse in a new abstract language, they risk being hoist by their own petard. Is it because Fisher intuits this that the Burglar's discourse can fall into an atomistic jumble of abstractions, collaged from a scientific article? To be sure the message gets across clearly enough that cellular discontinuities make for an abundance of life, emphasising the role of chance and unpredictability, thus ultimately fighting a world in which nothing surprising is supposed to happen – the assumptions of power and fascism. But a weariness can set in as the abstractions pile up with little variation and with perhaps too relentlessly *objective* a tone with a concealed voice, only occasionally thematised in the capitalised personae who announce endless externalities.

The paraphrase of the Deleuze and Guatarri world is not, perhaps, ironic enough, nor re-imagined enough, nor in my view comic enough, nor sometimes creatively distanced enough. However Fisher knows the dangers because his 'self' aims to distinguish between *types* of multiplicity as he again paraphrases Deleuze and Guattari:

> The self becomes an instantaneous apprehension of multiplicity
> In a given region not a substitute but an *I feel*
> Myself become animal, animal among others
> On the edge of the garden created in order
> To escape abstract opposition between multiple and one
> To escape dialectics and cease treatment of numerical fragment
> As lost totality or as an organic element in unity
> Instead to distinguish between types of multiplicity (83)

Of course, this passage should be read in the full context of the poem: itself a sequence of a treatise on the self, with its situationist credo, its fictional figure of the burglar and the visionary sense of oneness with scientifically-described natural order. The *distinction* however still does not address this vision of the 'nature' of number in its dismissal of the Platonic one and many. Is there, also, something a bit too desperately pedagogical about this otherwise quite accurate summary? How much is that 'Myself become animal' a graceful sense of the self in the world

---

[22] Paul Feyerabend, *Against Method* (London: Verso, 1975), pp. 19-20.

of nature, with an almost Buddhist sense of acceptance against the Christian-Capitalist psychosis, or how much does it dogmatically claim that, as seen from that alliance, the world is somehow scientifically orderly in the rhizomic perception? There are huge problems here, not least, apart from the obvious satiric possibilities and the points noted above, of what becoming an animal actually means. That Fisher senses this is obvious in this passage, where the pedagogical impulse, the announcement of a poetics, is neatly offset by a humorous recall of the lion head and Burglar. The effect is at once wistful and gently ironic. There's a beautiful variable rhythm throughout, a syntactical frame is acceded to, though the last phrase is too nervously added on as if the molecules couldn't be left out.

> In this multiplicity of writing, bye and barren themes
> are best fitted for invention;
> Subjects so often discoursed confine the imagination,
> and fix our conceptions into the notions of fore-writers.
> The lion-headed moves into sunlight squinting
> a purr ignores the Burglar begins to lick paws
> rubs them on the face and side of head occasionally
> biting at fur as if unwanted molecular difference (84)

There is a comic gentleness that haunts all Fisher's poetry when he is not so insistent with the way things are.

The aim is here is to suggest where both the strengths and the problems of this newish (though to a lesser extent it has always been there) turn in Fisher's poetry lie. It is an old problem that Whitman, too, could not get his head round, that in speaking for everyone in a revised general system, the self as a particle of the universe in Shelley-like creation and decay, you can lose the specific life, the specific consciousness of the self, the uniqueness and the anguish as well as the joy of a very different sense of the self of which the 'old' discourses and practices perhaps gave just as variable and rich a sense. That single dead ant in Deleuze and Guattari's always surviving ant-group might be worth noticing, even worth mourning and hanging you up for a bit in your rhizomic helter-skelter confidence, even if you didn't want to make a fetish of a dead ant.

It may be that part of the difficulty lies with the way sources are used, the very post-collagist procedures defamiliarise at the expense, paradoxically, of historical complexity and recall. Where is *the world of*

Marx, the world of *1848*, in the collaged fragment? Where is the world of Che Guevara on the t-shirt? It is simply obliterated in its *capitalist rhizomic* (because rhizomic structures have already been incorporated by the bosses) lateral connection with other signs, producing the always fashionable profit. There's a real problem of synchrony and diachrony here, scarcely solved, indeed, virtually created by postmodernism. If the fragment is to enter the new arrangement in full force, can it survive the lateral rearrangement with other signs, if that is the only thing that produces any real significance and if all representation and all narrative historical sense are taken as an absolute negative?

Coda

As a final thought, however, it might be useful to think less of philosophical matters than visual. Turning from the analytic to the visual, it has to be said that one of the biggest influences on Fisher's poetry is precisely the post-Surrealist world of mid- to late-twentieth century painting. Here the importance of the Fluxus group with which Fisher was very briefly associated might be recalled and also Eric Mottram's *Towards Design in Poetry* which was to a certain extent influenced by it.[23] In many ways, however, it is the American artist Kitaj who is as powerful an influence as either.

The key question, which is only offered here as a concluding open-ended thought, is how easily do lateral juxtapositions of the heterogeneous pass from visual to verbal practice. In an essay on Kitaj, Richard Wolheim spoke of three different uses of the 'fragment' in the painter's work.[24] The first concerned the relation of the past to the present – that is the use of past painting pasted as it were into the present work. Wolheim noted that in the re-presentation there was never a fixed amount nor a fixed proportion. There are various moods: 'loitering' figures from Doré for example 'are spies from the past, policing the present' (39). On the other hand, Michelangelo's sinner will dominate a composition like 'The Peril's of Revisionism', a title that clearly invites multiple meanings from the visual to the political. Then there are borrowings that do not reproduce obvious details like a

---

[23] See the discussion in Bush, *Out of Dissent*, pp. 449-457.

[24] Richard Wolheim, 'Recollections and Reflections' in Richard Morphet (ed.), *R.B. Kitaj: A Retrospective* (London: Tate Gallery, 1994). Further references follow in the text.

particular contour, or free brushwork or a kind of 'rhyming of forms' (39).

Second, there is a form of assemblage of past figures that make a sort of imaginary eternal city: 'where Baudelaire might have strolled with Svevo, and Walter Benjamin had a drink with Polly Adler, and John Ashbery written poetry at a café table, and where Cavafy and Proust and Pavese could have negotiated with Jupien for the sexual favours they craved' (39). Third, there is a use of the fragment to 'convey the darkness of the mind' (39). These bear witness to the figures who have had most bearing on his work, what Kitaj himself called 'Symbolist-Surrealists': van Gogh, Picasso, Giacometti, Miró, Balthus and de Kooning, who for him articulated the 'primacy of artistic craziness' (40).

Wollheim went on to talk about how these remarks merely referred to a kind of content, and, in a parallel spirit to that of Deleuze and Guattari, spoke of the actual painting as articulating 'new forms of coexistence' (40). The planar composition was obvious. The organization of the cubicles on the surface were not just configured but in themselves represented 'windows, or screens, or table-tops, or the panelled awning of a café' (41). In other words, geometric design was abandoned.

When we look, however, at, say, a picture like *Kennst du das Land?* (1962), where Kitaj refers to his 'collaged images', the multiplicities and the ironies reveal themselves immediately. We do not immediately say this is non-geometric or I do not see traditional chiaroscuro or perspective here. The relationships are immediately *there*. We hardly need Kitaj's own commentary to see this is Spain not Italy (though fascism is common to both), with the collaged drawing of Goya's whore among the four squarish images, 'cubicled' and lined off at the top. In the roughly three-quarters of the picture plane below, we immediately get the sense of the battlefield, the irony of the lemons on top of the cars ('*wo die Citronen blühn*'), the tonsured monk behind the machine gun, and the floating 'mitre' in full colours floating above a chilly white-grey field. Our eye moves from the whore to the monk (whose side is he on, a Catalonian or a Loyalist? it's not obvious), from Goya's sense of the immediate presence of the whore neither endorsing nor criticising, marginalised as a permanent sign within this lost-war against fascism. Modernity in the parked cars is as ugly as sin itself. Doubtless the contours and free textures of the deployment of white and grey for landscape and sky are part, too, of the collaged images.

Kitaj, however, is prepared to vary *his sense of what this form is*. He is delighted with his friend Julien Ríos's reminding him of an older convention of Spanish art called *canto y seña*. In language, in poetry, however, there has to be more work with the post-collagist fragments, because pure juxtaposition in language does not work so satisfactorily at the semantic level. The apprehension is not so immediate, the complexities of the same and the different are much greater, and there has to be, even in the most abstract juxtaposition some sense of a person, a history, a tension between the subjective and objective, the metaphoric and the metonymic, the syntactical and the 'object' it delivers.

Nonetheless I think Kitaj's reflexiveness and sensibility is there in Fisher's best work. Any of these three broad deployments of the fragment, for example, can be found in the latest work. I have merely pointed out the dangers as well as the pleasures in *some* current directions. Read as a whole, *Excavation* is extremely varied from the lyrical anti-lyricism of 'Jigwalk' and 'Jitterbug' (showing that 'darkness of mind'), to the meditation on time and colour in 'Lindy Hop', to the utterly charming sonnet, 'beginning of Mouse'. The permanent irony of the presentation of the self among internalised biological flows and sub-molecular structures skirting the dangers of consciousness, idealism and its perils is always lively. And perhaps the problems offered here are intractable. At one point, Fisher confronts the heart of the matter head on, in a prosaic aside:

> A self-conscious personality is perhaps like an organism whose structures or ideas are consciously self-imposed. But a reflective human being, by living out a certain self-conception and a set of goals and values, can also bring about changes in that conception, in these goals and values themselves. Therefore, a self-consciousness is not like an organism. It is far more like a unique process, which can survive radical changes in its complex electro-magnetico-chemical structure, and which initiates its own change independently. (110)

One wants more sense of that 'reflective human being' in the poems, and more saying of what 'its own change' is exactly. That 'perhaps like' and 'like a unique process' beg some of the obvious questions. How does the world of values exactly relate to that of its 'complex electro-magnet-chemical structure'? If it is not *like*, why is the same language used to describe it? The pseudo-objective eco-vision has its own unresolvable contradictions.

At the same time the models of nature that we have of course inflect our ways of thinking about ourselves. Historically, the consciousness of the self is represented differently in the ages of Ptolemy, Galileo, Darwin and Einstein, though there are certain extra-historical matters that ensure a permanent invitation to their worlds: ethics is one, the continuous investigation of science is another, systems of power are yet another, not to mention the slow movement of socio-anthopological systems and law. But no system fully constructs the sense of the self, indeed the self merely *suffers* structure. Neither is it coterminous with it, nor is there ever a final system. There are many other discourses, too, for these human conditions, and they too historically vary and adapt to the *Zeitgeist*. Fisher knows all this, but perhaps in the clear gleefulness of his subversive abstractions, what is now needed is a more variable tone to soften the plethora of enunciations, and a more variable discourse of the self in danger, in his endlessly engaging and daring Whitmanesque attempts to 'contain multitudes'.

The New Complexity:
Preface to Allen Fisher's *Imperfect Fit*

PIERRE JORIS

> *The cosmic myths and initiation legends suggest the existence of worlds that a timeless fluidity entangles, superposes and locates in hidden recesses where the most certain laws of our Aristotelian sciences and of our geometrical apperception, as inherited from the Great Watchmaker, are abrogated.* –
> Raoul Vaneigem

At the threshold of this, now already deeply scarred century, I wrote in *A Nomadic Poetics*: 'We will take the whole of the new century to finally read Allen Fisher's vast investigation into all our knowledges, the great serial constructive *dérive* he calls *Gravity as a consequence of shape*.' Did I exaggerate in terms of the time it would take to read his work? Do we actually have that much time left? I'm not sure on either count, though I know that the scintillating massiveness, the true-to-the-world, I mean true-to-the-cosmos, complexity, the rich strangeness – call it *ostranenie of all the in-betweens* – of the work and its imagistic and linguistic reaches, will ensure eye-widening pleasures and insights with discoveries galore for the long crossing. A quick bird's-eye view of the Fisher constellation: The core poetry work as gathered into two major assemblages – 400 pages of *Place* and the 800 pages of *Gravity as a consequence of shape* – is only the most visible/available part of the textual *oeuvre*. There are works that fall outside those two major processes, but that always in one way or another connect to, are informed by and in turn inform them, such as *Apocalyptic Sonnets* (1978), *Blood bone Brain* (texts & documentation of an installation and performance work, 1982), *Unpolished Mirrors* (1985). Then there is as a plethora of further writings in smaller, fugitive publications dating back to the late 60s and including textual, visual & conceptual works, audio cassettes, essays, documentation, investigations, etc. – among them the recent *The Marvels of Lambeth*, a volume of interviews and statements – not to speak of the man's vast life's achievements in various art fields, from Fluxus related objects to performance scenarios and installations, to drawings and paintings.

Imperfect fit, the volume at hand, is his first major gathering of essays on writing and art making – he prefers the word 'facturing' for both activities – and thus a most welcome aid not only to a deeper understanding of Fisher's own writing and art making practices, but it also offers us vital investigations into the present situation and the future possibilities of the aesthetic arts. A present situation I see as a major hinge between old human-centred civilizations – the culture of the anthropocene – and what is looming now, a moment in which the main energies shaping this world will probably not be human-centred, but where external forces, the effects of climate change, will radically impinge on the human position on spaceship Earth. We know, or should know, that what Jean-François Lyotard called the 'Grand narratives' – religious or profane eschatological tales be they of a Christian, Marxist or, as recently revived, Islamic order – have collapsed, revealing themselves a fraudulent power-grabs, after having paved the yellow brick road into the disaster area we now find us in. Unhappily humans seem incapable of functioning without such a grand narrative, unable as most of them are of staying in what John Keats called 'negative capability'. Yet it may now not only be possible, but essential and urgent to create such a grand narrative, but one that for once will not have let in those man-made excuses, god or supreme leader as single source of authority, transcendent or immanent paradise as driving force, but one that will try to think us from – and, why not, sync us with – the world that is both around and in us. Or, as Robin Blaser put this when he insisted that the 'real business of poetry is cosmology': 'The music of the spheres is quite real, but the sound of the earth must meet it.' The cosmic sense involved here is what Margaret Mead describes as a 'human instinctual need for a perceptual relation to the universe,' an idea Blaser illuminates, saying, 'this is the scientific basis for the proprioceptive process which Charles Olson speaks of.' And which Allen Fisher's work implements and extends via a range of concepts discussed in this book, such as decoherence; traps, tools and damage; or 'confidence in lack.'

I am deeply convinced that Fisher's work can be a major tool to think through and retool our old view of the world toward a new and more complex, more multi-dimensional vision necessary for the future – however much or little of the latter is left for our species. Not that it proposes a 'new, improved' model of the world that would finally be the accurate one. But it does offer what Olson called a *meta hodos*, a methodology for en-vision-ing an exemplary path towards – a term that originates in Foucault's last conferences – *parrhēsia*, truth-telling via aesthetic facture. It is, I would like to suggest, only this kind of cross-disciplinary work, encompassing a wide enough engagement with all our knowledge-fields as done by poets, artists and radical thinkers and activists like Allen Fisher, that will allow openings for paradigmatic change wide enough to entertain the possibility of a redeemed or redeemable anthropo-sphere.

Fisher's work as a poet combines a most powerful degree of formal invention (procedural structures crossed, bent, enriched and written through by processual activities) with a political and social radicalism and insight that is truly stunning. It is impossible to sum up this work, though here is how the British critic Clive Bush has tried to describe it: 'His poetry shows… a huge range of learning. His interests include ancient archaeology, western and non-western traditions of sculpture and painting, mathematics, the local history of the City of London and contemporary music.' Add to these: astrophysics, geography, theoretical physics from Lucretius to string theory, biology, systems of healing, contemporary theoretical thinking from Adorno to Deleuze, and so on. Bush then compares Fisher's enterprise to the ambition Shelley proposed for the poet's work in his *Defense of Poetry*: 'Poetry is at once the centre and circumference of knowledge; it is that which comprehends all science, and that to which all science must be referred. It is at the same time the root and blossom of all other systems of thought…'

William Blake's lines 'I must create a system, or be enslaved by another man's; / I will not reason or compare; my business is to create,' could stand as motto for Fisher's work. But, of course, there always are a range of other men and women's work that stand behind even as complexly idosyncratic a system as Allen Fisher's. Clive Bush again, proposing the American connections: 'Fisher shares with Pound the breadth of cultural ambition; with Williams the sense of place, the local as a complex of occasions, and of science as a co-eval creativity analogous at least with the poetic act; with Olson a visionary view of the transformations of the earth's structure, the patterns of trade, and a fascination with ancient and pre-socratic culture; and with Oppen a concern for critical philosophy and the victims of oppression.' Of course, a wide number of further connections, through the centuries and continents, could be mentioned. Fisher, in a very meticulous way, indicates these sources, for both the poetry and essays, usually under the title of 'resources' at the end of the given work. One of the great pleasures of reading him is that his texts – poems or essays – via these resources open up into further adventurous readings. The work operates as/in an open system of process-showing where writing that may seem difficult on the surface is however never and in no way wilfully hermetic.

Fisher is exactly what Robert Kelly suggested the poet as last generalist of the whole needed to become: a 'scientist of totality… to whom all data whatsoever are of use, world scholar.' Fisher belongs to the tribe of poets who 'do not have hobbies/ they eat everything,' with the proviso that 'the poet is then not the encyclopedia' but as 'discoverer of relations, re-integrator, explorer of ultimate connection / & connectedness in among & all.' Here, from his Introduction to *Brixton Fractals,* is how Fisher himself puts it succinctly: 'Imagination and action. My knowledge of the world exists validly only in the moment when I am transforming it. In this moment, in action, the imagination functions, unblocks passivity, refuses an overview. Discontinuities, wave breaks, cell divisions, collapsed structures, boundaries between tissue kinds: where inner workings are unknown, the only reliable participations are imaginative. The complex of state and control variables. The number of configurations depends on the latter: properties typical of cusp catastrophes: sudden jumps; hysteresis; divergence; inaccessibility. Boiling water's phase change where the potential is the same as condensing steam. Random motion of particles in phase space allows a process to find a minimum potential. What is this all about? It's a matter of rage and fear, where the moving grass or built suburbia frontier is a wave prison; where depth perception reverses; caged flight. With ambiguous vases it's as if part of the brain is unable to reach a firm conclusion and passes alternatives along for a decision on other grounds. The goblet-and-face contour moves as it forms in your seeing.'

Sad to say, but the vast majority of contemporary art – poetry or visual art – even while paying lip-service to current technological advances (integration with or references to computer-age machines and machinations) remains firmly caught in a classical 19C Newtonian vision of the world, oblivious of how the various sciences have paradigmatically reshaped our 'vision of the world' into what could be our 'vision of the multiverse.' And that means that it perpetuates the age-old schism between the 'arts' and 'sciences.' And yet, to quote the German poet Durs Grünbein, author of *Im Schnee*, a long narrative poem on Descartes: 'Why shouldn't we be able to think the likes of William Blake and René Descartes together? Only because the former has been hailed a visionary while the latter has been branded an obstinate rationalist? Imagination is a hybrid, it avails itself of many different methods in order to attain its goals.' An imagination that, however, also needs to take into account the advances in quantum physics, biology and the other fields enumerated above that constitute Fisher's reading as much as the fields of art and poetry.

All of the information thus gathered is however not used as a hammer to drive home (wherever that may or may not be) some ideological nail. It is allowed to enter an open field in which the essential (maybe the only?) advance of 20C art, namely the technique of collage/ montage, mounts temporary assemblages in which self-referential (inside their own fields) discourses are broken down, cut-up, juxtaposed with others into new co- and de-coherences, always exhibiting the vulnerabilities necessary for *parrhēsia*, truth-telling. This field remains open also at another level: the reader/viewer has to participate in and contribute to the works' facture. As Fisher puts it: 'the production of any artefact is the consequence of two activities: aesthetic facture and aesthetic reception.' What helps to keep the reader engaged and on her toes in these essays in their search for (an always to be questioned) *parrhēsia*, is the slight but necessary strangeness – a version of *ostranenie* – of the prose itself (beyond the vocabulary visible in the required work of/on syntax), willed by the author but also by the matters addressed or addressing author and reader.

The 'age of poetry,' or so the French philosopher Alain Badiou suggests, extended from the 19th century to about 1960, starting with Friedrich Hölderlin (I would add William Blake) and ending with Paul Celan. The French poet Michel Deguy – in a recent conversation – suggested that what superseded Badiou's age was an 'age of poetics.' And indeed, as I have shown elsewhere, how in the last decade of his life – from 1960 to 1970 – Paul Celan's work exactly straddled this 'age of the poet' and the proposed 'age of poetics' in that his poems became process-showing (to use Allen Fisher's term), i.e. externalized their poetics while attempting to define and explore the new reality of the post-19th-century cosmos. Less inclined than the French to make such claims, I would suggest but we are at the moment where poetry and poetics have to conjoin and show themselves in simultaneous actions while opening up the aesthetic field of endeavour to be fertilized by a wider range of human endeavours and investigations. Celan's work, for its own historical and autobiographical reasons, remains at the threshold of our century. If in him (as in, say, Artaud or Olson) there are intimations of both the coming disasters and of the poetic and aesthetic methodologies needed to address them, these are beginning to come to a head only now. Under that purview the work of Allen Fisher is and will remain core to our attempts to locate a way forward through the arts. With this book we have the perfect guide to his work. Let's start reading – there is no time to lose.

Resources:

Alain Badiou, *The Age of the Poets* (London New York, NY: Verso, 2014).
Durs Grünbein, *The Vocation of Poetry* (New York, NY: Upper West Side Philosophers, Inc, 2010) 36-37.
Pierre Joris, *A Nomad Poetics* (Middletown, CT: Wesleyan University Press, 2003)

Artefactu(r)al Logic In Allen Fisher's *Sputtor*

CALUM HAZELL

Remark on Method

The operative distinctions between a typical critical analysis of a poetic text, and the reading strategies employed by a poet, firstly concern *the type of knowledge or truth* constructed through engagement with the text, and secondly, the ways in which these knowledges or truths come to be applied. Allen Fisher, whose 2014 work *SPUTTOR*[1] is the focus of this essay, summarises this interrelation of reading and writing, describing 'research' as 'the work in poetry and painting that is *carried out in parallel* with work in the factory, in the laboratory, and in the facturing process... *The results from the research sometimes directly feature in a poetry sequence or painting... [s]ometimes they directly feed each other, sometimes their parity is incidental.*'[2] In this sense, then, we can consider reading or researching as a writer as an activity that runs 'parallel' to the experiments of poetic composition or 'facture'. The relationship is marked by a particular positionality: a spectrum is established out of the research materials running from 'direct' to 'incidental' in terms of the sense in which they come to be 'featured' in or incorporated into a creative work. Thus, the arrangement emphasises the generative potential of research as a consequence of its constructed distance from the project in hand. It is this distance that facilitates the selection of researched material and determines the sense of its possible incorporation and *the conditions under which it is true*- perhaps in relation to other found or researched materials – *for the creative work*.

There are also ethical and political implications of research insofar as these activities take place in a creative project. As Adorno warns, '[t]hose who brag of having "got" something from an artwork transfer in philistine fashion the relation of possession to what is strictly foreign to it.'[3] Whereas we might tentatively assign this notion of 'possession'

---

[1] Allen Fisher, *SPUTTOR*, (Veer Books: London, 2014).

[2] Allen Fisher, 'The Poetics of the Complexity Manifold' in *boundary 2*, Vol.26, No.1: 'An International Poetics Symposium', (Duke University Press: North Carolina, 1999), 116, (emphasis added).

[3] Theodor W. Adorno, 'Paralipomena' in *Aesthetic Theory*, (1970), (Continuum: New York, 2004), 345.

as a constitutive feature of critical analysis – claiming, as is its tendency, aspects of an 'artwork' or poem in order to substantiate and advance a particular argument – a practical project negotiates its research materials in a different way. Thus, rather than 'getting' or 'taking' something from the texts that are the objects of research, practical work enters into a correspondence with these items that establishes a textual complex as a form of exchange. The research materials are refashioned and mutate as a matter of this correspondence.

Taking heed of these remarks, this essay will explore certain aspects of Fisher's *SPUTTOR*. I shall firstly investigate Fisher's incorporation of text and image in *SPUTTOR* in reference to its use of quotation and collage; I shall then consider the attitude in *SPUTTOR* towards established forms of knowledge, and ultimately nominate *SPUTTOR* as a textual site for the establishment of an innovative poetic knowledge. I will begin each section by devising a speculative conceptual framework.

Collage and Quotation

One of the great achievements of *SPUTTOR*, that, unlike other aspects of the text that require a different kind of attention, can be observed as soon as the book is opened, relates to the sheer viscerality of its arrangement. The correspondence and interface that *SPUTTOR* develops between its vast array of pasted images, poems, notes, esoteric markings, graphs, and tables suggests an affective compound and textural richness which bely and distort the level surface of its pages, gesturing towards the tactility we might imagine of its pre-digitised rendering. Juha Virtanen notes that the 'poems, images, and commentaries' in *SPUTTOR* 'mutually permeate each other's pores and interstices.'[4] Whilst the phenomenon Virtanen describes is apparent throughout *SPUTTOR*, it is particularly striking in the intermittent double-page spreads, such as we find on pages 56-57. Here, we are faced with an interpretation of a passage from Michel Foucault's *The Courage of Truth* concerning the 'responsibility' of the 'Cynic philosopher',[5] which

---

[4] Juha Virtanen, "Writing on: Context and Visual Culture in Recent Works of Allen Fisher and Ulli Freer" in *Journal of British and Irish Innovative Poetry*, 8(1), e3, (May 2016: http://dx.doi.org/10.16995/biip.20, accessed 28/04/18 at 15:18), 12.

[5] Michel Foucault, *The Courage of Truth: The Government of Self and Others II, Lectures at the Collège de France, 1983-1984*, translated by Graham Burchell, (Palgrave Macmillan: London, 2011), 299.

'permeates' a washed-out image and textual fragment from Andrew Wilson's *Space Shuttle Story*, which are partially obscured by a poem (that appears again, enlarged, across pages 118-119), which is in turn associated with the cut-out of a foreboding headline on the subject of a 'gas cloud' heading towards a 'supermassive black hole', which itself functions as a subscript, grounding the assemblage.[6]

Conceptualising Fisher's compositional strategy, Pierre Joris notes that '[a]ll of the information... gathered by the poet... is allowed to enter an open field in which... *the technique of collage/montage articulates temporary assemblages* in which self-referential (inside their own fields) discourses are broken down, cut-up, juxtaposed with others into new co- and de-coherences...'[7] In this sense, it is possible to associate the agglomeration of textual and visual artefacts in *SPUTTOR* with notions of locality and scalability. *SPUTTOR* establishes a nexus of 'temporary' 'fields' or territorial degrees for the interface of assimilated items. This interface can be observed on the macroscopic level of the book-object, through the districts consolidated under separate chapters, through the enclaves formed out of double-page spreads, through the thresholds of single pages, to the micro-signalling exchanged between one item and another. Consequently, *SPUTTOR* articulates a conceptual continuum of time and space. The local assemblages are 'temporary' because they endure and cohere for as long as they are attended to: they are momentarily discrete, they accumulate and they collapse, they are intervened upon and they bleed out. In this way, *SPUTTOR* arranges and performs a spatial sequencing out of its component parts that plays out over (readerly) time.

It is possible to associate these remarks with a more focused consideration of Fisher's integration of textual and visual objects. Whilst the 'breaking down' and 'cutting-up' of 'discourses' in Joris's account suggests a violence recalling Fisher's notion of 'fracturing research',[8] it is important to note that strategies in collage and quotation do not indicate a complete dissociation of the artefact from the environment, field, or context in which it was found. As Lawrence Rainey argues, '[e]very quotation bears an imaginary map... that charts a... discursive

---

[6] Fisher, *SPUTTOR*, 56-57.

[7] Pierre Joris, 'The New Complexity' in Allen Fisher, *Imperfect Fit: Aesthetic Function, Facture and Perception in Art and Writing since 1950*, (University of Alabama Press: Alabama, 2016), xvi, (emphasis added).

[8] Fisher, 'Complexity Manifold', 116.

topography plotted both spatially and temporally. This map graphs other quotations… with appropriate genealogies and relations to culminate in the moment of its own understanding…'[9] Hence, irrespective of the degree to which a quotation is adjusted or preserved, and however a visual item is treated or prepared, that quotation or image neither constitutes a simple 'reproduction'[10], nor is it disengaged from the site of its previous transmission. Rather, in the manner of James Williams's 'processual sign', it 'plays out… forward and backward along a suite of intensive changes'[11] upon its transplantation into a new textual domain.

As such, techniques in collage and quotation can be seen as establishing a transformative textual event involving and augmenting the 'discursive topography' of the item(s) in question. This textual event articulates a tension consisting in the material violence of the extraction of an artefact from its previous context, and the paradoxical sense in which the artefact endures in that context. In this way, the 'genealogy' of a transplanted artefact, like the artefact itself, is subjected to both 'fracture' and expansion. *SPUTTOR* can be read as disclosing this dynamic: the images and fragments obscured, smeared, spliced, chopped and screwed, precede a 'Shuttle Flight Summary' cataloguing the resources absorbed or engaged.[12] In this light, Fisher's notion of the 'productive' and 'positive' aspects of 'damage'[13] and 'fracture'[14] names this middle ground: it is one part maim, and one part embrace.

An important implication of these remarks is the association of the compositional practices of collage and quotation with a fundamental heterogeneity. The array of artefacts establishing the textual fabric of *SPUTTOR* each bear witness to, and each embody, the immanent 'genealogy' of their discrete transmissions. It is this initial discrete embodiment that prepares the ground for the 'permeation' of textual items as they come to imbricate and interact in the text. In other words,

---

[9] Lawrence S. Rainey, *Ezra Pound and the Monument of Culture: Text, History, and the Malatesta Cantos*, (University of Chicago Press: London, 1991), 61.

[10] Ibid.

[11] James Williams, *A Process Philosophy of Signs*, (Edinburgh University Press: Edinburgh, 2016), 78.

[12] Fisher, *SPUTTOR*, 124-125.

[13] Allen Fisher, 'Traps and Tools or Damage: Inventive Perception and Transformation' in *Imperfect Fit: Aesthetic Function, Facture and Perception in Art and Writing since 1950*, (University of Alabama Press: Alabama, 2016), 172.

[14] Fisher, 'Complexity Manifold', 116.

these items are not incorporated *en masse*, nor do they produce a ragbag arrangement. But rather they are carefully woven according to the sense (maintained and intended) particular to each thread. Crucially, this notion demarcates a distinction between Rainey's formulation – which describes the movement of an *inherited transmission* – and that which concerns the decisional process of an *intended transmission*.

As an extension to the extract above, in which he articulates the 'direct' and 'incidental' degrees that a research material might 'feature' in a creative work, elsewhere, Fisher describes his employment of the term 'negentropy', so far as it appears in his critical and practical work, as a "developmental" or figurative use of [its] origins.'[15] This is important because it allows us both to conceive of the authorial moment, in its 'parallel' relation to a research activity, as a transformative space in which the *sense*, *logic*, and *extent* of a particular artefact is determined, and also because it accentuates the heterogeneous nature of collage and quotation. Put otherwise, that the 'genealogy' of every item integrated into *SPUTTOR* is unique to that item, expresses a truth concerning the reception and *inheritance* of research materials in general: they are, in Williams's words, 'asymmetrical in their concurrent operation',[16] they are exclusively the same. Conversely, that every artefact taking place in *SPUTTOR* reflects a conscious or nonconscious determination of its *sense* or *logic* (by the author), expresses a truth concerning the point of its integration: the *intention* for each object incorporated, and the aesthetic conditions under which they are installed.

In this way, it is possible to consider the heterogeneity intrinsic to collage and quotation techniques as determined across two interrelated trajectories. Every artefact installed into *SPUTTOR* is marked by the material and contextual 'genealogy' of its previous transmission, and also by the intention or sense of that installation, as determined by the author. The researched artefact, and its history, undergo transformation as a matter of an initial isolation, a following extraction, the conceptual conditions under which it is incorporated into the new textual site, the particular treatment of the artefact in the 'laboratory', and the correspondences it enters into with other textual artefacts. The researched artefact, and its history, are augmented according to these

---

[15] Allen Fisher, "Testing and Experimenting: A Personal View of Aesthetic Practice and Reception" in *Imperfect Fit: Aesthetic Function, Facture and Perception in Art and Writing since 1950*, (University of Alabama Press: Alabama, 2016), 35.

[16] Williams, *Process Philosophy*, 78.

degrees or stages of transformation, which build upon and mutate that which the artefact reveals and retains.

Fisher's collage and quotation techniques in *SPUTTOR* also imply a series of permissions: the permission to build textual assemblages out of a wide array of different media, the permission to incorporate and draw upon research materials from various fields of study, and the permission to experiment with the design of the codex form. These techniques, at the same time, raise certain questions: What is at stake conceptually in the incorporation of research resources into a new textual environment? What is the relation between the material presentation of a poetic project and that which the work establishes conceptually? How can the material and conceptual aspects of a bookwork be aligned, so as to produce a new aesthetic dimension of the work?

The 'Space Shuttle Summary' in *SPUTTOR*, like the pages documenting the 'resources' drawn upon and integrated into *Gravity as a consequence of shape*[17] and *Place*[18], are particularly important in this context. In one sense, the particular relationship that Fisher constructs between *SPUTTOR* and the books, objects, and vocabularies informing its establishment, depends on the referencing and documentation of these resources. This is, above all, a question concerning the construction of a readerly access: through the 'Space Shuttle Summary', *SPUTTOR* facilitates a deliberate and direct negotiation of its source materials. It is clear that this negotiation would play out differently if the reader was not supplied with bibliographic information.

Poetic Knowledge

It is possible to connect Fisher's collage and quotation strategies in *SPUTTOR* with a distrust of established forms of knowledge. Through these strategies, *SPUTTOR* can be seen to attack the totalising gestures of inveterate fields of study, in order to prepare a space for the development of an innovative poetic logic. There is a sense in which Fisher's scepticism towards established fields of knowledge necessarily follows from the 'breaking down' of 'self-referential… discourses' that Joris attributes to Fisher's collage technique. We can also read the

---

[17] Allen Fisher, *Gravity as a consequence of shape*, (Reality Street: Sussex, 2016), 574.

[18] Allen Fisher, *Place*, (2005), (Reality Street: Sussex, 2016), 409.

'damage' and 'fracture' that Fisher associates with his treatment of research resources as delivering a material violence upon the artefact in question, and as a broader opposition to the context and discourse in which the artefact has been found.

In *SPUTTOR*, this opposition is perhaps most keenly felt in relation to the 'self-referentiality' of scientific discourses. *SPUTTOR* includes extracts from Albert Einstein's description of his general theory of relativity,[19] Galileo's 1st Theorem concerning uniformly accelerated motion,[20] and poem fragments referencing vocabulary and concepts associated with quantum mechanics, such as 'quantum systems',[21] and 'decoherence'.[22] Whilst these phrases and concepts - drawn from a range of scientific fields – can be seen to populate *SPUTTOR* throughout, the aesthetic strategy is perhaps most striking in the poem fragments, such as we observe on page 23. In this fragment, the quantum mechanical notion of 'decoherence' is referenced alongside 'Euclidean geometry'[23], to produce an intensification of the 'fracturing' and remodelling of 'discrete' scientific discourses.

Fisher's compositional strategy in *SPUTTOR*, then, can be seen as liberating a series of scientific concepts and terminologies from self-referential fields of study and, in so doing, establishing new connections between them. In turn, these scientific items are placed in juxtaposition with concepts from philosophy, architecture, mathematics, music, politics, and poetry. In associating scientific concepts with concepts from different fields of science, and associating scientific concepts with concepts lifted from different fields altogether, *SPUTTOR* organises a new form of poetic knowledge, that is marked by its polyvocality. This innovative knowledge collapses the ratiocination particular to scientific experiment and research and, in the process, *liberates science from itself*. This strategy is compounded in the couplet 'self-liberation in motion an entrapped power aesthetics/ leaves the harp to choose its own theme'[24] from the poem fragment on page 41. If we read 'the harp' as a symbol for the aesthetic arrangement of *SPUTTOR*, we are able to conceive

---

[19] Fisher, *SPUTTOR*, 54.

[20] Ibid, 15.

[21] Ibid, 22.

[22] Ibid, 23.

[23] Ibid.

[24] Ibid, 41.

the book as 'liberating' the collaged artefacts from their 'entrapment' by the contexts and discourses of their previous transmissions. In this way, the 'theme' of *SPUTTOR* reflects the continual organisation and reorganisation of these liberated artefacts as they combine to produce new experimental knowledges that are mobilised, or put 'in motion', under the observation of a reader.

Thus, Fisher establishes a poetics in *SPUTTOR* that draws upon a series of disparate discourses and concepts, without being reducible to any of them. *SPUTTOR* refuses the ratiocination of evidence-based science, the modes of 'truth' and 'logic' propagated in various philosophical investigations, and the expectations of text-based poetic form. Instead, just as John Keats's concept of Negative Capability recommends 'being in uncertainties, mysteries, doubts, without any irritable reaching after fact and reason...'[25] as the basis of an innovative poetic method, Fisher's notion of 'confidence in lack' grounds his own poetic system.

In one sense, Fisher articulates 'confidence in lack' in terms of the 'self-delusion' involved in the 'public' reception of scientific discoveries. Fisher suggests that these discoveries are translated into 'figurations', metaphors, and analogies in order to satisfy the public need for 'coherence'. This analysis is extended to include the development of the 'specialist vocabularies... used in the public sector by commerce, education, and the war machine.' These specialist figurative vocabularies dilute and repackage our reception of the 'decoherent' truth of scientific researches, because we do not, or cannot, engage directly with the results of these researches, and because, more broadly, we tend erroneously to consider scientific research as a unified and holistic endeavour. Likewise, the operative and contingent decisional processes of our state institutions are rendered as 'coherent' and manageable soundbites. As such, our comprehension is mediated by a blackbox that we have constructed ourselves, albeit under duress.[26] The question for an innovative poetic practice, then, concerns the possibility of utilising and incorporating a corrupted language-material without simply

---

[25] John Keats, *The Complete Poetical Works and Letters of John Keats*, (Cambridge Edition), edited by Horace E. Scudder, (Boston, MA: Houghton, Mifflin, and Company, 1899), 277.

[26] Allen Fisher, 'Confidence in Lack: Logic, Coherence, and Damage' in *Imperfect Fit: Aesthetic Function, Facture and Perception in Art and Writing since 1950*, (Tuscaloosa, AL: University of Alabama Press, 2016), 20-21.

regurgitating the 'violent' measures of its state-sponsored, or capitalist, or fascistic, or big-business, or otherwise 'deceitful' manipulation.[27]

SPUTTOR can be considered as intervening upon this state of affairs by revealing the productive possibilities of confidence in lack. Virtanen describes Fisher's confidence in lack, in relation to the aesthetic developed in *SPUTTOR*, as 'a processual continuum where the poet may speak through convictions and contingencies, asserting their anger and resistance towards manifold injustices without adopting the imperative modes of an oppressive ideologue.'[28] In this way, Fisher's concept eschews the pernicious manipulation of public language by 'speaking through' and occupying the sites of 'oppressive ideologue' and discourse, without 'adopting' or propagating them. Recalling Keats's Negative Capability, this negotiation is ultimately built out of a repudiation of the corrupt and corrupting logics and rationalities grounding dominant forms of discourse. In short, Fisher's 'confidence in lack' arranges a vicious, yet potentially efficacious, circularity. The oppressive prescription and determination of public measures of 'truthfulness', that produces our 'lack' of knowledge, is nominated as the precise context for a 'confidence' in the subversive powers of poetic in(ter)vention. *SPUTTOR* can be seen as a vehicle for this generative aspect of confidence in lack, according to the tension it articulates between its integration of 'specialist' vocabularies, and its occupation of dominant conceptual paradigms.

Conclusion

Fisher's incorporation of a 'Shuttle Flight Summary', that we have discussed above, is but one example of shaping the reader's engagement with the resources that *SPUTTOR* draws upon. We might also consider his integration of various media as establishing an aesthetic logic that produces a material polyvocality. In turn, this material presentation of *SPUTTOR* appears to encourage an innovative reading strategy. As Craig Dworkin suggests, '[h]owever naturalized they seem, the strategies we normally use to activate written language as signs... might

---

[27] Ibid, 29.

[28] Virtanen, "Writing on", 5.

be substituted with other techniques of engaging a text…'[29] As such, the formal and material presentation of *SPUTTOR* can be considered as marshalling an innovative 'activation' of its 'signs' by an imagined reader, that reflects the poetics developed in the work. A new poetic logic, and new forms of discursive knowledge, are reflected in the particular materiality of their textual embodiment.

Works Cited

Adorno, Theodor, W., 'Paralipomena' in *Aesthetic Theory*, (1970), (Continuum: New York, 2004).

Dworkin, Craig, *Reading the Illegible*, (Evanston, IL: Northwestern University Press, 2003).

Fisher, Allen, 'Confidence in Lack: Logic, Coherence, and Damage' in *Imperfect Fit: Aesthetic Function, Facture and Perception in Art and Writing since 1950*, (Tuscaloosa, AL: University of Alabama Press, 2016).

Fisher, Allen, *Gravity as a consequence of shape*, (Hastings: Reality Street Editions, 2016).

Fisher, Allen, *Place*, (2005), (Hastings: Reality Street, 2016)

Fisher, Allen, *SPUTTOR*, (London: Veer Books, 2014).

Fisher, Allen, "Testing and Experimenting: A Personal View of Aesthetic Practice and Reception" in *Imperfect Fit: Aesthetic Function, Facture and Perception in Art and Writing since 1950*, (Tuscaloosa, AL: University of Alabama Press, 2016).

Fisher, Allen, 'The Poetics of the Complexity Manifold' in *boundary 2*, Vol.26, No. 1: "An International Poetics Symposium", (Duke University Press: North Carolina, 1999).

Fisher, Allen, 'Traps and Tools or Damage: Inventive Perception and Transformation' in *Imperfect Fit: Aesthetic Function, Facture and Perception in Art and Writing since 1950*, (Tuscaloosa, AL: University of Alabama Press, 2016).

Foucault, Michel, *The Courage of Truth: The Government of Self and Others II, Lectures at the Collège de France, 1983-1984*, translated by Graham Burchell, (London: Palgrave Macmillan, 2011).

---

[29] Craig Dworkin, *Reading the Illegible*, (Evanston, IL: Northwestern University Press, 2003), 76.

Joris, Pierre, 'The New Complexity' in Allen Fisher, *Imperfect Fit: Aesthetic Function, Facture and Perception in Art and Writing since 1950* (Tuscaloosa, AL: University of Alabama Press, 2016).

Keats, John, *The Complete Poetical Works and Letters of John Keats*, (Cambridge Edition), edited by Horace E. Scudder, (Boston, MA: Houghton, Mifflin, and Company, 1899)

Rainey, Lawrence S., *Ezra Pound and the Monument of Culture: Text, History, and the* Malatesta Cantos, (London: University of Chicago Press, 1991).

Virtanen, Juha, "Writing on: Context and Visual Culture in Recent Works of Allen Fisher and Ulli Freer" in *Journal of British and Irish Innovative Poetry*, 8(1), e3, (May 2016: http://dx.doi.org/10.16995/biip.20, accessed 28/04/18 at 15:18).

Williams, James, *A Process Philosophy of Signs*, (Edinburgh: Edinburgh University Press: Edinburgh, 2016).

Imperfect Fit: on Allen Fisher's painting / Allen Fisher on painting /

ALLEN FISHER, PAIGE MITCHELL, SHAMOON ZAMIR

They are works that explore and innovate both aesthetic and non-aesthetic functions and rely on a slow production of meaning in the viewer. Joseph Beuys's exploration can be shown to compress these functions, and a part of his innovation has been to transform this compression into sculpture with social resonance. Another part of his innovation has been to allow the non-aesthetic functions to direct his facture. This tension between the non-aesthetic and aesthetic promotes an imaginative meaning. It never fixes but allows the enigma, that Beuys's work often creates on first viewing, to remain as a potent residue for meaning to accrue. It is also meaning that, by Beuys's method of constant self-referral, informs each subsequent work.

Beuys's enigma is a consequence of this tension between functions and the interrelationships of his works. The non-aesthetic functions create for the viewer a spread into research and the aesthetic facture provides a coalescence to which the viewer refers. The meaning continually being produced by the viewers in their energetic processes of comprehension, enjoyment, and disquiet, creates a social resonance informed by Beuys's spiritual and other concerns as they change, at least potentially, the viewer's interaction with the world outside the gallery. In both microcosmic and macrocosmic senses Beuys's world-view can be simplified as a concern to present transformation,, and begin the process of transforming those involved.

from Allen Fisher, 'Monuments to the Future:
Social Resonance in the Art of Joseph Beuys,' (1986, unpublished)

*

Allen Fisher is an internationally known poet whose painting is now also becoming recognised. The poet-artist of such seriousness is rarely encountered, and Fisher's undertaking links him to William Blake and David Jones. The endeavour of the long poem, transparency of plastic image arising from transparencies of language, reordering of time and space through literary and art historical reference, the discovery of the extraordinary in the ordinary, and thus an emphasis on the role of the imagination in the real, are shared features in the work of these artists. Blake drew on the Bible, Milton, Swedenborg, 17th- and 18th-century aesthetic theory and science and his romantic contemporaries. David Jones combined Christian mysticism and the experience of war with classical poetry and Arthurian legend. Fisher collages and factures the conceptual fields and lexicons of Blake, 20th-century physics, molecular biology and mathematics, post-structuralist hermeneutics, perception theory, art history and his literary contemporaries.

Fisher's beginnings as a visual artist are in the 'anti-art' movement *Fluxus* whose protagonists included John Cage and Joseph Beuys. His re-acceptance of the art-object – ultimately, the picture plane and figuration – proceeded via the development of a complex narrative of deconstruction in his poetry and the formal study of art history. During the 1970s Fisher had gained wide recognition as a poet with his long poem, *Place*, an imaginative excavation of South London as the grounding for a systematic consideration of knowledge and desire. In the 1980s, the period of his formal art training, he began work on another long poem, still in progress, *Gravity as a consequence of shape*. With this work, the cycling of thematic material between the written and the drawn or painted surface became obvious. The collage drawing, 'Lifting from fear' (illus.1) is an example of an image first appearing as language and later presented visually.

More recent paintings which arise as interferences with texts are those in the 'Views of the City' series: the 'Savage', 'Barbarian' (illus. 2) and 'Civilian' (the deliberately retrograde terms employed with characteristic mischief). The subjects of these paintings are the Badger, Beaver and Hare, introduced as 'three kinds of perception', from the poems 'Ditty Bop Walk', 'Dixieland One Step' and 'Double Shuffle' in the *Gravity* series.

> "…The productive potential of every Badger in Western society transforms the environment into ends useful for Badgers and not for the society that burns them." Long noses sense out the coming devastation…The Badger-soul strides forward in an ever-increasing alienation from *all* Culture. The fight is hopeless and fought out to the bitter end.
>
> Beavers seek out the period's most avant-garde texts… Projects propel each Beaver forward. The discovery of a spectral reality, a skeletal City, the sodden awareness of chaos and war.

> The pride of consciousness facing the world, origin of their absolute freedom, a special relativity.
>
> Give Hare a place to stand and the earth moves. Culture, democracy and economics are funds of society. The Hare insists upon self-administration rather than state monopoly or private capital… "Now we speak of the invisible sculpture, the ideas of creativity and self-determination in an alternative social situation." That is the wider understanding and only a beginning.[1]

Fisher's work often opens to multiple interlocutors as the passages cited above show, with Joseph Beuys speaking directly in the last. The use of the Hare as the exemplary Civilian serves as a tribute to this artist.

The contrasted constructive means of these paintings illustrate Fisher's approaches, especially in the juxtapositioning of diverse source materials. They are unified by their backgrounds – analytical horizons derived from different periods of European painting. The Badger-Savage is directly based on a photograph in a local newspaper. The Beaver-Barbarian takes up the central position from Carpaccio's portrait of St Augustine writing his philosophy of Love and Beauty, with a cheekily adjusted nimbus, and commentary in the form of later Beavers, de Beauvoir and Sartre, who inspired fashionable 'existentialists' sent up by Tony Hancock (shown retreating). The use of such multiple reference may be no more problematic than similar assemblies in classical painting – Raphael's 'The School of Athens', for example – but the condition of being 'post'-common referents and shared general knowledge is a serious preoccupation of Fisher's. The Hare-Civilian, finally, is abstract, a 'deconstructionist' re-defining of elements initially seen as an assemblage of items found in the painter's studio (a funnel, siphon, jug and piece of wood with two holes in it). For Fisher, the Civilian is in the process of becoming. 'Civility', the basis for principles of co-operation and participation in a desired culture, has been a concern since the early poems of *Place*.

The animal-humans of 'Views of the City' make multiple references extending from Hogarth's transformative caricatures to ancient Egypt and Greece and the world of children's stories. But they also allude to shamanic cultures which Fisher has studied in researching the roles of consciousness and the imagination in healing. These cultures

---

[1] Allen Fisher, *Gravity* (Cambridge: Salt Press, 2004), p.217.

are iconographically present in the *Dispossession and Cure* series. The concern with healing is directly evoked in the 'Stress' series of 'animated abstractions', improvisations where collage is manipulated to break pre-existing sets of associations. Fisher uses the term 'Warrior' in the sense of overcoming stress and thus restoring calm. The figures in these paintings derive from objects used quantitatively to measure stress and strain and such objects have been motivic in Fisher's work since the late seventies. Form, colour, investigation of balance and transformation of the motifs contribute the playful elements of healing.

The grounding of civility and healing in consciousness as a subject of art is implicitly discussed by Fisher in 'Breaks Margin', an article about the work of two artists: the painter, sculptor and collagist, Harry Thubron, and the poet, painter, musician and performance artist, Ulli Freer:

> …perhaps art is for survival. The predominant function in art, the aesthetic, is concomitantly one of the functions of consciousness. Consciousness and aesthetics share the summary of their activity as patterns of connectedness, which are patterns necessary for life. They are patterns that provide the structures for ethical, moral, and social understanding and efficacy, and they change, can be changed. Loss of renewing and changing capacity of this patterning… amounts to loss of significant life.[2]

An underlying matter-of-fact handling of materials, complex forms of reference and multiple directions, invocations of the anonymous and the famous, evocations of healing, the mischievous rigour of rhyme and pure exuberance of colour-play as process are all preoccupations of Fisher's art. Fisher works at the nexus of vision and language, using iconic and conceptual rhyme to meditate on existence and the uncertainty of a projected new consciousness at once questioning and joyful.

Paige Mitchell, 'A Projected New Consciousness,'
text originally written to accompany Fisher's single-artist show,
'Lifting from Fear,' King's Manor Gallery, York, England, 1993

*

---

[2] Allen Fisher, 'Breaks Margin,' *First Offence* (1993).

(The following is an edited collation of conversations and written exchanges which took place from March through May 2007.)

AF: This group of four is called *Meditation Traps* (illus. 3-6, c.31 x 23 cm, ink on paper) and is linked to a larger series called *Meditation Studies*. The works' visual information derives from work on and research for *Dispossession and Cure* (1994) in the late 1980s. These particular four studies date from around 1995 and the specific research that informed them was to do with the way in which some Japanese groups wishing to meditate, wishing to put themselves in their own personal space, wherever that actual space was, would encircle themselves with a string or a rope and hang from it pieces of paper which signified that somebody was in a private state, or a state which we might call meditation or contemplation. That's where the initial image is coming from, of pieces of paper hanging off of almost horizontal lines or strips. So that's one way to talk about the image. Leaping off from the fact that it's a meditation space, this leads on to the fact that you're involved therefore in a meditative activity when making the work.

The work goes through a number of processes. They're not one offs. The processes involve painting with masked areas and then removing the masks and making decisions about whether that's left in place or whether you then add more ink or not. As it happens, with these four I don't think anything more than that was done but there are others where it's more complex than that. There are others which involve colour and there's greater complexity in how the composition has come about in terms of the number of processes gone through. There are three examples of the coloured version of the process at the front of the book *Stroll and Strut Step* (2004).

As a consequences of the method, as a consequence of the process, you actually get a record of a visual process going on, and therefore there's a developmental process of seeing and of analysing what repetition and difference mean and how you use repetition to engender new work but then don't repeat, you move on, you transform it from the repetition – and so the repetition you might say is the masking that is moving around in simulation of the rope and the meditative paper hanging but it's not simulation in the sense of making it look exactly like it, it just becomes a shape which you use iconically, and you say that's what that stands for me as I'm doing it. Internally so to speak, mentally speaking.

This work linked into the trap material because of its visual form and some of the research but you can't actually see the evidence of the trap research in these particular pieces.

SZ: Knowing your visual work from over the last two decades or so, working in series is clearly something you do again and again. Your sense of that, the way you've just described it, is that the sense that has remained from the start, or has your sense of working in series changed in some ways?

AF: I do work in series. I started working in sequence in the novels I was writing in the 1960s. I planned a sequence of six novels and never completed them, abandoned them in fact. It's partly to do with planning, that is to say it's partly to do with conceptions or preconceptions. It's partly to do with an energetic function – it gives me the confidence to just move on so to speak because it gives me the material to work with. So that I'm ahead of time, I know what I'm working with in terms of materials. And because I'm involved in more than one activity in my life, it allows me to come in and out of different activities and pick them up because I can recognise which particular sequence I'm involved in. That's a sort of simplistic way of saying it but that's a rationality for it.

SZ: The notion of abandonment is important within the idea of the sequence.

AF: Yes, it is. It's a quite complex question that really, because it relates initially to a move philosophically or in preference of the kind of work I'm making, but it also has much more to do with composition, in the sense that there's the debate that Baudelaire sets up when he's discussing Courbet's work as the difference between finished and complete, and that overlaps with the discussion about abandonment. When I initially set up to write *Place*, I set it up to abandon the work after ten years. So I started the writing in 1971 and completed it in 1981, literally completed in the 'abandoned' sense. But, actually, completion in the sense that it has always been critiqued in my work, the debate about finish and complete coherence so to speak, that's been around for 150 years. Through different elaborations of that complexity, right the way through from negative capability, through the uncertainty principle, through to a book I'm currently working on which is called *Confidence in lack*, lacking, knowing that you lack beforehand gives you the confidence not to worry about lacking. And so abandonment has been quite a prominent feature but it's not abandonment out of despair or as a negative activity, it's abandonment as a positive.

SZ: *I was thinking of de Kooning – there's an interview in which I think he's asked how or when he knows that a painting is finished, and he says he doesn't, he just knows when to walk away, to abandon it. It's that kind of sense you're talking about?*

AF: Yes, it is. There's a philosophical understanding in de Kooning which accepts abandonment before he carries out a work. There's a difference here in so far as I've actually planned it, as in *Place* for instance. There, on the first or second page, it tells you when the work will be abandoned. So that's a planned abandonment, which is quite different from de Kooning's. But there's a philosophical affinity to de Kooning in so much as he accepts abandonment philosophically before he necessarily carries it out.

SZ: *Looking at these four images, you've explained how the white strip structures relate to the meditational string used within Japanese culture, and in other paintings and watercolours from this period related to these we actually see a Japanese figure in a state of meditation behind a string. This fluid and complex movement between figuration and abstraction is characteristic of a lot of your work. Motifs from the figurative work get, as it were, abstracted. Yet anyone who knows the figurative work, or knows the poetry, can often see the continuity and therefore cannot simply say that these images are figurative or abstract--one is aware of the other image bank related to them. At the same time, most of the people who see these pictures often remark on being moved by them, without of course having any knowledge of you or your work, and without recognising the meditational structure or the string structure.*

AF: Two things that come out of that: one is the question 'do you need to know the prior set in order to understand this set, do you need to understand the figurative set in order to understand the abstract set?' One answer to that is you don't – they are autonomous so to speak. I would hope and expect that you could appreciate these four studies without having seen some of the work that it's derived from. But I don't at the same time want to discount the fact that you might get some pleasure by making a pattern of connections between this cycle from around 1995 and another cycle, more figuratively made in the late 1980s. I also think that there are figurative elements in this work in front of us which aren't the initial figuration, if we think of that in terms of the rope and the paper indicating meditation space. If that's then displaced, I think you're then involved in a different subject. You're then involved in a subject which you might not be able to name, but you see this shape here and you see it moving, albeit slightly, changing through the four, so I do think these four work better together than they would do individually, and that narrative, you might say, or that series of connections, that series of patterns of connections is an intention which I prevail upon quite a lot. Yet you could still take the autonomy of the single piece and work from it. It's just that it's quite clear that you would get a different richness or a different set of complexities from it in series. Now if we just think about that in a larger frame outside of what *I* do, that's actually likely to be the case in any artist's work. So that you would benefit from seeing a single collage by Georges Braque but you would more than benefit by seeing five of them from the same period. And although he's not intending you to see the series as such, or he may not be, you would benefit from doing so. You benefit from seeing the development of somebody's work, or the way in which somebody's work has retained some shapes and forms and discarded others over periods of time. But you don't necessarily need to know that sequence in order to appreciate the single work and so I think it works both ways.

Viewing 'Meditation Traps' I-IV intrinsically involves a visual experience of shapes and tones of black, white and grey. At times, the tones encourage spatial depth – encouraged by apparent 'opening' into clearings, by apparently overlapping shapes. There is a kind of horizon that gets broken, or shifted like a geological cross-section recording damage in the landscape. There is also a simulated sensation of ink spilling and ink flow. Part of these thoughts could be applied to other paintings like 'Before the Pain of Return' and 'Mr. & Mrs. Thubron' which are discussed later.

Viewing 'Meditation Traps' extrinsically involves (a) recognition of a sequence, (b) recognition of other studies or sequences using similar or comparable shapes or motifs, and (c) recognition of elements derived from my earlier work.

Recognition of a sequence leads to a kind of narrative that is both exploratory of processes of facture and sequence, where a pleasure accrues from recognition of a narrative presented both sequentially but also, so to speak, visually all at once.

Recognition of other studies or sequences using similar or comparable shapes or motifs produces a broader pattern of connectedness, using the shapes, the narrative, the title of the work, its series title (such as, in this case, *Dispossession and Cure*) and a process of discovery with indications of organisation and decision-making. The opening or window motif becomes figuratively more tangible like a memory flashback or an insight into a fresh scene. Recognition of elements derived from my earlier work leads to an iconographical pattern of connectedness, to, for instance, the paintings in the *Dispossession & Cure* series. Particular to the meditation, roped off space and hanging papers associated with elements of Japanese and Aïnu cultures. This further provides for links to Zen calligraphy and ink graphic practice and Heideggerian ideas of 'clearing' (*Lichtung*) and contemplation of the idea of self and other or becoming in the producing viewer.

PM: One thing a series says is that there is intention over time, so it immediately raises the issue of where the artwork exists because clearly it has to rely on reference to that intention to do something and to repeat and change it. That's something you've been dealing with for a long time. Planning. It's in the poetry, too. It's questioning the existence of the artwork, where it is and what it is.

AF: I continually think that the actual artwork is made by the person looking at it, and the consequences of that are that you move from a word like 'making' to a word like 'facture' ('making' or 'creating' often imply completions or finished products). So what I do as an artist is to provide the means for seeing something, and it's not a fixed means of seeing something because we all have a different perception and a different understanding, a different way in which we arrive at knowledge and meaning. Which isn't to say that it's just completely loose. It does have its parameters and the artist's work is providing the parameters or the set of limits from which to make perceptions possible. Now if we think of the idea of the sequence here, what I'm also trying to do is provide sets of connections which are patterns and shapes, or whatever they might be; I'm providing 'information' for somebody who comes into it cold, comes into it without prior knowledge, which is one of the things Shamoon's indicating. So as you might walk past these four, you might appreciate and take them into yourself and understand them in a way that I've never understood; in a way I will never understand I should say.

SZ: That's partly what I was getting at with the sequence issue because it seems to me that so much of your work works best when it is seen in sequence as it's intended here, which is different to seeing a retrospective of an artist where of course you gain a certain knowledge because you're seeing work from an earlier period next to work from a later period and you can see a development. As Paige says, here there is a different kind of intentionality involved. And I think one of the reasons why people react to these immediately is because they are seeing the transformational structure played out for them.

AF: Yes, which is also what you can get from some parts of *Gravity as a consequence of shape*, the writing. You can see how one text leads into another or the other way around, how one text is drawn from a previous text and made a transformation, made a change of whatever it happens to be.

SZ: This may be too big an area to get into straightaway but behind my question about how one group of images might link to another set of images which are more figurative and so on, is really a question about the larger body of your work. I think it is fair to say that many more people know your work as a poet than as a painter. But anyone who's seen the visual work realises that almost right from the very start, the two things are inseparable—they are inseparable in the way you've constructed your work and in the way you think about your work. So there's a larger issue about what the relationships are between the visual and the written work. Clearly the work goes back to figures like Blake, who's been a major presence in your thought. Can you say a bit about that? I'm just conscious of addressing an audience which is most likely not very much aware of the body of visual work. I understand that you can read the work without looking at the images, and certainly you can look at these images without having any knowledge of the poetic work at all, yet in your own thinking and process of working the two things have been almost indissolubly linked in some ways. Could you reflect on that linkage?

AF: It has initially to do with my own integrity, my own wish to be cohesive within my own practice, and that's to do with how I generate energy, enthusiasm and the will to go on, so to speak. In other words, it's not viable to just separate them off as two different activities, although they are two activities in one physical sense. In a proprioceptive sense they're not separate. In the 1970s I was writing and not making visual work in the normal sense; I was making conceptual work which used some visual elements, like *Blood Bone Brain* (1981-2) used jars of things in it and photographs of jars. And I would involve myself in performances that made my understandings vulnerable to the audience. Then there was a kind of personal crisis with regard to Elaine, my first wife, who had started to undertake dialysis at home, and I found that I couldn't concentrate in my writing processes and found that energetically I was better off making something physically, more physical than writing was and that's when I started painting. It wasn't simply for that reason but it was at that period. (It was contemporary with having seen a large retrospective of Jasper Johns's work at the Hayward in the late '70s). What that indicates is that as human beings physiologically we're better at one thing than another at different times of the day, and I find that I have better periods during the day when I can think, and better periods of the day when I can practice something, doing something. That doesn't mean I'm not thinking when I'm making things, but it's a different kind of process, or rather a different way in which energy is used. And I find therefore that I'm making better use of energy that way because I can draw on resources that wouldn't work for writing but would work for something else. That's rather vaguely put actually but…

SZ: There's a difference between you and let's say a poet who might also paint, even though those two bodies of work would be linked in some way obviously through the concerns and interests of such a poet-painter. In your case it seems to me that there's a much more enmeshed and close link, for instance in the Traps *or* Dispossession and Cure *series, so that the coherence or the integration of the two seems to be quite intense and consistent, at many levels – titles, subject matter, resources and so on. And therefore, although the two can stand separately, I'm just trying to get a sense of what in your view might be gained by taking the two together.*

AF: I think there's a creative interaction between the two. If we separate them out as being visual and non-visual, visual and written, which is not unfair to do, I think there is another relationship which I'll just bring in in a second. But if we just think of visual text, if we think of the text and think of the visuality, they are linked for me conceptually; I do think of one and the other so to speak, in and out of the other. There is another interface, which is illustration, which is typically not the case in my work but, in fact, with a small amount of analysis you could probably attribute some illustrative aspects to it, by which I mean that some visual images might be enhanced or re-seen when a text, when certain parts of a text, are put with it and vice versa. And some of the writing might benefit from seeing some of the visual work. It's not that they rely on it in either case but they could be enhanced in both cases. The way in which that sometimes crops up is that illustration becomes a book cover or becomes pictures within a book. *Dispossession and Cure*, the book, has one of the paintings from the *Dispossession and Cure* series on the cover. The *Stroll and Strut Step* poems have got visual pieces from the meditation series, and, although that's not obviously related in the sense that 'this equals that,' there is a relationship of period of time when made, relationship of overlapping processes when making, and so on and so forth. At some times that's more obvious than at others.

PM: But I think there is something here that you actually have to dig down to, because Place *is conceived as a moving object, you're describing a sphere, it's very carefully planned according to something which is in fact in 3-d, and so is* Gravity, *and you've used collage so your written work, its deep structure, is very much related to art, in the sense of painting and even sculpture. You also have the issue of recurring themes referring not only to people like Blake but also to the character of the Painter in* Gravity. *So they do seem to me to be kind of very much adjacent, and you can look from one into another.*

AF: You *would* have to dig that out to show how explicit you are about that or not. It's just that it's not set up that way in my thinking. Well, let's just think of it at least on two different levels. One level would be that process showing has been part of my work for a long time, certainly since the beginning of *Place*, and so you not only partake in a process but you show it in the process, during the process. I think Olson said something about letting some of the dirt hang on when you're pulling the vegetable out, so it's that, and you can see that sometimes in the visual work. Typically, I don't over-correct visual work. I either accept or reject. I'm inclined to do that rather than change or alter to meet a certain requirement, and that's because I accept the process as part of the work. I don't mean it visualises, it illustrates process showing, I mean it is part of that.

PM: *You're using very similar processes in a lot of your work. As I've already said, you use planning, you structure it. You use deformation, you use internal rhyme, as well as having a departure from the plan, so that there's an element of the work that's unplanned, and those are consistent processes in both your written work and your visual work.*

AF: Now there's another level at which it works, and I'm just trying to grab how to say it really. Well, for example there is poetic work which arises out of the theory of civilisation and being civil, to do with the figures of barbarian, civilian and savage – I elaborate and partly parody that in part of *Gravity as a consequence of shape*. But as I say this you might be reminded that there is a series of paintings called Civilian, Barbarian, Savage as part of the 'Views of the City' series. And so it is quite clear that that thinking has contributed both visually and textually, and although one doesn't illustrate the other, in the process of writing or in the process of making pictures I've been influenced by the fact of both of them, or they've both been influenced by a single thought. Something like that.

SZ: *In fact, that is the example I wanted to turn to. With essentially abstract pictures the link with the written seems to me less of an issue in the sense that they have a kind of independence, but in the 'Views of the City' triptych the imagery is so enigmatic and so referential and complex, not only because it's referring to so much else in the visual tradition, or indeed in the cultural and intellectual traditions, but it's also so closely tied to a specific body of poems.*

AF: I just have to agree, but that's nothing I could anticipate because in the process of making one doesn't think about entirely the process of reception and so that's the difficulty there. And the paintings are too large to be seen by any one person at one time because they're just in geographically different places, and to get them you need the three together, plus you need to know some texts in the way that you do when you're looking at some works by Renaissance painters of mythologies. If you don't know the mythology, you wouldn't get some of it. If you look at some Kitaj paintings, you wouldn't get them, and that has to be the case for a whole range of works by different people. So, although I'm disappointed by that fact, I can't do anything about it really, effectively. One of the ways that Kitaj dealt with it, for instance, was to put a text against the pictures, and initially he did it literally, physically in the gallery, by the side of the painting. Eventually he started to put it into catalogues. And there's been a lot of criticism of that. One is it's thought that the pictures are therefore illustrative of a text, therefore you cannot see the picture without having read the text. It's interesting that it's that way around. I think typically you don't have that problem when reading the work, you're not looking for the picture. Not in the same kind of way, because you kind of make your own picture of what I might mean by a civilian, or of what a hare looks like. That's probably a consequence of the medium, I think, the use of figurative painting.

SZ: Shall we have a look at the 'Barbarian' (84 x 126 cm, oil on canvas) from 'Views of the City'? (illus. 2)

AF: Let me just do what I did with the previous one which is to talk about what's in front of me and then move on from that, because partly what we're trying to do is build up a text. Here we're looking at a painting which is part of a triptych, and the underlying subject was different kinds of perception that people have within a particular society. I took some rather overarching, mundane archetypes in the form of the Civilian, the Barbarian and the Savage as proposed by a number of different writers. So that's one level, and it comes out of a discussion that was going on in part of *Gravity as a consequence of shape*. 'Three kinds of perception' is one of the subtitles for that piece. It's in the book *Dispossession and Cure* I think. There are two others canvases which go with this one. There's a central one, subtitled 'Savage,' which just shows a badger, or a human figure with a badger's head, walking across a field with a rifle. And there's one of a hare running across a part of countryside which might be a meadow or something like that, which is gradually being destroyed by a heap of discarded cars and other detritus, and the hare has got some of the detritus caught in his or her physical being, something like a plastic jug jammed onto it and so on and so forth. In the background there is a landscape of the Lugg Meadows mills. So that is part of a debate that was going in Hereford to do with thinking of putting a road across the Lugg Meadows, and that's a debate that also crops up in *Gravity* because the debate in that particular book or set of poems moves from London to Hereford.

With this particular painting, 'Barbarian,' we could start by talking about how the content has been arrived at. The central figure and the overall set of ideas for the design come from a sixteenth-century picture by Carpaccio from the Church of St George in Venice, a Dalmatian church. Carpaccio's painting shows St Augustine in his study writing his philosophy of love and beauty, receiving the voice of St Jerome from heaven as a ray of light through a window.[3] The figure is sometimes misidentified as St Jerome because it is like a St Jerome in his study. One of the elements in the Carpaccio painting is what some people might call St Augustine's familiar, or certainly a small little dog which is looking up in a sort of diagonal eye line – if you set the eye from the dog you get a line of the light coming through the window, through Augustine to the animal. The platform on which St Augustine sits is typical of the kind of platform that Renaissance scholars are shown standing upon, and there are additional elements to do with the book and the table and the pen and so on. And in the background there are these ghost figures, figures that are coming from the thinking of the person involved.

I use or transform many of these elements in my painting, with the head of St Augustine having become the head of a beaver. In the related written texts there's some debate about the beaver which comes from me reading Simone de Beauvoir and Jean-Paul Sartre, 'Beaver' is what Sartre used to call Simone de Beauvoir, and in English in any case the idea of the beaver is of the person hard at work, as typically the animal is always seen to be. On the left of the 'Barbarian' there are also some ghost figures coming through. The initial figure is Sartre on a protest march walking through the streets with papers, giving them out to the people that he passes by. And behind him is de Beauvoir. And in a further distance there are figures to do with Tony Hancock. Hancock made a joke of simulating or imitating Sartre at one time in his *Hancock's Half Hour*, dressed in a black pullover and being existential. So there's a kind of a double, there's a nonsense going on as well as serious thought in the work.

There are also some small design elements to do with playing with the golden section and shifting it around a bit. That's to do with Euclid and Fibonacci measurements, which I have been playing with for a long time. I played with those measurements to structure *Gravity*. I took one of the Fibonacci series, marked it out on a cylinder and then crushed it

---

[3] A reproduction of Carpaccio's painting can be viewed at: http://www.stanford.edu/~mgorman/STS123/week3images/carpaccio1503.jpg

so that it had to be reread in a damaged sequence...

SZ: You've given a rich description of the complex structure of referentiality in the painting and you were saying earlier on that in some ways you're not thinking about reception in the process of making, of facture. But can it be that when you're doing a painting such as this you're not thinking about reception? I mean, to be totally literal-minded about it, nobody would know that was Hancock. And though I've been pushing on the links between the visual and the written, it is also the case, isn't it, that there's a lot in the painting around the issue of the Barbarian which is not in the poetry and there are materials in the poetry which are not in the painting. So there's a more complicated dialogue. But really, in making a painting of this kind (and this is the most referential piece in the triptych), how can the issue of reception not be an issue in the process of making?

AF: Well, it's not an issue in the sense that I can't do anything about it because I'm in the process of making. You're saying, how does somebody looking at this who doesn't know that that's Sartre get this work? And I don't know. I don't know whether they can and it might be that that's a critique of the work.

SZ: I'm interested in your own sense of the term in which you are addressing the viewer.

AF: One mode would be to create enough intrigue to make them go and find out more. Perhaps I can give you an analogy, however crass this might seem. When I was at school, I picked up Pound's *Cantos* and I read through the first five or six. What I got was what was written in English. And what I didn't get was what was written in Chinese and Greek and Latin even, or maybe even in French. One choice would be, 'I can't read this, I'll dump it, I can't be bothered with this.' But there was something in it which made me say, 'there's enough energy and information in this for me to want to find out more', which I then did, and so then I had to go away from the work and then come back to the work. That is the example that I would use, though not all my work is like that, as you're indicating. And maybe this is an extreme case of it. And now the question might be, 'that being the case, what is the route that somebody would have to use?', and the route would involve *Gravity*, I think, and you could find a trail in there because I give bibliographical references in there, at least partly I do, and some of the work is implicit in the writing in there.

SZ: *That's in part what I was getting at because, in this instance, I* did *find myself having to go back to the poetry as the route. Hence the earlier issue about what the dialogue between the two is.*
You did a number of small watercolour studies in preparation for the 'Barbarian' in which you explored the geometry of Euclid through a number of rectangular blocks in various arrangements. These were also studies of colour and horizon lines.

AF: 'Landscape Studies' is a set of graphic analyses of vertical and horizontal divisions within a rectangular form (the analyses didn't use the usual 'landscape' format). The analyses derived from historical demonstrations evident in paintings. Vertical divisions used trees or building edges, or curtains to provide a doorway, or proscenium arch with theatre wings or entrance, into a deeper space. Horizontal divisions used horizons and divisions of landscape terrains (traditionally since Rubens into three areas). Many of these analyses used Euclid's *Golden Section* ratios.

The stylised or simplified divided blocks were coloured in strident lime green and cadmium reds, oranges and yellows. When facturing *Views of the City*, the studies were selected from and used to make decisions and divide the background colours. *Scattered Studies* used the measurement of geometric divisions simulated by Poussin's originals, but the sequence *Landscape Studies* was also used to inform some of the decisions.

My use of proportionate divisions and scaled blocks of colour have been informed by the analytical work of Juan Gris, Paul Klee in *On Nature*, Josef Albers in *Interactions of Colour*, Wassily Kandinsky's Bauhaus work and Mark Rothko's interviewed discussion in terms of weight and the Sublime. These structural and constructionist ideas were further embellished by theories of 'Realism' and 'Romanticism', particularly with regard to horizontal banding and land-sky horizons (August Weidman), and my own development of a theory of diagonal dynamics derived from eighteenth century aesthetics. Both kinds of embellishment were informed by Kant's theories of the 'Mathematical and the Dynamical Sublime' and Meyer Shapiro's theory of semiotics. I did about twenty of the small studies in order to arrive at what it was I would use for the paintings that ended up as 'Barbarian.'

SZ: The 'Barbarian' is a painting where you've worked, as many other painters have, with earlier painters and transformations of their works in very complicated ways. I think that has been, at least since the '80s, a consistent practice for you. Perhaps we could consider this aspect of the work through the 'Scattered' series.

AF: The 'Scattered' studies come from a request from Clive Bush to make paintings in response to a series of poems he'd written, poems which were direct responses to, or made use of, a number of Poussin paintings from the 17th century. The works are large watercolours of varying size. The series was planned as a series of twenty-four works, two of which were abandoned. Six appear as a portfolio is Clive's book, plus one on the cover.[4] The series title was derived from Clive's early working title, itself derived from Pound's essay 'I Gather the Limbs of Osiris.'

I took the same works that Clive had used, and for each work made a geometric analysis. I think that's the easiest way of describing it. And, from the geometric analysis I drew up proportionately pictures on watercolour paper, a whole series of what I'm calling studies because they were meant to be stepping stones to something else, although that may never be the case. So in front of me during the process of making these paintings I've got a reproduction of the Poussin painting and I've got my geometric analysis and I've got the lines drawn with light pencil on watercolour paper. And I then start transformations or start translation.

SZ: Adequate transformation or translation in the dialogue between you and the earlier model is something we've talked about in the past. How do you think about that, or how does that work in your painting? Maybe it will be easier to pin down if we look at an example from the 'Scattered' series. Let's take the fourth in the series, 'Et in Arcadia Ego' (c.54 x 75 cm, 2001) (illus. 7) which draws upon Poussin's 'The Arcadian Shepherds.'[5]

AF: On one level the work, like a lot of the work from this period, is involved in formal transformation from one set of parameters and

---

[4] Clive Bush, *Pictures After Poussin* (Hereford: Spanner Press, 2003).
[5] Poussin's 'Arcadian Shepherds' can be seen at: http://www.artlex.com/ArtLex/p/images/poussin_arcadian.lg.jpg

geometric descriptions and other kinds of description into another. This particular work I've labelled 'Et In Arcadia Ego' from the text which appears on the sepulchre in Poussin's painting. It is a subject he uses more than once. Several elements from Poussin's works are quickly recognized: the staves used by the shepherds – they are structurally important in Poussin's painting, although when you look at his painting that's not what catches your eye because there are human figures being depicted; the central yellow rectangle provides casual rhyming with the tomb in the Poussin; also the trees that appear in the background – I've picked some indicative trees which have been geometrically placed in the horizontal plane.

What's improvised in my work, or what is in this particular work, or what is not derived from the Poussin, are the colours, the tones, the incompletions and so on. I'm using, therefore, a strict set of parameters or structures in order to move, make something different, in order to transform. So it's clear that the 'blurred' forms in the foreground, if we call them that for now, might indicate human activities, or activities which move.

Because I'm both using a ruler and not using a ruler, there are accidents. I use the deliberate accidents that that produces, or the deliberate inaccuracy that that produces, to add vibrancy to the work. It's really a proprioceptive response to geometry. The works are made on the flat. They're made on a table and therefore typically don't show drips. They don't show a movement of water in that sense. The water is a movement on a flat plane made by a large or small brush, or both usually. Washes of water and colour. This particular piece uses watercolour and pencil and so some of the hard lines are in fact a coloured pencil which mixes graphite and oil and pigment. The rubbing on the 'blurred' shape on the left is simply the paper peeling as I've moved a sponge or something.

SZ: What are you getting out of this series, how is your engagement sustained in a series like this?

AF: There are at least two ways in which I make a demand on the work which precedes me and which I am interested in. The first demand has to do with the subject matter, just simply that. And the second demand has to do with its formal accuracy for me, the way in which it formally activates my interest. There's also something more complex than that which I can't quite articulate just now. So I'm likely to pick an artist who does both of the things at once. In fact, that's not the reason I chose Poussin. But I think that's the reason that Clive chose me to help out with the Poussin, because he would know that that's the situation for me. And the next set of work I'll do, when time allows me to, will be [Jacques-Louis] David, because that seems to be the next stage after Poussin for me that has got a formal structure that is exciting and has at the same time a referential content, in his case, to do with civic duty and such like that has a lot of interest for me.

What I find is that I work best out of a study of what I'm doing. One could say you could take any geometric arrangement. One could, but I couldn't. I would always want to have an investment in what I'm doing, interest, a whole elaborate set of interests. That isn't to say I require that of anyone looking at it, but that's what I need in order to do it. And part of that has to do with the actual physicality of doing something, and that physicality is how the engagement is bringing about a transformation. And so, what are the transformations for then, or put it the other way around, what is the geometry for? The geometry is there in order to give me the engagement that I first need; I'm using that geometry, therefore, as a way in which I can hold onto my own confidence, and that confidence allows me to make the improvisation without worry about it. I can just get on with it, because I know I've got something to hold onto. Even though I keep falling off each edge I've got something to hold on to.

The depth of the engagement comes about because I don't just look at the picture by Poussin, measure it up with a ruler, and then get on with it. I study the picture that's about to be transformed, and I try to find all the other nuances that might be of use to me in the process of the transformation to come. With this particular work, I researched 'The Arcadian Shepherds' extensively because it's got a whole range of ramifications from aesthetic to spiritual to quite mundane and so on. And that kind of investment or study area is something I prefer because it gives me then the energy I need, so to speak, within me.

Before I start the painting, the diagram of the painting, the plan of the painting is somehow allowing me to remember, that might be the way of saying it, my study and I'll drop into it elements that are encouraging that memory. Now I don't remember all the nuances of this particular piece at this moment. Neither do I require anybody to do so. I'm just asking them to look at the picture, but I'll leave clues lying around and I won't hide the title here. Or the fact that it's from Poussin, although it doesn't mention that, but, I mean, I'm not hiding the fact that it's from Poussin.

Now that's different from many of the other works because the text that I've used is much less evident, unless one knows the works that people have written about Poussin, including Clive, of course. Whereas before we've talked about a text which typically I've written, and you may or may not relate it to the visual work. And what we need to bear in mind is that the texts I've written have also often come about from study that precedes the written text. So you know there's a whole complexity of thoughts to do with what the processes are.

SZ: Is the Poussin series the first series in which you've gone through a number of works by a previous painter? I mean, in contrast to the Carpaccio which is a one off.

AF: If I say 'yes' we might find that's too categorical, but I think it's the most overtly evident.

PM: I'll say 'yes.' It is the first time. There are allusions elsewhere but not done in the same way, not analytical which the Poussin series is.

SZ: You said earlier that having done the Poussin series, the next figure would be David. Why David?

AF: I think that the next painter after Poussin to provide that geometric complexity that I'm interested in is David. I don't mean he's the only one but he's one of the ones that follows. Not only does he do that, but he's also carrying with him a subject matter that I've got a deep interest in, which, in David's case, has got to do with the discussion of duty to friends and duty to country, or moral duties and ethical duties at different levels. He's also got the debate going about liberty and freedom, which I'm interested in. So there's philosophical substance there that I'm interested in, and in some of those that he's reading also. Not simply Corneille or people from the 17th century but also people who are his contemporaries around the French Revolution, the Enlightenment. That's why I think David's the next person I would pick. It wouldn't be such a big series. I wouldn't need so many. But I'm thinking of, the substantial works of David that I'm particularly interested in, like 'The Oath of the Horatii,' or the Brutus painting.

SZ: Since you indicate subject matter as one key area of engagement with the visual work of predecessors, was this a problem with Poussin? We've been discussing one of his works with classical subject matter, but you've also transformed or translated several relating to Christian themes.

AF: And a completely strange Christianity for me… No, it wasn't a problem because I knew so little about that side of things. And what I did was to take it, give it the respect that I can give it, which is to do with my own humanity and understanding of the need to be self-reflective, contemplative and meditative and so on – which I get, whether or not I fully understand why. I get quite an emotional experience from looking at many of Poussin's paintings even though the subject matter leaves me dead. I just don't get the subject at all and I don't have any deep reading of Christian or other texts that he's used from the Golden Legend or from the Old Testament.

SZ: As we began to talk about the Poussin and 'Scattered' you indicated there may be a further level of transformation, although you haven't undertaken this yet, which in your case usually means moving some of the watercolour work into oil.

AF: Yes, these are 'studies' for that reason, and I haven't given myself, or had the continuity to do that fully or properly. It's only happened in one case, and I'm not fully sure that it works at all. What I'm trying to do is bring together two contemporary studies to make a new work. And the new work is based on the geometric understanding that I've derived from this, and some of the transformations that have come about, together with a set of drawings which are based on something else. There are hundreds of very small drawings, no bigger than A6, no bigger than my hand, and they were done every morning, one a morning. I would turn up in the studio and draw without looking at the paper. And as soon as what I was drawing visualised in my head from the physicality of having done it, I would stop. So as soon as I recognised that was a straight line, that was a curve, it would stop.

SZ: So the way you're using the term 'study' in relation to the watercolours is not in the traditional sense, making a watercolour study of a particular view in landscape painting, for example, which then gets translated into an oil version of that same view.

AF: No, that's right. It's just catalytic. It's not the idea of the sketchbook in order, in Turner's case, to make something else which is more monumental, more significant and more finished. It's Monet's sense. In for instance 'Impression Sunrise' in 1873 and works like that he's not looking to take that to another work but he recognises that that was done there and then. Full stop. It's the French idea of *ébauche*, an idea of something being in between. So this is a work in itself, I'm not thinking of this as something you put in a drawer as a study. It's something you look at for itself, and in the next work you will see a relationship to this but you don't need to know about it.

SZ: *Let's turn to an earlier series,* Dispossession and Cure, *and look at 'Before the Pain of Return' (75 x 94 cm, 1988) (illus. 8).*

AF: This was quite an elaborate set of studies over a number of years looking at dispossession and different meanings of the word 'dispossessed,' whether it happened to be whole groups of people or individuals. And dispossession overlaps for me with ideas both of contemplative thought and ideas of deprivation, ideas of despair. So there's a whole range of different issues linked here. The central figure there, the human figure is partly from a portrait of Nietzsche. The bridge that leads off from the table on which the toad that Nietzsche's looking at is sitting derives partly from Edvard Munch's work, like 'The Scream,' of which he produced nine different versions, and also from Van Gogh who also uses bridges as disappearing elements. It's a diagonal element that you get structurally in a lot of painting, but it's used frequently in expressionist painting because it's got a very dynamic pull since it's coming diagonally across what is ostensibly a horizontal structure. I was writing *Gravity* at the time. The book *Dispossession and Cure* from the *Gravity* sequence was contemporary with some of the paintings that were being made. Most of the paintings are black, white and grey and are different tones. They're typically made of collage and ink drawing, although there's some crayon and pencil drawing also.

SZ: *There's a lot of pasting of bits and pieces of paper all the way through, some of it photocopies.*

AF: Here's a figure walking along carrying a dead animal, and it's almost as if that dead animal has become a mask on the top of a man or woman's head. To the left and right are copies of photographs of garter snakes over rocks moving around in serpentine ways. Further up here are seashells that have been opened and discarded after the contents have been taken from them, like oysters and such like. The figure in the bottom left is partly taken from one of the figures in the 'Last Judgment' by Michelangelo, a figure of despair. Two of the figures above are from figures of despair in Giotto, partly from *his* 'Last Judgment,' partly from the 'Massacre of the Innocents.' There are other elements from Giotto too. At the back there are sedimentary or maybe metamorphic rocks that are highlighted by the fact that the black and white has made the ridges caused by the sedimentary construction stand out as white lines almost. What I've just done is fragment the whole into bits for you. There was a whole study of natterjack toads going on at the period that I was making this and I had a lot of interest in them. It also comes from a Basho poem about a frog that jumps into a pond. And this is also of course a bridge for jumping from, for suicides. So there's that side of despair as well. I cut up various pieces which have been photocopied from magazines like *National Geographic* and *Nature*, and have been enlarged or reduced on photocopiers and sometimes blackened up with ink, or made darker by washes of grey.

SZ: What about the figure with what looks like an animal on his head, where the animal's legs mirror the woman's uplifted hands.

AF: This is an image of someone carrying a dead animal like someone delivering to the butchers would, which links in part to the idea of poaching, like you might carry a deer, so that's to do with the extinction of animals through poaching and it also partly has to do with mis-identities, but their face is being concealed by the animal, so you misidentify and you mythologise the figure, that's how the badger and civilian and the savage come about to some extent. I mistake the person walking down the road as having a badger mask on. In fact he has braided hair, and I am being deliberately playful but that's how mythologies occur in a sense. It's like that whole analysis of Greek mythology which looks at fossils and the way that past civilisations have put the fossils together in the wrong way and created a mythological animal. But there are also references and links here which I've now lost for the moment.

SZ: On an occasion like this where we just stand in front of it and start talking about a picture, it's understandable enough that you're saying I can't remember x y or z, but my feeling is that's not an occasional problem; it is intrinsic to the work itself, the structure of memory and forgetting is part of what you do. And your own forgetting is essential to the work. It's there even at the level of immediate facture in as much as erasure and damage are included. So you don't keep meticulous notes of where this image came from. You were using the example of Kitaj and the texts with which he sometimes accompanies his works: you don't pin it down that way, so there's a certain losing of the work from your own self.

AF: That's very true. It's not a worry. I haven't destroyed the sources. If I have them around, they'll still be around somewhere. I just haven't methodically linked them so that I don't have a notebook marked '*Dispossession and Cure*, here are the references'. What this piece means I can't tell you; all I can say is that this person here appears to be meditating on or studying this animal in front.

PM: Well, sorry, the painting is about extinction. The natterjack toad was going extinct. You've got Nietzsche ('Man and Superman'), you've got a man down below who's sort of part-man part-animal in a very strange way. There's references to the geological record in terms of extinct species and changes in the earth and then a kind of apocalyptic response in terms of using religious painting to refer to these various expressions of despair which you know include suicide.

SZ: That's a good reading.

AF: It *is* a good reading.

PM: I just remember what he was doing when he did it.

SZ: We've been talking about a work which is monochrome, as many of your works are, but one of the most striking aspects of your work is the very distinctive command of colour, and there are certain colours which seem very prominent, certain types of purple, yellow…

AF: That's very true

SZ: I know that you have made a study of colour (you've often spoken about Albers in this regard).

AF: Maybe we come to this and to some ideas of facture through the 'Mr and Mrs Thubron' picture (see cover illustration, c.55 x 68 cm). Elma Thubron and Harry Thubron taught me drawing and colour, amongst other people, so the painting will act as a catalyst to talk about what it is we've just raised, because two of the issues I'm interested in, making visual work, are colour and drawing.

This painting is dated 1983 to 1994 and what it takes me back to remembering is that, when I first started making it in 1983 I'd just joined University of London's Goldsmith's College and had started on a programme of work with many tutors, two of whom were Harry Thubron and Elma Thubron. The initial painting was made with oil sticks which is particularly obvious from the pinks and the oranges and the browns. And one of the debates in making the painting was involved with Harry Thubron's view of how one makes decisions about colour, which effectively became Elma Thubron's view as well after Harry died, which he did whilst I was at Goldsmith's. She continued his philosophy of colour. It's quite difficult to describe without making this like a course in colour, but what it's partly about is how do you tell whether or not you are putting in a colour that is interfering or one that is compatible with the colours that you've got there. And you might want either and you might want both, but you need to know that you're making those decisions when you're using the colours. So when I first started this painting, if we exclude the horizontal figure up front in the picture, you can see the browns and the pinks and the oranges are the first painting. It's all very liquid. Although I'm using oil-stick, I'm, using it with turpentine – so, if we looked at the back of this picture, you'll find it's stained with liquid turpentine which is an oil that causes the stick to be very fluid. It's as if you were using a brush. The overall idea or exercise was that it was tonally equal. And that tonal equality was brought about by squinting the eyes, or if you're short-sighted you take your glasses off, so that no image is interfering with your decision making, it's purely to do with tones, and that was one of the things that they taught me so that's really one of the issues that was involved there.

However, this didn't really get completed as a picture in 1983. It got put aside as an exercise. It got put aside as something I didn't want to use, to take any further, but I didn't want to lose it, because it had this signature of having been made with Harry, because it was one of the last things I did with Harry, and I remember his walking stick. He walked with two walking sticks and a bottle of vodka in one pocket. He'd already had a couple of strokes, and I remember him hitting the canvas, not intending to be violent but just so that he could make a movement with his arm and pointing out different aspects of where it was working, where the difficulties were, because some of the difficulties that occur with colour are that, if the colours don't merge across each other, you're creating a shape, you're creating a line, or you're creating what might be thought of as a drawing effectively.

In 1994 I found it while looking for something else and it gave me the inspiration you might say, or it made me respond to it in response to my memory of Harry and Elma Thubron. I think Elma's still alive. So what I did was to find one or two fragments of paintings by Elma Thubron that I had slides of, all of which were very poor slides available through the Goldsmith's slide collection. And I started to build up a painting which then took off in what you might call an improvised way, or a way which has to do with visual connections inside the frame, in memory of the vividness of her colour. That vividness is partly coming about from the way in which she recommended you would mix on a palette, and it is partly to do with the fact that she was coming out of a Caribbean tradition – they taught for some while in Jamaica. So instead of talking about subtleties of red, it would be red in your face and very strong colours, and that's where that contrast to the previous experience is. And that's where this deliberate almost crudeness or rudeness of colour is coming about. So it's a medieval idea of colour, it's not the subsequent ideas of colour that impressionism and later thinking have brought about, Ben Nicholson and so on. It's actually much more medieval. Tonally speaking, it's light or it's dark; there's no difference between that blue and that red in those tonal colour senses. Looking at it now, I can still think of this as being one surface floating on another surface, one surface in front of another surface. And that crops up a lot in collage production because clearly what you are doing is putting one sheet with another sheet against another sheet, at least if you're doing it as Rauschenberg did or somebody of that kind.

The image in the bright coloured top surface is from Elma Thubron and her assimilation of Caribbean and African sculpture. The under surface loses iconographical efficacy. The painting's success is not an outcome of its extrinsic recognitions, but its internal patterns of connectedness and their imperfect fits to expectation. That is its æsthetic. The layering, the overlapping and the occasional glimpses of a surface beneath, the allusion to figuration and its non-figurative alternatives in terms of decorative and geometrical shapes and implied forms feed the potential expectations. The paint application emphasises the different layers from turpentined oil crayon and brush to graphic application of oil stick and crayon giving the top surface a rugged feeling. There is a tension emphasised by the use of colour that combines constructive and expressionist use of colour, both measured applications and contrasts.

The second thing it reminds me of is that both of them, together with other people that were working at Goldsmith's, tackled drawing very very severely and strictly and with interest, and I was a mature student so I was fully engaged and wanting to do that. And my life drawing experience before that had had many shortfalls, I would say, and had been based on rather poor life-drawing classes, or rather life drawing classes where there was very little instruction, classes which were based on simulating techniques, techniques where you would copy from photographs and make drawings that were outlines of aspects of photography. What the Thubrons did was to deal with what strangely they were contemporary with, their thinking was contemporary with what Charles Olson and people were doing. It was to do with proprioception. It was to do with how you felt in gravity, how you felt about the sky being above you. Paul Klee is also somebody who talks about this and he is somebody they used. One of the aspects that interests me about their drawing is the way that they talk about the physicality of drawing and the proprioception of that is that it is to do with your heart and your lungs as much as it is to do with your senses, as much as it's to do with your eyesight and perception. So in life drawing they would talk about the weight of a figure and how the figure sits or stands in space because of gravity. For instance, me leaning on this mantelpiece at the moment indicates to you that some of the pressure involved in my structure proprioceptively is that my weight is here and not there. What that leads on to understanding is that the lines in a picture as they leave the rectangle of the picture are actually being held by that. And it turns out that human eyesight will return to pictures through these lines. In other words, they're not taken away outside the picture by these lines, they're brought into the picture by these lines and the more you do that, the more that's evident. It's used a lot by abstract painters like Franz Kline, Willem de Kooning particularly, very strongly. But, actually, it's used a lot by Renaissance painters and Baroque painters fully aware of that, or incidentally aware of that, where they put a foot over the edge of a rectangular part of their picture, or they'll put a frame within a frame and then break the inner frame just slightly with something like a ray of light entering in an annunciation painting. It adds dimensionality, three-dimensionality, to the picture, but it also makes the picture dynamic, it makes it much more proprioceptive in the sense that, as the viewer's looking at the picture, the viewer unconsciously, if that's the right word, understands the gravity of it.

Now that whole debate got turned around in the 1940s and '50s and is still underway because Pollock took the picture off of the vertical plane, where this debate takes place, onto the floor. So the whole business of gravity shifts. Now it had already shifted with painters like Kandinsky who had been painting on tables and turning the picture or walking around the table. In other words, the top of the picture is in debate, the position of gravity is in debate in an abstract picture if it's been made from above on a flat surface. I'm trying to indicate the relationship between the physicality of the making of the work and the dynamics of the drawing of the work, which is where both the Thubrons were very powerful.

They also, particularly Elma, were very powerful about drawing figures that were moving so that you recognised that there was no precision in the drawing of a human being, if all you get was a fixed line. And the fixed line became more and more evidently an expression line; it was a line of expression because the line doesn't exist in actual physical relationships. If I look at your bodies at the moment, there are no lines around them and there are movements around the body, but the body is continually moving, my eyes are continually moving, thousands of times a second. The idea of a fixity is in fact to do with ideas in the brain, it has to do with ideas and not to do with perceptions as such, and so their idea of proprioception is just to pull that around and articulate it. They're not saying you don't use lines. They're saying that, if you do, you recognise what it is you're doing. The idea of natural drawing is therefore scuppered at this moment. When one sees a Pollock painting, you clearly recognise the physicality of Pollock as well as your experience of that through the painting. You don't have to see him doing that in order to understand the physicality of movement in the picture. Because you're proprioceptively understanding how it's working. His difficulty and yours is to understand why it is this way up and not that way up. And those decisions are not arbitrary, but they are subsequent decisions made about where he might cut the canvas, decisions about where and how he's hanging it at a subsequent occasion. And there might well be occasions where you could actually have the painting hanging up either way. And that's certainly the case with some abstract work for that reason, because it's not made vertically. It's made on the horizontal plane.

SZ: In an essay on Larry Rivers' 'Washington Crossing the Delaware' (1953)[6] you've written: "Rivers' painting, in the context of its New York milieu, demonstrates heroism in a new age. It is in the face of monumental paintings and public gestures by Jackson Pollock and many of Rivers' Cedarbar compatriots. It flies in the face of abstraction as in danger of retroaction. This is partly because Rivers demands to address a different strand of the western tradition, one that embraced iconography in which meaning was substantially derived through a recognition of images. He makes clear the strand he is addressing through his title and its association, he makes clear the damage through his own facture and unrepaired damage, particularly as this is informed by abstractionist facture. He becomes heroic in his daring to do this in a milieu where more comfort would have come from a range of abstractionist options." And you continue by adding: "In the larger cultural sense, Rivers' achievement lays the ground for a considerable range of changes in U.S. American, British and French painting in which the iconography of image production in the viewer leads to a new appraisal of modernist hope and melancholy, a reappraisal of the potentials for social change." I find this description pertinent to the return of figuration or the iconographical in your own work and also to some aspects of facture in that work, especially in the 'Views of the City' triptych. The three canvases joined together as a horizontal cross are certainly monumental in their own way, and they too combine iconographic and abstractionist forms and explores damage. Could you speak about the turn to figuration or the iconographic in your work, and perhaps also something about the area towards which the above commentary leads, i.e. 'social change'? I'm thinking too here of what you refer to as 'social resonance' in Beuys's work—in that commentary, as in the discussion of Rivers, there is a broad and recurrent concern with the relationship of the aesthetic and the ethical as an organizing nexus for some of these issues.

---

[6] Allen Fisher, 'The Hero in New York' (2006), available at http://www.e-space.mmu.ac.uk/e-space/handle/2173/4090

AF: Having looked at the work of Larry Rivers and RB Kitaj in various close ways, I've recognised in their work that they've understood abstraction, or understood how you can make work derived from other work and at the same time that's not all they want to do – they want to continue participation in a tradition which you call iconographical, which I think is a useful way of looking at it, rather than figurative, which is to say that they rely on some of the image structure from earlier visual examples, whether in art or elsewhere, as being recognisable. The second thing to say is that they're both aware of the proprioceptive consequence of figuration which is that they are human beings standing on the ground with paintings that are vertically in front of them and they recognise therefore there's a weight issue which is to do with the fact that you are in a rectangle, there's gravity, light is coming from above, that's what I mean by proprioceptive. They take into account, therefore, that even though they might be making abstract marks, those abstract marks are not divorced from the fact that they are human beings making the work, they're actually part of the world in other words, so that's why they are figurative in other words, they are relying on a human existence. So those two complexes I take on board as already in place for me to work from.

In the 'Views of the City' triptych, I'm recognising those two, you might say, traditions. One of which is a geometric plus propioceptive engagement with what's in front of me, which has to do with the colour and the shapes and the measurements. And, secondly, an iconographical tradition which uses images such as Hancock, Sartre, St. Augustine from the Carpaccio and therefore has a double reliance, really. A reliance one that you have recognitions that reference back to some of those figures, recognitions of who they are, and the other reliance has to do with your physicality, the fact that you're a human being also experiencing shapes and geometric forms that are proprioceptive as likely to be linked to you as they would be to me. And so, in the first instance, the philosophical idea behind that is that you can experience the painting and appreciate it just on a physical level but then if you're drawn on that level you subsequently potentially then have an intrigue to know who these characters are, or you already know. If you don't already know you might then take some pains to find out. So it complexes and deepens your appreciation of the painting, and, actually, I think improves the painting as a consequence because you go back to it more than once. And with all good painting you do that.

SZ: A lot of people who know your poetry or know your association with Fluxus and that early work might find the turn to easel painting and figurative work surprising, especially in the current artistic climate where it's seen as unfashionable. So I was just wondering whether there was any point pursuing when and how that came about.

AF: One circumstance, as I've already indicated, was the situation with Elaine and her dialysis. Now contemporary with that almost, around 1978 I think, Jasper Johns had a retrospective at the Hayward Gallery which completely bowled me over, absolutely knocked me out. And as you know, his work is, I mean we've talked about Rivers and Kitaj, but Johns would be another seminal figure who uses or combines both iconographical and geometric almost decorative shapes at times. And so those are the two crucial reasons, both for my life and the life out in the context of the world that changed. I also found, I think this is part of the same discussion, that I was doing performances and found that without written material, if I tried to do them as extemporisation there and then, I found that I was too emotionally involved in the dialysis problem and found that I just needed to pull off from this, I just didn't need to expose this to anybody.

SZ: Your dialogue with Kitaj has been a very long and sustained one. I know you wrote your dissertation on Kitaj when you did the MA in poetry and painting at Essex in 1986, but when did that engagement begin?[7]

AF: I still have a copy of the TLS, November 15, 1965, with a Kitaj cover, and I have the catalogue of the 1977 Kitaj show I went to at the Marlborough. My connection is both literary and directly viewing the paintings, with a twelve-year development through graphic works and reproductions in books until 1977. Looking at his *Graphics* catalogue (1963-1969 in Berlin) you can see the prints of MacDiarmid, Olson, Benjamin, Creeley, Dorn, Duncan, Rexroth, Wieners. I was interested in the fact that Kitaj had this relationship to poetry in the first place, that's where I would have first encountered it, I think. And there would have been book covers and so on. He did the cover for Ashbery, he did

---

[7] Allen Fisher, 'Necessary Contradiction: Facture, Function and Context in the Art of R.B. Kitaj at the Marlborough Gallery, London, February 1963,' *Talus* 2 (Autumn 1987), 65-87, is derived from the dissertation.

the cover using Creeley's picture, he used Olson's picture, McDiarmid, a whole range of poets he did pictures of, a much bigger range.

PM: In the Kessingland series (1978)[8] you have the representation of seascape, pier, etc, but the first place where you actually used representation was where you had Cosi and Genesis in Throbbing Gristle in one of the frames of the 'Melody Chambers' sequence (1978-83).[9] What happens is that some how it opens up, and you begin to incorporate figurative work which begins to relate to narrative. You don't go out and start to do portraits of your friends.

AF: What happened also was that, in order to join Goldsmiths, I went with a portfolio of mainly 'Melody Chambers' and 'Kessingland' and got in on their fine art course but was offered the alternative of taking Fine Art with Art History. And then I found out who was teaching on the latter course, which was the Thubrons and a whole group of systematic artists that I knew very much more about, that is to say they were completely non-figurative, they were conceptual artists, and I thought that was far more interesting. What Tony Collinge said, who was one of the people who interviewed me and who was one of the people running the course that the Thubrons were teaching on, was that I must do some life drawing between being interviewed (it must have been summer) and joining Goldsmiths, which is what I did. I don't remember where I did it, but I must have joined a class and done it in the evenings. That would have been 1983. Paige correctly remembers that Kessingland was early drawing, and it was preceded by some stuff that was a simulated kind of drawing, or graphic related drawing.

PM: What I'm trying to get at is that you go from representation, something

---

[8] Four canvases bolted together, the first using Kessingland Studies made on the beach then developed using some of the ideas in René Thom's structural morphogenesis (shorthanded as catastrophe theory).

[9] A set of 16 oil and collage triptych paintings (shown in the 1994 Hereford retrospective), abandoned after 16 studies and 6 triptychs; all initially 3 feet high x 9 feet wide, using three schema (conceptually derived from Pierce and Jacobson's analysis sometimes summarised as 'icon index and symbol') developed through (1) narrative and figurative representations linked to work in *Faust Undamned* and *The Apocalyptic Sonnets*, the use of a sculptural and iconic pattern of connectedness (e.g. wooden forms bolted to the canvas in the form of an energy diagram and a bone) and a measured out, geometric design using strings and drawing. In addition, a set of notes, fragments of which were published as *Atherapy Studies Q*, Writers' Forum, London, 1978.

which is representational though clearly abstracted, to figuration; you show the figures and they're actually quite realistic, and I think they might have been from a poster or photograph.

AF: The Cosi, that's correct.

PM: And I think they were in there because one of the panels in these triptychs was to do with performance.

AF: Yes, it was to do with drama.

PM: But that's different from what you then started to do where we see it in things like the Nietzsche and that whole series, which is where you imply a very complex narrative structure and you need the figure, you need figures in the painting, in order to have that.

AF: Yes, you do

PM: The way you were building narrative in the visual work was similar to what happened in Becoming and in Place. Place *began to pick up narrative elements toward the end – it was always there implied, but it really came in* Becoming, *where you took mythic figures, you described their setting, what they were doing, and then where you developed allegorical figures like Moneta talking to Newton.*

AF: Absolutely.

PM: So you were beginning to create these characters in your poetry, and there was just a sort of lag between that and when they translated across the visual work, and I think the lag was probably to do with you doing life drawing and getting more confident with that kind of stuff.

AF: The *Dispossession and Cure* series was preceded by the *Frenzy and Self-Control* sequence (1986-87), a mix of paintings on canvas and on paper including portraits of Merce Cunningham, John Cage, Albert Einstein, Julia Kristeva, Eleanor Burke Leacock, Eric Mottram, William Burroughs, Jackson Pollock, Ezra Pound, Charles Olson. For this series I used photographs of dancers as well as my drawings of movement. One of the things the Thubrons taught was moving figures, so you would do life drawings of figures that were moving, and this was contemporary with me seeing Cunningham and all sorts of people like that. *Frenzy and Self Control* relates to dance and movement as much as anything else.

PM: It is very interesting that you go to this from stuff which is incredibly reduced and spare gesture. One of my favourite pieces from when I first met you was 'Printing Days', which was just dabs of cotton squares from cleaning down a printing machine. I have it in my mind that somewhere there's actually a statement to the effect 'I'm completely rejecting the picture plane and vertical display of painting'. It's a 'painting is dead', a Duchamp type of statement, which I used to show him after he got to Goldsmiths. And there's also the art historical stuff, to be fair, looking at the whole history of art, and suddenly it opened up this whole potential range of meanings and things and so that was also very powerful.

AF: My paintings and poetry takes on the recognition that consciousness and cognition involves a complexity of functions. Human consciousness has many functions, including the æsthetic function. The use of the frame (the rectangle) has a long æsthetic history that includes or overlaps with human proprioception and the questions of how the world is experienced or known, both in terms of natural phenomena and in terms of inherited practice.

There are clear occasions when my work has visually or verbally derived from work that already exists and is in that sense abstracted. The work also, however, never loses its proprioceptive underpinning or its deliberate, planned or improvised, disruption of expectation. The pattern of connectedness that is the æsthetic for the work in painting and poetry is also an æsthetic that relies on imperfect fit for its efficacy. The concept of imperfect fit involves the relationship between consciousness and aesthetics. In this relationship a pattern of connectedness between an object and its image in the perceiver's perception can almost match, and this near-match has the capacity to produce a more significant aesthetic effect than, for instance, a perfect match and identity, or a complete mismatch and distinction. That fit is part of the viewer or reader's production.[10]

*

---

[10] For a first elaboration of the concept of 'imperfect fit,' see Allen Fisher, *The Topological Shovel* (Ontario: The Gig, 1999).

Twombly's constructed praxis is signified by his references to, and quotations from, the mythologies made literature and art by Greek, Roman and Renaissance writers and artists, and through them by Charles Olson and Robert Duncan. Twombly's use of measuring aligns to Jasper Johns and Leonardo da Vinci and is presented through metonymic displacements of materials as referents for activities. These displacements lead to understanding of Twombly's art as both post-Romantic and post-Expressionist. Such terms do not, however, give proper pertinence to his most significant function as an artist. In the presentation of works that signify the process of their facture and the sensitive-thinking this insists upon, Twombly emphasises his dimension and stance: his work is both non-Aristotelian in its critique of the cultural singularity it confronts and yet relies on that cultural crowd-out to operate and effect its critique. The insistence in this process is upon his experience as an artist who factures patterns of connectedness that provide a basis for a discourse to the producing-viewing that may then say that Twombly's stance is that of a post-experiential innocence. In the face and façade of the cultural malaise he is exposed to, Twombly is revealed as nervously involved in crowd-out, yet negatively capable of holding on.

from Allen Fisher, 'The Crowd: momentum, energy and the work of Cy Twombly' (2007), available at http://www.e-space.mmu.ac.uk/e-space/handle/2173/9747

The facture of groups of associated clusters and the ability of some models of information storage and recall in the cortex are radicalised, as perpetuation of conventions and expectations are distorted or left incomplete…
Ibid.

Many artists and very many more others recognise the weakness of human memories and the frailty of imagination, and if we can devise an art which encourages our brain to remember many more things than usual, we alert our attentions.
from Allen Fisher, 'The Sitting Room,'
in *The Sitting Room* (Manchester: Righton Press, 2007).

Philly Talks 19

KAREN MAC CORMACK & ALLEN FISHER

MARJORIE WELISH, MATT HART & ROB HOLLOWAY

*

"One has to set up conditions for a vortex to occur; that's the PhillyTalk."
– Louis Cabri

*

Contents:
– Karen Mac Cormack / Allen Fisher, Email correspondence
– Marjorie Welish & Matt Hart, pre-event response to correspondence
Event: Kelly Writers House, Philadelphia, 21 October 2001
– Rob Holloway, post-event response

*

As* the invited guests of the reading/talk series *PhillyTalks*, poets Karen Mac Cormack and Allen Fisher held a four-month email correspondence prior to the event, sharing new writing and sketching the networks of research underwriting their work. The correspondence was published as an edition of the *PhillyTalks* newsletter, to which Marjorie Welish and Matt Hart responded with critical prose and poems of their own – also prior to the event. Live video of the *PhillyTalk* itself was webcast by Aaron Levy for the Slought Foundation. A discussion followed the reading, with questions including some phoned in from the virtual audience. Rob Holloway responded to these exchanges with a reading around the first stanza of Fisher's poem WADDLE.

This sequence of texts crystallizes a distributed *deposition* gathered down (held fast even) against what winds whipped from mid-summer 2001 to 1 February 2002. Documentation of *PhillyTalks* 19 is online at the Slought Foundation website – <http://slought.org/content/11082/> – which houses downloadable audio of the event and full texts of those presented here in an edited form. The edit is intended to maintain the programmed music generated by Cabri's vortex, though a more generative transect might measure x) the degree of discursive efficacy established as a function of the interaction between n) the resources available at the sites of the writing's production, and z) the limits imposed on the conversation's emerging ordering principles. Such a diagram would log the *facture* of the discourse in all its different tunes, dislocating in the nano-political oil-mine an automated canary of the poets' own devising*. Or maybe that's already history. See below materials.

Justin Katko, 10 May 2007

*

1) FISHER / MAC CORMACK CORRESPONDENCE

Mac Cormack to Fisher #1
Wed, 27 Jun 2001 10:04:06

Dear Allen,

I'm wondering if you've revised and/or continued with your 'Decoherence and Crowd-Out' of which you sent me a tantalizing glimpse some time ago? – 'the quantum physics discussion of the step-like micro and the apparently different macro-experience ... and the overlapping discussion about consciousness, perception and focus' – (your initial description).

I'm considering in what ways your 'investigation' might relate to my exploration of 'innovative architecture' and how such investigations and explorations inform one's writing practice...

Here's something on gravity from the French architect Bernard Cache:

> We normally think it is gravity that makes us stand upright, and we therefore forget that it is diagonalization that prevents us from falling down. As if we were nothing but a weight. But our everyday actions and reactions take place within frames of support that prevent any evasion. (Cache, 59)

Karen

[*Here Cormack includes "Thirteen" [from Implexures]. See following pages.]

historical letters 10

'I' is only a convenient term for somebody who has no real being.
      – Virginia Woolf

Following the implied direction of possessions, environment is a room more specific a person. – Diane Ward

Description as a partial view – this side of the building visible presents itself as a form of re(a)d. Ruptures in the membranes of circumstances close by, successively overlapping … what is interaction? A mutual touching within the same instance. If the fall is 'free' then the trajectory knows no bounds other than contact or its delay.

> 'Between an empty space or landscape and a still life properly speaking there are certainly many resemblances. But … an empty space is distinguished above all by the presence and the composition of objects that are wrapped up in themselves or become their own container.' (Deleuze, quoted in Vidler, from *L'Image-temps*, 27)

I enjoy travelling solo. There are problems, but they're not insurmountable. The Italian and Greek men are totally perplexed by single women going around the world & it seems to unnerve them that there are so many.

On Tuesday the Italian government, by a vote of 156-154, vetoed a bill legalizing abortion. It's saddening to say the least.

Athens is more expensive, harsher, more tired in every sense. BUT, it is GREECE, goddammit it, it's Greece & it's the beginning of my trip & I'm thoroughly enjoying myself. love, love, love (Saturday 12 June 77 Athens)

'The medieval mason combined the skill of the modern contractor, engineer, and designer. The separation of the art of design from the knowledge of building is a post-medieval development. The design and construction of medieval buildings were rooted in the mason's craft.' (*Medieval Crafts/ a book of days*, 24)

> 'A strange effeminate age when men strive to imitate women in their apparell … on the other side, women would strive to

be like men, viz., when they rode on horseback or in coaches weare plush caps like monteros, either full of ribbons or feathers, long periwigs which men used to weare, and riding coate of a red colour all bedaubed with lace which they call vests, and this habit was chiefly used by the ladies and maids of honour belonging to the Queen, brought in fashion about anno 1663, which they weare at this time at their being in Oxon.' (*The Life and Times of Anthony Wood*, 1663, 153 [The Literary Companion to Fashion])

To write a work structured not as an architectural blueprint but as if exploring an architectural surround (known or unknown?) length of a line or sentence concurrent with number of steps toward a wall, punctuation as door or window perhaps … to write as one would explore a city, so a map would produce routes of numerous lines of a poem or the range of sounds heard in a given setting.

Weight of snow becomes icicles in a temperature change. Evergreens deeper colour against winter morning. How temperature affects sound. Deer in the woods the train track interrupts. How a man looks when sleeping on his birthday morning. Seeming touch of darkness against dermis but ether sustains both our day and night. The sealing wax of earlier centuries a brittle membrane informed by touch, different from callous. "Public Guidance Systems" for orderly queues in the temporary train station adjacent to the one being replaced, now detonated.

Perhaps the summer when tent dresses fluttered in lime and hot pink swirls if there was a breeze I watched her sketching the sailboats and painted a single butterfly on my own cheek. The lobby represented "inside" surrounded by floor to ceiling plate glass windows (no curtains) with the single option of door. Waiting for grandmother's social exchange to give way to a girl's anticipation of lunch the delivery man appeared as a mobile distraction to the adults' conversation. Noon. The brightness moved into one's pores, though air-conditioning terminated what should have been heat. He was a big man. The sound of glass breaking all around his trajectory through the expanse of window covered us all. Repeatedly shaking his head and arms he attempted to shed the shards adhering stubbornly. The superintendent appeared. No one thought the man should drive but he refused to be taken to hospital. Amazingly, there seemed to be no cuts as a result of this newly dangerous portal.

Fisher to Mac Cormack #1
Thu, 28 Jun 2001 08:47:14

Dear Karen,

My research [on] crowd-out, decoherence, traps and damage continues, became delayed by the British Library's loss of Physics papers (they never did find them). In any case I had to jump back to review my torn comprehension of quantum mechanics and revisit the methods and practices in calculus and field theory, two areas of practice I have never used enough to be entirely familiar with. I'm very struck by recent work on the subject reflecting on John Bell's work after his death in 1996. Remember my worry over the Gödel idea that truth cannot be demonstrated and then that whole business of quantum phenomena being beyond perception, except through machines of electronic nerve gas, that continuous reliance on the 'confidence curve' for decisions about accuracy.

This also impinged into the gene matter of mistakes and evolution, brought to the fore by local issues (in Hereford, England) of genetically-modified food contamination, the consequences of using 'confidence curves' in genetic engineering. I completed WATUSI last month. I started WADDLE and a reappraisal of freedom and misery via Fichte and Simone de Beauvoir.

This sounds eclectic, but that's simply an illusion. The architecture of the micro-cellular spacetime, the impossibility of personal, human perception of part of the activity and the reliance therefore on prediction, expectation, confidence and the reliance, always unnamed and hardly ever signalled, on mistake.

We may need to pull out some texts already written, to help new readers to this get some of it.

Allen

There are influences going faster than light, even if we cannot control them for practical telegraphy. Einstein local causality fails, and we must live with this. The orientations a and b are not independently variable as we supposed. Whether apparently chosen by apparently independent radioactive devices, or by apparently separate Swiss National Lottery machines, or even by different apparently free-willed experimental physicists, they are in fact correlated with the same causal factors as the A and B (the outcomes of the measurements). Then Einstein causality can survive. But apparently separate parts of the world become deeply entangled, and our apparent free will is entangled with them. The whole analysis can be ignored. The lesson of quantum mechanics is not to look behind the predictions of the formalism. As for the correlations, well, that's quantum mechanics. (Bell, 1980)

Fisher to Mac Cormack #2
Wed, 4 Jul 2001 08:54:41

Dear Karen,

leading off from back into your use of Carruthers…

> Patterns, of simple words and stories (text) and of decoration … become incised permanently in the brain, like the ruts that kept cartwheels on medieval roadways. (Carruthers 1998)

Carruthers' description of pattern reminds me of Waddington's idea of chreods (necessary path) and this leads into the discussion of mnemonics, architecture, maps and locations. (I remember the memory theatre and places and the Fluxus Memory Jars carried in transit and the idea of the city as dynamegopolis where all roads leading to and from the metropolis are the city) (I don't think Freud and Derrida on magical writing pad and trace have quite got this.)
    In Carruthers' *The Book of Memory* discussing Quintilian, Quintilian defining the 'places' of argument laid down in memory, likens a skilful orator to a huntsman or fisherman who knows exactly the habits and haunts of his game… The metaphor in the word (for example Aristotle speaks of how people recollect … 'hunt successfully') error, both 'error' and 'wandering,' is an aspect of this same idea, for the one who wanders through the pathless silva (meaning both 'forest' and 'disordered material') of an untrained memory is one who has either lost the footprints … that should lead him (sic) through…

Not to mention:

> Along the journey of our life half way,
> I found myself again in a dark wood ... (Dante and now
> Caroline Bergvall, from "Via")

Anyway, the recall complexed as I noticed your architectural links to person and senses and started* in again on the first *Implexures* in *The Gig* 7 (Nov 2000) and prompted by the wonderful new small book taking from *Implexures* 7 onwards, and the memory plastics in that work 'in progress'. I came back from Belfast last week, with its mixture of heavy colonial pressures (massive Victorian architecture for instance), and its world fashion culture, that is the same high street in Leicester, Cardiff, Hereford and Belfast serving the same cheap-labour made goods from US/UK designed SE Asia.

Standing in the garden, aircraft above, a car buzzes by, a bird, a fox I'm thinking about a bruise on my leg taken out by outside the garden, trip up again. How the memory journey is that but more interesting, inventive even.

The de Beauvoir I was alerted by came via Steve's discussion, ethics and my crowd-out worry about the dialectic (the latter used I also note by J.H. Prynne and Steve in their exchange in *The Gig* 6 & 7). The rejection of poetry by Sartre in his later work and the whole discussion about ethics without belief in essence and what I would insist upon (probably influenced by Mukarovsky and Marcuse) that is esthetics as redolent of ethics.

de Beauvoir writes: 'a being who is at a distance from himself and who has to be his being' (*The Ethics of Ambiguity*). and her openness in: 'To say that (existence) is ambiguous is to assert that its meaning is never fixed, that it must be constantly won.'

Architecturally that can mean an understanding that fixities are involved in shifts, that doors open, glass cracks, walls move, but also our comprehension of where we are shifts with weather, temperature, the presence/absence of others, that is we move through, tarry, move back.

Allen

Mac Cormack to Fisher #2
Fri, 06 Jul 2001 21:27:52

Dear Allen,

Carruthers ... again ... into ethics ...

> The choice to train one's memory or not, for the ancients and medievals, was not a choice dictated by convenience: it was a matter of ethics. A person without a memory, if such a thing could be, would be a person without moral character and, in a basic sense, without humanity. Memoria refers not to how something is communicated, but to what happens once one has received it, to the interactive process of familiarizing – or textualizing – which occurs between oneself and others' words in memory. (*The Book of Memory*, 13)

Writing itself was judged to be an ethical activity in monastic culture. (156)

Perception – Medieval mnemotechnique treated

> 'the memory as though it were a flat area divided linearly into columns within a grid,' whereas 'Roman mnemonics were not as closely tied to the grid ... the classical mnemonic ties the "places" to an architectural setting.' (129)

Now for me what is fascinating is the probability (?) that this changed understanding of the nature of the mnemonic 'locus' – from a three-dimensional room, in which perspective changes as one 'walks' through it mentally, to a two-dimensional cell within a grid on a flat surface – may account for some of the confusion medieval writers had in understanding Tully's rules about the making of backgrounds. (ibid)
In your *Sojourns* there's the wonderful poem SHEAR (STRESS):

> Deformation occurs where parallel planes in a body remain parallel, but are relatively displaced in a direction parallel to themselves. Contact usually includes a tendency to slide over each other. A rectangle becomes a parallelogram, a conversational stretch.

And so to Bernard Cache's *Earth Moves* again: 'our perceptions are inscribed on the surface of things, as images amongst images,' (xviii) I just finished reading *A Selection from the Works of Thomas Swan*. Do you know this seventeenth-century poet's work? (His 'Colours that do correspond not to the outward aspect though in truth I do see them so' is quite extraordinary, and impelled me to reread your *Sojourns!*) To quote again from SHEAR (STRESS):

> 'Focusing theorem' concerns bundles of rays and plays a crucial role in blackhole physics, in the theory of singularities, and the poetics of mobile collage.

Now referring to a poem in my *Straw Cupid* (1987) I quote:

pattern is an overlay on disparate elements

how many

desperation's continual distribution of complexities
singular and present

voices speak a simultaneity distance holds hostage
a precedent of impulse in intervals of letters (87)

Karen

Fisher to Mac Cormack #3

Sat, 14 Jul 01 14:12:57

Dear Karen,

Thinking about crowd-out I remember M.R. James's story 'Count Magnus'. 'It is curious,' he notes:

> how on retracing a familiar path one's thoughts engross one to the absolute exclusion of surrounding objects. Tonight, for the second time, I had entirely failed to notice where I

was going (I had planned a private visit to the tomb-house to copy the epitaphs), when I suddenly, as it were, awoke to consciousness, and found myself (as before) turning in at the churchyard gate, and, I believe, singing or chanting some such words as, 'Are you awake, Count Magnus? Are you asleep, Count Magnus?' and then something more which I have failed to recollect. It seemed to me that I must have been behaving in this nonsensical way for some time.

I was following up a check on Aristotle's last work *Ethics to Nicomachus and the Politics* for a talk on Raphael's *School of Athens* and I started looking at an analysis by John Gillies in 1893 and reminded of Mary Carruthers' investigations and your *Implexures*, partly because of the hunting metaphor in medieval vocabulary, which I'm not sure I go for, and partly the struggle with description of perception of another's perceptions and your own memory and vocabulary generated from encounter with the vocabulary of another connected other.

For the perceptions of imagination and memory, though not rigidly governed, like those of sense, by the power and presence of external objects, do not, however, float at random [I think I prefer phased in distinction or crowd-out against], but are subjected to a certain order and progression, conformably to established laws of association [and laws now jars the door of it], which Aristotle was the first philosopher that attempted to investigate, to enumerate, and to explain. He investigated them in analyzing the complex act of reminiscence or recollection, in which the principles of association [this analysis written contemporary with William James excitement about the stream of it and Freud the narrator's will to completion] operate under the immediate direction of the human will [which Nietzsche burgled from their sleep]. He enumerated them, as far as seemed requisite to the subject which he was then treating [an indicator of Aesclepian intrigue], by saying that they might be reduced to the four following heads: proximity in time; contiguity in place; resemblance or similarity [which I would now need to unravel in terms of spacetime and aesthetics or consciousness and patterns of connectedness]; contrariety or contrast; and he explains them by showing that in every act of recollection we are conscious [somewhat emphatic in an age that precedes Cubism] of *hunting about, as it were, among our thoughts,* [his emphasis] until we hit on some one which is intimately connected with that which we wish to recall; or in other words, that we produce in succession a multitude of vibrations ['A Singular Plurality' (*Straw Cupid*, p 39)] or motions in our organs [this business of the momenergy] ['Sometimes the words arise from the outside and lips form around them' (*Straw Cupid*)], until we hit on some one of them intimately connected with that of which we are in quest [relabeled in an era when the mobile video-phone reports from the war crowd to the city war zone almost before it happens, unlike say Tennyson reading *The Times* after the event and collaging a poem into his peer's recent rhymes recited from a woollen helmet], and which has the power of reviving this last, because the one motion is either excited nearly at the same time with the other [or exactly simultaneous but not observed at the same time it is measured and is anyway decohered by any semblance of measurement], or is entirely the same in kind with it, or so nearly the same [a notion of simulation and simulacra in John Gillies' contemporary Aby Warburg later to be revived by the Catholic pain of Jean Baudrillard's Reformation], that the minute difference between them is speedily overpowered and lost and from near agreement finally reduced to perfect coincidence [much, no doubt, to the awakening of Jung's jaded followers]…

> Another matter to do with freedom as it recurs in WADDLE (underway) when Aristotle quotes 'the poet': 'None choose wretchedness, or spurns delight' (205).

Which preceded (in the sense of not remembering or apparently knowing this passage first, 'freedom includes the decision to be miserable' and this is accounted for by what precedes it, 'mis-scribed by origin of freedom / the decision to be in misery made by someone else.'

Leaders are those members who gain control of any given group. (*Straw Cupid*, 40)

Or back with crowd-out:

> If words are not things, or maps are not the actual territory, then, obviously, the only possible link between the objective world and the linguistic world is found in structure, and structure alone… (Korzybski, 61)

and:

> In fact, in structure we find the mystery of rationality, adjustment, and we find that the whole content of knowledge is exclusively structural. If we want to be rational and to understand anything at all, we must look for structure, relations, and, ultimately, multi-dimensional order, all of which was impossible on a broader sense in the Aristotelian system… (ibid)

Allen

Mac Cormack to Fisher #3
Fri, 20 Jul 2001 18:10:47

Dear Allen,

I would like to introduce Robert Musil's *The Man Without Qualities* into this discussion:

> Most people relate to themselves as storytellers. They usually have no use for poems, and although the occasional 'because' or 'in order that' gets knotted into the thread of life, they generally detest any brooding that goes beyond that; they love the orderly sequence of facts because it has the look of necessity, and the impression that their life has a 'course' is somehow their refuge from chaos. It now came to Ulrich that he had lost this elementary, narrative mode of thought to which private life still clings, even though everything in public life has already ceased to be narrative and no longer follows a thread, but instead spreads out as an infinitely interwoven surface. (709)

(Remembering that *TMWQ* was set in 1913 and that Musil worked on it after WWI to his death during WWII (it was unfinished) the above seems 'contemporary' to me.)

Now this from the Spanish architect Ignasi Solà-Morales's *Differences* (which resonated for me regarding *crowd-out* and *Implexures*):

> Contemporary time – today's fragmented reality of overlapping virtual and 'real' times that was artistically anticipated in the writings of James Joyce, Robert Musil, and Mario Vargas Llosa – is presented precisely as juxtaposition: a discontinuity; something that is in complete contrast to a single, unique, closed and complete system. Time in the architecture of the classical age could be simply reduced to zero (as in the experience of Renaissance centrality) or at most constitute a controlled time – a time with a beginning and an orderly and ordered expansion (which was entirely the experience of baroque temporality)…

Eugenio Trias, in his book *Los límites del mundo*, speaks of the untimely nature of the contemporary situation and contemporary art; untimely in the sense of sudden, unanticipated coagulations of reality, events that are produced not through linear and foreseeable organization but through folds and fissures, as Foucault himself sometimes says, that in some way afford the refuge, the tremulous fluttering of a brief moment of poetic and creative intensity. (66-68)

Karen

Fisher to Mac Cormack #4
Tue, 24 Jul 2001 09:06:51

Dear Karen,

Here's WADDLE as it is today, more response to your last soon. Love Allen.

1.

I focus on a bridge form
as it moves
releases pinches releases
pylons lift in sunlight from grassland
catch sky base a range of cloud shapes
cirrus interrupted by striations
A figure embraces and unfolds in rhythm

it could be a bird, trapped to the ground
attempts to free from this instructs its
unseen other in operation beyond view
Gender unspecific but questions are raised
regard for freedom
About situation
between edges of perception, now
reaches between strata:
a state of uplift:
a new freedom.
This celebrates an increase in existents
a multiple self, enhances embrace.

2.

In simulated light surveillance I lift
heat coil and appear alienated
up from a bird screech marked by wing beats
Listen up, an overhead
pours a neon spread pathway
shut against an actual road
serpentine from animal wander
felt pushed in the back lost footing,
stammered, loose metal bushes burn
exactness and expectation. Dice clenched, apparency,
return in to light shafts
recorded in blind stripes or
exhausted definition in measured speed
Somehow, it's difficult to know,
I prove my shell metal mossed wrath
vivify flight indoctrination
through hector lime hash robbery's guise.

Ponderous eruption
shakes London
Named in laws of interaction
break them
Named jubilance and speak of joy and worry,
a net released and tightened, a sparrow chick

simulates flight in fledged flurry
on gutter edge
capital's main street the Banker
sharpens his steel it skins a chance replaced
his finesse. Can you imagine his loss
shaken. The Banker chances with
his speculation
"free to arrest transcendence" stolen in conscience,
cell wrapped and
unwrapped stingray
Beaver's ontology
condemned to be free
without value judgements
authenticities.

3.

Who the I is confuses the narrative
tossed in translation
eroded her language like a kid
with a trick
this common individual
the inert limit
of freedom
In keeping with my intention
maintenance of close relations
between ideal and real measurements
now a collective observation
in which decoherence occurs. For as long
as the struggle lasts, always
to others that the very contingency
of events and the qualified freedom
of individuals express the conflict itself
always possible to put an end to it
a sort of comportment necessary
an individual pleroma, imagined
virtuality, normative and catalytic,
gratuitous play, ascetic
expressions of sadness, joy, love

in very limited particulars

4.

always the historic and circumstantial
result of conditions outside
the domain of knowledge
to get away from it
and destroy it where
freedom includes
the decision
to be miserable.
The Banker
studies complicated
by extreme variation
in substitution rates
between sites the
consequence of parallel mutations
difficulties in estimations of
genetic distance
Constantly before the reader
an accidentality of any
surface stricture
chosen as realisation
of underlying thought
told spelled tould
to rhyme with would.

5.

the discrepancy a prediction error
demonstrated by observation
that learning is blocked
a dreadful state of misery
may overtake the
in uncertain hope of annihilation
simple temporal contiguity
between stimulus and reinforcer
Presentations of surprise generate

positive prediction errors
encoded neuronal messages modify
synaptic connection in snares
of reason, absoluteness and knowledge
the decision to be
in misery
made by someone else.

Fisher to Mac Cormack #5
Sun, 5 Aug 01 16:52:49

Dear Karen,

One plateau of discussion invites linked together realities, our work, on various occasions, uses linking and/or demonstrates a range of realities that overlap, sometimes blur into each other, sometimes erase one over the other, sometimes crowd-out the previous instant until itself crowd-outed and sometimes this is fleeting and initial reality returns. This pressure recognises that reality proposes representation of an actuality, what is happening, has happened, represented, presented again.

 A syntactic or paratactic continuity that provides a ground for demonstration of sudden change – characterised in the vocabulary of 'quantum leap,' René Thom's catastrophe theory where smooth process jumps into new spacetime (new reality) like a phase shift from wet to boiling, in the larger scheme: the punctuated equilibrium of step-like change in animal evolution.

 The underlying discussion is epistemological and thus about truth and freedom as well as knowledge, about will and natural expectations, as well as information and structure and how structure provides (facilitates) the necessary pathways as well as the auto-habits, the chreods, (Deleuze and Guattari call the crevices made by the run-offs) for representation.

 This requires research and experiment, drawing on a range of vocabularies from pre-Enlightenment as much as Enlightenment and post-Romantic – from Fichte as much as de Beauvoir and Sartre as much as Deleuze and Guattari. pasting the geneticist's enterprise onto the capitalist method. shifting the burglar's ingenuity into the realm of both, where the singular purpose of the latter crowd-outs any difference with the other.

Other plateaus would then discuss intake from scheduled outsides, connections to a larger spread of connectedness without immediate, apparent patterns, but with innuendo and rhyme to early tracts in the same sequence complex A >> Z but not in that order.

Allen

Mac Cormack to Fisher #4
Sat, 11 Aug 2001 12:10:02

Dear Allen,

There's been an ongoing heatwave here, during which time I've been reading Joseph LeDoux's *The Emotional Brain*. (Carruthers referred to it, along with Damasio's *Descartes' Error* in *The Craft of Thought*).

Compare the following to the 'lost' 'narrative mode of thought' in Musil's character Ulrich:

> We concluded people normally do all sorts of things for reasons they are not consciously aware of (because the behavior is produced by brain systems that operate unconsciously) and that *one of the main jobs of consciousness is to keep our life tied together into a coherent story, a self-concept.* (LeDoux, 33; emphasis mine)

And not losing touch with Carruthers (and in response to your 'connections to a larger spread of connectedness without immediate, apparent patterns") she writes:

> We tend to make a firm division between reading and creativity now, but it is clear that medieval scholars did not. ... every verse ... becomes a gathering place for other texts, into which even the most remote and unlikely matters are collected as the associational memory of the author draws them in. Associations depending upon opposition and contrariety are just as apt to end up being collated as those of consonance and likeness. (Carruthers 1993, 892)

And so to Cache:

> A sort of cubist sculpture of the city of Lausanne could then be constructed through the combination of these four basic figures: cone, prism, dihedral, and plane.

This sculpture is a mnemotechnical object. One must also remember that the surface of the territory is mobile and fluid as it is given to the continual distortions of memory...

In the exercise of their profession, architects can choose to ground their practice in the concept of site. The work of architecture then becomes the expression of the specificity of the site that is to be built upon ...But this position runs the danger of falling into a mistaken notion of site, equating all too easily the notion of specificity with that of identity. The case of Lausanne demonstrates clearly enough that the identity of a place is not given, and that if the expression 'genius loci' has a meaning, it lies in the capacity of this 'genius' to be smart enough to allow for the transformation or transit from one identity to another ... [there] are gestures through which an architect can position him or herself with respect to a site. But in no case does the identity of a site pre-exist, for it is always the outcome of a construction. (*Earth Moves*, 10-15)

and Cache:

> In mathematics, what is said to be singular is not a given point, but rather a set of points on a given curve. A point is not singular; it becomes singularized on a continuum. And several types of singularity exist... (16)

and Cache again:

> If we wish to define architecture as an operation on space, we must then define the nature of this space more precisely. Classical philosophy saw it as a form of coexistence or simultaneity. It was contrasted with time, which was seen as a form of succession. But architectural space is not this general form of simultaneity; it is a space where coexistence is not a fundamental given, but rather the uncertain processes of separation and partitioning. The wall is the basis of our coexist-

ence. Architecture builds its space of compatibility on a mode of discontinuity. (24)

WADDLE's intensities recombine with each reading, providing multiple "grounds for sudden change."
  Is there room for Agamben with Fichte, de Beauvoir, Sartre, and Deleuze and Guattari?

Karen

'Imbalance is a porthole.' (*Quill Driver*)

Fisher to Mac Cormack #6
Sun, 12 Aug 01 11:55:56

Dear Karen,
this matter of continuity, narrative (Musil & co) and impertinence: the issues of post-collage; for instance in *Quill Driver*:

> Then it was crashing. Film technology has advanced since Stein's use of 'cinematic' technique. But embroidery done by machine still lacks desire. If the object 'to move' insists on being 'still the subject' there is always a room for a table.

and patterns of connectedness along with multiplicity and the energy of shifting truths as you point out via LeDoux: 'one of the main jobs of consciousness is to keep our life tied together into a coherent story, a self-concept.'
  but as you say, also where poetry 'builds' its space on a 'mode of discontinuity.'

We both use the complexity of transformations a lot. In *Quirks & Quillets*, for instance from proven to heaving:

Combination or weaving the influence of
literature on sunsets with a proven space for
heaving anything at all through windows
where aeroplane numbers are without…

or in *MultiPlex*, 'Oval Value': 'an option positions opposition "just so" …'

put the trash out
leads to
put the trash out, Darling
which gets realigned in
put the trash out, Darling,
it's on fire,
but the impertinence is better attained in
put the trash out, Darling,
fired the lot of them.
The expectation from sense and syntax
leads to a new syntax, or a new plateau of conscious/unconsciousness,
an alternative in asyntax
could provide the occasional realignment shift
but this cannot be continuous if it is to work
put the trash out, Darling
nails it (closure)
whether in the storm or waits
for the can to
put the cat out
before it eats the trash.
Somehow the break from expectation
needs to also provide enough shift
to be beyond a single collage
change in direction
plane over plane
and somehow demand a rereading
of vocabulary in the process of reading it
where the vocabulary "trash" becomes
verb and trash out like
thrash about shifts
put the trash out into
something like 'do the funky chicken'.

Allen

Mac Cormack to Fisher #5
Wed, 15 Aug 2001 10:34:34

Dear Allen,

Here's another definition of architecture, this one from Ignasi Solà-Morales:

> It seems more and more that we are confronted not so much with a work of architecture as a point of intersection, the interaction of forces and energies proceeding from diverse locations whose momentary deflagration explains a concrete and particular architectural situation, action, and production... (16)

Giorgio Agamben informs us:

> The usage of the word 'stanza' to indicate a part of the canzone or poem derives from the Arabic term bayt, which means 'dwelling place,' 'tent,' and at the same time 'verse.' According to Arab authors bayt also refers to the principal verse of a poem composed in praise of a person to whom one wishes to express desire, and in particular the verse in which the object of desire is expressed. (*Stanzas*, 124-125)

[and] suggests that:

> Poetic language takes place in such a way that its advent always already escapes both toward the future and toward the past. The place of poetry is therefore always a place of memory and repetition. (*Language and Death*, 76)

Here's a recent poem (that having read 'put the trash out, Darling' seems a response of sorts)

Karen

somehow the weather intrudes (not only in the month of February)
it's not as if one writes "best" simply when impelled

(far from it) the temperature declines repeatedly
and a slip takes on connotations other than
not even "slides" is equivalent in this environment
language means itself across and through such seasons
to remember is a reference the act of printing
points to an action continually revised

another month (of May) and I join *raining* in the act of
going out into itself along the swerve of
leaf-green these minutes hinge a subject with a walk's
duration, process a recognition of how pacing
affects degrees of density (as in "is this surface durable
enough to write on?") reworking what occurs
in the words familiar new realizations understood

to determine or undermine sequence
disrupts middle into where-to-when occurs for whom
the instance of what advertising is why
lifestyle is how recent a term

Fisher to Mac Cormack #7
Thu, 23 Aug 2001 08:51:42

Dear Karen,
I've returned to some simple concepts to bump into more recently, in response to the use of texts by architects and their proposers, like Cache as well as Agamben's stanza design, with a view to:

> hold the matter of speech at becalmed points of place as such
> on all fours three ways… ("Oval Value" in *MultiPlex*)

I've been making a map of my room in Roehampton so that I can keep track of where various projects and books are. I already keep such data on what's in Hereford and in my studio. Something about the activity brings me to some of what we have been saying. To begin with take typology, for instance, Will Kunz (1998):

> 'The established principles of typography could be likened to the principles underlying architecture or music – necessary for craft but insufficient for art.
>
> ...
>
> Typographic design can proceed from two types of structure: an optically improvised visual structure, or a predetermined structure – the grid system.
>
> ...
>
> For complex, extensive assignments, a predetermined structure – the grid system – is necessary.
>
> ...
>
> Depending on their placement within a given space, the same elements will assume different visual aspects of weight and movement.

and then a colleague at Roehampton, Alan Read, "Walking west from Hammersmith Bridge, along the north bank of the Thames..." notes:

> Here is a speech site where a history of orality reveals something more than oral history, a location where locution might be amplified in order to discern an ethics of speech for an emerging metropolis...

He concludes:

> Between these two apparent poles, [modern and older architecture] is a spectrum of positions from which one might construct a politics of the location of locution, that neither lionises stability nor celebrates the insecurities of hybridity. Walter Benjamin understood this tension when, in speaking about the art of the storyteller, he characterised the archaic representatives of the genre: ... ('Speech Sites')

One of the understandings from what we've been exchanging is that specialist practice is secondary to aesthetic necessity, and that any specialist practice needs interaction, however framed or broken, with another practice and more. Of course, once we grab aesthetics as a requirement, but not a precedent nor a simple outcome for active consciousness.

Allen

Mac Cormack to Fisher #6
Tue, 28 Aug 2001 22:47:56

Dear Allen,

You refer to "simple concepts" but in the context it seems to me that you bring a welcome swerve to such concepts (structure, maps . . .). And the first excerpt from *Implexures* that I sent to you at the end of June included a reference to maps (indeed, that work is full of them). Thinking about typology and typography I offer a further spin (the following quotation appears in the section of *Implexures* I'm currently working on):

> Writers between 1500 and 1650 used all of the marks of punctuation in use today, but with observable differences. Semicolons will be met with only rarely, colons far more than today. Question marks were used then as we use them, but also they were used where we use exclamation points. These last were latecomers, being almost unknown before 1650. Quotation marks were seldom used before 1600, and then rather to call attention to a phrase or a sententious expression than to mark direct quotation. (Dawson & Skipton, *Elizabethan Handwriting 1500-1650*, 18)

The choice of word lists, sentences to learn by, and the exercises in these respective manuals reflect not only the ongoing changes in North American English for this period, but also the shifts in educational, business, and technological terminology.

Here's a sample from GWAM:

Tab a full size otherwise
Take the brakes off your fingers and let them explore new stroking patterns.
5 minutes
reach the centre of hold
to do it or if is by it and can . . .
Skill Measurement II
in a similar manner do not stop, let it go; just keep on

at any easy, controlled rate
now think the word, not the letters
(instead of o r, or) word-recognition response
"It can be done if you do not pause . . ."
accuracy, shifting for capitals
stretch as you make the reach
Place movement touches
"Let us do big things if we can or small things in a big way."

Indeed, the more I consider these issues the more I think in terms of the plural. "Architecture" is no more an homogenous 'given' than "language" is, yet both are too often taken for granted in the discussions to which they are central.

Karen

Fisher to Mac Cormack #8
Mon, 3 Sep 2001 19:06:01

Dear Karen,

I want to quote at length from the very bright introduction by Deleuze & Guattari to their *A Thousand Plateaus* in Massumi's translation. I came to this late, I had read the terrific last chapter first in semiotext(e) and somehow dropped into the book in an appropriately non-linear way. I'm engaged with their principles throughout, but let me example from 5 & 6:

> Principal of cartography and decalcomania: a rhizome is not amenable to any structural or generative model. It is a stranger to any idea of genetic axis or deep structure. A genetic axis is like an objective pivotal unity upon which successive stages are organized; a deep structure is more like a base sequence that can be broken down into immediate constituents, while the unity of the product passes into another, transformational and subjective, dimension. This does not constitute a departure from the representative model of the tree, or root...

continues:

> It is our view that genetic axis and profound structure are above all infinitely reproducible principles of tracing...

and:

> What distinguishes the map from the tracing is that it is entirely oriented toward an experimentation in contact with the real...

Now the idea of the 'real' needs to be unpacked, but I was encouraged by the drift. Later they note: "The map has to do with performance, whereas the tracing always involves an alleged 'competence'."

and then we get to something else that you and I have been engaging regarding the inside outside architectural discussion:

> Drives and part-objects are neither stages on a genetic axis nor positions in a deep structure; they are political options for problems, they are entryways and exits, impasses the child lives out politically, in other words, with all the force of his or her desire.

Allen

Mac Cormack to Fisher #7
Wed, 05 Sep 2001 23:48:19

Dear Allen,
historical letters 4 Contrary to a tracing, which always returns to the 'same,' a map has multiple entrances ... A map is a matter of performance, whereas the tracing always refers to an alleged 'competence.' Gilles Deleuze & Félix Guattari (from *On the Line*, p. 26, quoted in *Implexures*)

Just as there is no universality of language there's no 'universality' of architecture, i.e. 'architecture' should not be construed as a blanket term any more than 'poetry' is some singular, neutral 'form' ... how this does or doesn't work re: quantum mechanics I don't know – thoughts

on this?
To allow D & G to continue:

> A rhizome is made of plateaus. Gregory Bateson uses the word 'plateau' to designate something very special: a vibrant and continuous area of intensities that develops by avoiding every orientation toward a culminating point or external end. (ibid, 49, and in a footnote on p 64 re: Bateson's *Steps to an Ecology of Mind* D & G state: 'It should be noted that the word "plateau" is used in classical studies of bulbs, tubers, and rhizomes: cf. the entry for 'bulb' in Baillon's *Dictionnaire de Botanique*.'

Walls as crowd-outs, windows as frames within crowd-outs?

One more trajectory before I send this off to you, from Michael Camille, concerning Romanesque art:

> But whereas in the ancient world triumphal arches and amphitheatres articulated the centrality of imperial rule, for medieval people they became gates and passageways between psychological, rather than political, states. Romanesque art is one of entrances, doorways, westworks, narthexes, porches, capitals and cornices... (56)

Karen

Fisher to Mac Cormack #9
15/9/01

Dear Karen,
One of the extraordinary results from the exchange has been the way in which it has opened out some of the complexity, given energy to the complexity to encourage better application. The terminological shifts from concepts of phase spacetime, catastrophe theory, punctuated equilibrium, quantum mechanics finds new ground in Lawson's *Closure*, flips to and from agreement. I've been researching *Traps or Tools and Damage* and this begins to impinge and contribute here to your extended work on architects' terminologies and that of linguistics (to

give 2 examples). This, as promised previously, is from *Closure* looked at last week:

> A mousetrap for example, can be regarded as having two discrete states: it is either set, it is ready, or it has sprung, it has gone off. Many different causes may have led to it being in one state or another: it may have been sprung by a mouse, but it could also have been knocked by someone or something, or someone could have deliberately set it off. In the context of the mechanism all of these variations are of no consequence, it is either set or it has sprung. The diversity of the immediate environment is thereby reduced to single state and its absence: it is either set or it is not set. Any mechanical arrangement that enables a system to alternate between two or more discrete states is thereby capable of providing the basis for preliminary closure... (30)

or what I might have called 'crowd-out'.
Lawson on page 31:

> It can be seen that closure provides a new outcome, which is not the same as the circumstances from which it was realised.

Thus when you say, 'Contrary to a tracing...' and 'There is ... no universality of language, but an encounter of dialects...' or a multiplicity of spacetimes (and again Bateson's pleateaux) which are necessarily unique or complete or separate from each other, but as quantum mechanics indicates, more complex, not open to the simplicities of measurement, which may over specify, which may be determined by the kind of measurements being used, which may require remote or virtual measurement, which may not be measurable in the usual sense at the level of phenomena and perception, but rather relies on hypothetical blur.

It is that blur, which has to be presented as measurement, or as a description of how subatomic activity or macro-universe-wide activities occur, that relies on the 'confidence curve', a kind of Boltzmann decision about spectra (which could have enlightened, but in fact confused some colour vision 'science')

Walls become decisions, and thus become 'crowd-outs', and as you say, 'windows as frames' within these and this is contiguous with your note on, for instance the Romanesque, that art of memory that cannot exclude the copulating couple or mooning saint or the dancers in the rafters of, and given the solemnity of, the sanctuary.

In medieval Chartres, in the late Romanesque, a floor carved into a labyrinth around which pilgrims crawled on their knees until, at the centre, they stood up to see the rose window before them, and were, presumably sent into another spacetime or certainly given a perception lift that becomes a crowd-out to the labour of getting there.

Allen

Mac Cormack to Fisher #8
Sun, 16 Sep 2001 23:08:52

Dear Allen,
thank you for your latest, particularly after the events of Tuesday, 11 September 2001. In terms of trying to process such a plethora of 'information' concerning those events, and being unable to discern anything contributing to clarity in that regard, so as to make some 'sense' of them.

As you stated 'blur … as measurement' … I hope to take up this discussion with you in Philadelphia on 17 October 2001

Karen

2) Pre-event Responses

Marjorie Welish

'For Them This Brochure is Unnecessary'

1   .

Sequences implicate sets corresponding. Contemporary societies… we at once began; the future will likely consum-

tion of a representation. Anyone else, anyone else's litter
making literal his "tion" of a representation to impregnate
blue and green matches (after hav- –after that date, never–
ing its tides). From the left, a predicate out of breath
delays category, and sometimes not.
Histories of the subjugated read otherwise
than do those of the victorious.
                        And rising is 1913, almost always
being coextensive with 1690, the 9th century pending and within sight of
an inch of water in a basin. Minutes in a neolithic settlement.

2.

We at once began corresponding; the future will likely strip-search,
                                      will likely anthol-
tion of a representation. Anyone else, anyone else's litter, the book's first half
making literal his "tion" of sonorous velocities permeated and said,
unfailingly blue from green, origin of (after hav- –after that date, never–
ing its tides). From the left, a predicate short of breath, the hand lifted
"skeptical" and "agora" together, and sometimes not.
Histories of the subjugated read other's dicta
than do those of the victorious.
                        Your uppermost story is 1913
much of the time eclipsed in 1690, the 9th century pending … and felt it
writing in a basin. Minutes adapted to a neolithic settlement.

3.

tion of a representation. Anyone else, anyone else's litter
making literal his lay launderette for "tion" of "imitation" to impregnate
ultramarine and/ or cobalt (after hav- –after that date, never–
ing its tides). "Prefabricated wiring with insulation and terminals" left a
                                  predicate breathless, territory
together with category transposed sometimes, as
histories of the subjugated read edgewise and are dusty, other
than those of the victorious.
                      Uppermost is 1913, immense, simultaneously
being read with 1690; the 9th century took place within sight of
an inch of anathema. Minutes passed a neolithic settlement.

4.

making literal his "tion" of "imitation" to impregnate
two blues: scarcely red, in being green (after hav- –after that date, never–
ing its tides). From stage left and clockwise, what is said of a fan
ventilating category, quantity and number, and sometimes
histories of the subjugated reverse. Speak through it, thickening. If you....
than do those of the victorious.
                      Theory of 1913 is as a fresh start, and uppermost is
your being multi-linear. In 1690, the 9th century took place and caused/
                                                  was caused by
an inch of anathema, the basin as such, a split-second neolithic settlement.

5.

blue and green aspects (after hav- –after that date, never–
ing its tides). From the left wing, a predicate retaliated and walked out,
territory rewritten in category, and sometimes
histories of the subjugated read as vernacular
underestimated, its entablature
reserved to describe a serious scatter of tubing above a disposition.
                                            Particles of 1913,
teenth century being read with 1690; the 9th century will burst
an inch of a thing done. Day passed a neolithic settlement.

Pre-event response to *Philly Talks* 19: Fisher / Mac Cormack

Throughout their intoxicated conversation, Karen Mac Cormack and Allen Fisher delight in a superfluity of telegraphic messages that refer to texts, texts concerning form and the representations of mentality which such form indicates. In other words, their shared excitement is not in referring to people, places and things in the intellectual's equivalent of a Grand Tour of cultural concepts, but in finding points of contact through rapid mention via non-proscriptive means. Of the messages sent and received concerning their poetics, Mac Cormack is especially interested in setting forth certain concepts regarding alternative or neglected visual and verbal schema for representing architectural space in historical time and what may be salvaged in understanding these interpretive schemes; for his part, Fisher is interested in setting out the possibilities of cognitive poetics through what the sciences reveal about organizing an entire gradient of phenomenal interactions, especially those that save complexity. In more general terms, what interests Mac Cormack is textual representation of spatiality and temporality and what interests Fisher is the structural basis of systems construed in functionally exhaustive array – this in order to be as intelligently discriminating and conceptually ramified as physical and ecological systems themselves require. For that the logic of ideology will not do.

It is possible to say that an encyclopedia of the subjective domain informs Karen Mac Cormack's *Implexures*, and that representations of this ordering of space and time in past rhetoric and literature help make *Implexures* specific as it now stands. On the cusp of modernity, meanwhile, sits Robert Musil, endowed with an excess of microscopic knowledge and a macroscopic comprehension of ignorance. The epochal disintegration of self-justifying empire which in Musil's work plays out in excruciatingly intelligent hyper-consciousness is a perfect citation for this project of Mac Cormack's.

May I offer this? Pierre Boulez, a systemic thinker of discontinuity if there ever was one, has volunteered that *The Man Without Qualities* was an early favourite book.

My question for Mac Cormack would be how the laws of association informing the subjective domain of events and their surrounds necessitate invoking the particular mapping configuration of a Deleuzean sort.

A possible answer may be advanced. Some passages in *Implexures* display a topic through an aggregated vocabulary of causes displaced onto effects, or episodes discrepant in scale. Death of a household pet in time present reconfigures itself a few sentences later as extinction, as such, which then modulates toward being the implied retrieval of subject through palaeontology. Topics are then not vehicles of subject matter but markers of historical coordinates expressed through the individuation of sentences. Meanwhile, the detained vocabularies offer specific events rather than evidence valorized through overcoding in reference to a system, adhering to the order of a heap. Aspects of her topic throw connectedness into relief in ways remote from coherence.

Similarly, for Allen Fisher: to what do we owe decoherence that is not already a familiar representation of simultaneous superposition?

Possible answers are these: the superposition of incommensurate objects interacting with their environments is now to be acknowledged as having infiltrated the quantum minutiae of our worlds, in effect. Yet on a macroscopic scale as well decoherence applies, such that there exist tenuous reciprocating influences between objects or systems and their environments.

So in this way chaotic poetic objects may be seen to be self-monitoring situations. This would seem especially true of Fisher's insistence that poetic equivalents of reciprocating influence be hard-wired in time-space objects.

Thinking of this, it is tempting to hypothesize that Fisher sustains a poetics in which a lexical farrago allows for sensitized science and brute social science. I wonder whether I believe this. I wonder whether I believe this now that I have reread *Sojourns*.

'The Crowd,' however, does represent Allen Fisher's own sensitized cognition articulating the taxonomy of facture in Cy Twombly's painting through the instrumentality of science.

Written a few years ago, his piece does not take cognizance of my own articles. (Of my writings on Twombly, the earliest came about on the occasion of 'Fifty Days at Iliam' (1978), on its debut at the Dia Foundation in New York to coincide with the Twombly retrospective at the Whitney Museum in 1979, for which Roland Barthes had written the catalogue; the most recent, 'Narrating the Hand,' considers work by him and by Mary Kelly in a comparative study of writing as a developmental set of motor and cognitive skills assumed by both him and Kelly to be the basis of language acquisition.)

And what Fisher and I independently realize is that the deliberative semantics informing Twombly's mark is posited on something other than optical twittering and, rather, 'is factured exactly,' to quote him on this.

Even so, cognitive science is an instrumentality too restrictive for Allen Fisher's poetics, which refers to and samples thematic predictive functions from ecology to quantum mechanics, and derives much of its poetic matter from these realities as a language of thought. Or rather, as languages of thought, which, superposed, animate each other in the process, or as he says, 'Collage can be defined as more than one plane of reality presented in one plane of reality, a kind of cubist enterprise ... a range of realities that overlap, sometimes blur into each other, sometimes erase one over the other, sometimes crowd-out the previous instant...' Admirable is his incessant investigation of blur, erasure, crowd-out and other unkempt structures not found in handbooks devoted to literary form.

Matt Hart

Wrong'un: A Pre-event Response to *PhillyTalks* 19

1. A problem.

Consciously, in a rush of reference and aspiration, Karen Mac Cormack and Allen Fisher's exchange raises one of those hardy perennials of aesthetic debate. It's a problem so persistent that we can easily lose touch with its many names. Call it, using Mallarmé's title, the 'demon of analogy.' Or resort to a more conventional rhyme and talk about the 'problem of homology.' At what point does the relationship between two putatively separate fields of knowledge escape metaphor? When is such a relationship not reductive? Consider what weight to put on the words 'as if' in the following phrases from Karen Mac Cormack:

> To write a work structured not as an architectural blueprint but as if exploring an architectural surround (known or unknown?) length of a line or sentence concurrent with number of steps toward a wall, punctuation as door or window perhaps ... to write as one would explore a city, so a map would produce numerous routes of numerous lines of a poem... (from *Implexures*, quoted in 'Mac Cormack to Fisher #1')

Here's that question again, described by Fisher as a problem of disciplinarity that, in his terms, defines the horizon of aesthetics itself:

> One of the understandings from what we've been exchanging is that specialist practice is secondary to aesthetic necessity, and that any specialist practice needs interaction ... with another practice and more. Of course, once we grab aesthetics as a requirement, but not a precedent nor a simple outcome for active consciousness, the momenergy, subsequent on the impertinent, imperfect fit, becomes the wonderful...
> ('Fisher to Mac Cormack #7')

The implication here is that 'specialist practice' not only 'needs interaction ... with another practice and more' but that such interactions define 'aesthetic necessity.'

2. Parallel lines; or, How did we get here, so fast?

Deformation occurs when parallel lines in a body remain parallel, but are relatively displaced in a direction parallel to themselves. Contact usually includes a tendency to slide over each other. (Fisher, from *Sojourns*, quoted in 'Mac Cormack to Fisher #2')

Could parallel lines, here, stand for disciplinary 'fields' – those fantastically discrete areas of enquiry, all going in the universal direction of truth, but never or rarely touching? Reading these poets, we learn quickly to avoid the fictions of parallelism, learn to see and examine the deformation of the singular. Here's the opening to the third stanza of Fisher's 'Winging Step':

> Tendency to perceive connected regions
> uniform image properties
> different from the neutron trap
> luminance, colour, texture,
> motion and disparity
> stops responses
> adapts, but retinal blood not
> perceived sees what she expects
> experience on the basis of edge information
> lost focus, reception dependence
> shape largely invariant over similarity transformations
> underlie internal representation
> conscious perception of texture segregation
> requires attention
> suggests expectation
> as an important component of inattention's blindness.

We can read these lines as medical description and diagnosis. There might be a patient here ('but retinal blood not / perceived sees what she expects'), deep in the language that signals a future without 'edge information,' 'texture segregations' – a future newly dependent on 'internal representation.' Or blindness might be metaphor, not referent. Fisher writes, after all, of 'inattention's blindness.' Blindness, then, is a property of 'inattention' and 'expectation.' The patient, losing her sight, has a 'tendency to perceive connected regions,' to join the dots and fill-in those spaces where sensory expectation is thwarted by sensory degradation. But the patient is not a person, or not singularly so. She is rather a mobile epistemological barometer: a weather-vane for a way of seeing the world, not seeing the world.

This practice has its problems, not least of them the seeming necessity of polymathia, which looms as large in this exchange as it does, for instance, in the biblioholia of a modernist like Hugh MacDiarmid. The poets' exchange suggests that 'interaction' entails the deformation of mastery, rather than the mastery of multiple forms (Baker).

Unanswered questions and malformed connections are inevitable: Just as there is no universality of language there's no 'universality' of architecture, i.e. 'architecture' should not be construed as a blanket term anymore than 'poetry' is some singular, neutral 'form' ... how this does or doesn't work re: quantum mechanics I don't know-thoughts on this? ('Mac Cormack to Fisher #7')

I'm also full of questions. Indeed, quantum mechanics seems most relevant to this argument precisely because it admits the necessity of uncertainty. Biology, memory and pattern are other poetic analogues, and not for some synaesthetic 'correspondence' – as Baudelaire has it in his famous poem of that name – but because (as we learn in Fisher's second letter) they lead us to appreciate the necessity of error: 'pattern is an overlay on disparate elements / how many // desperation's continual distribution of complexities / singular and present' (Mac Cormack, from *Straw Cupid*, quoted in 'Mac Cormack to Fisher #2').

3. Just be wrong.

I want to end by emphasizing error. I began with ways of talking about a problem of metaphor or homology: When one writes a poem that employs the language of chaotic physics (e.g., Fisher's *Brixton Fractals*[1]), how does one avoid identifying poetry with physics, telling us little about either? It seems we must go in the direction of wrongness, a *via mismatchia*, as in this comment from Fisher:

This sounds eclectic, but that's simply an illusion. The architecture of the micro-cellular spacetime, the impossibility of personal, human

---

[1] [Collected in Fisher's *Gravity* (2004).]

perception of part of the activity and the reliance therefore on prediction, expectation, confidence and the reliance, always unnamed and hardly ever signalled, of mistake. ('Fisher to Mac Cormack #1')

As I understand it, 'mistake' is central to the vision of poetry outlined in this exchange: the brilliant but erroneous analogies through which one makes a path in the intellectual forest (a stanza is not a room, after all). The grand mistake is the monomania of "crowd-out" – of hacking-away, not hacking-through, those nuggets of difference and confusion that define aesthetic objects.[2] The theoretical road for this sort of journey might be found, these poets argue, in analyses like Deleuze and Guattari's distinction between a 'map' and a 'tracing.'

But there's one more mistake at issue. And Mac Cormack's poetry describes it quite brilliantly. Here's the opening to 'At Issue III,' a poem you can find in full via the Electronic Poetry Center:

> Putting shape into getting without perfect in a culture that doesn't think, pumps up, the two traits go at the face of rate themselves, cropped by impasse, express your monochromatics from within, discover it blushes, reduce the signs to surface, sharing space in a new high-tech fabric, the pale face extra – prevent every day year after year, retreat returns by filling out advance notice, since seeing is oxygen more supple, sways, just take graceful, tilt feature-controls are big, stable rattles accept different speeds sing, sprawl-moguls seized a story, raking in celebrity,heat-activated genre, hands full turned, loops removable gusseted, postpone television, revelations, introspection, an assemblage not incidentally imposed, crossover success, so many boxes yet smashes toward toward...

Here's a poem that takes on the central problematic of what Fisher calls 'a syntactic or paratactic continuity that provides a ground for demonstration of sudden change' ('Fisher to Mac Cormack #5'). Despite the absence of periods, the poem's clauses are paratactic. Though 'putting shape' and 'pumps up' are both redolent of the gym,

---

[2] "Singularity in the sense proposed here involves an over centralised view of artistic production. This overcentralised view, derived from the crowd-out of semiotic analysis, can only provide an incomplete analysis of material production. To provide a fuller analysis of practice it is necessary to include pragmatic description with semiotic analysis." (from Fisher's 'The Crowd')

any hypotactic relation soon wanes. (It's possible that 'tilt feature-controls are big, stable rattles accept different speeds sing' still plays on the image and argot of work-out machines, but I won't bet on it.) Could *Implexures*, or WADDLE, be a 'crossover success,' will their endless will-to-interact end up mimicking the noisesome eclecticism of the 'sprawl-mogul'? The answer suggested by [the Fisher / Mac Cormack correspondence] is a cautious 'no,' so long as we keep our eye on error. So long as we write from the house of mistake.

*

3) Post-event Response
Rob Holloway

First to register the specific importance of Karen and Allen's correspondence, whose areas of attention Allen summarises at one point: –

> the underlying discussion is epistemological and thus about truth and freedom as well as knowledge, about will and natural expectations, as well as information and structure and how structure provides (facilitates?) the necessary pathways as well as the auto-habits, the chreods … for representation ('Fisher to Mac Cormack #5')

This highlighted to demonstrate the ambitious scale ultimately intended by both writers for their work, one that the collaborative research opportunity provided by the *PhillyTalks* correspondence allowed them to constructively enact.

I stress the conditions of the collaborative process here because they map closely what both writers would hope to create as the conditions for response of their readers: to suddenly be alert within new patterns of connectedness / transformation. In Karen's work, the potential for this recently through her 'perplexing' of corrupted discourse in e.g. *At Issue* and *Vanity Release* or, in *Implexures*, offering textual representation of inventive memory at work. In Allen's, due to the superimposition of a becoming-interactive array of 'languages of thought' (Welish, 'Pre-event response') previously voided as 'eclectic', that bring forth potentiality through complexity; with all environments intending to catalyse break-out from habitual 'truth'-frames and the knowledges they institute. This their proposed efficacy, their ethics.

The Trap of Ethical Ideology

Ethics as the point where ideology disappears, thus making the difficult realisation that ethical ideology is a contradiction in terms despite the fact that its promoters use it as the means for generating awareness and activity regarding the protection of fundamental human rights. Unsurprisingly, seeing those rights eroded, they figure the human as a victim, in 'misery'. This ideology enhanced at present by the increasing appearance on the world screen of the 'refugee'. We're asked to bandage the wound.

    A present form of freedom is that, while enacting our complicity, we can keep thinking. In relation to this focus, help perhaps from Agamben in *Homo Sacer* (1995) who sees the 'refugee' as limit of the 'citizen', and thus an unmasking of the alibi of 'nation' maintained by sovereign powers beneath which they seek to exert increased control over the 'common individual'. And sure enough, we're seeing increasingly clumsy attempts by countries to hide or deny refugees, specifically therefore to maintain 'nation'-status. As suggested therefore, such action an attempted masking of their own already institutionalised intent: to reduce and so control the human at the level of raw material (this being Foucault's now familiar analysis under his term 'biopolitics', rightly raised by Steve McCaffrey during the *PhillyTalks* 19 discussion to identify what Ron Silliman was blocking, along with ontology, by his prioritisation of the 'geopolitical'). The recognisable, ongoing dynamic: roll-over of politics to trade liberalisation and its institutions, legitimising global Capital to the extent that it is not held responsible for the chaos it creates, combined with recovery of sovereign power through permanent militarism. A dynamic that is restricting increasing numbers to that state of alienated raw material ('…capital's main street the Banker / sharpens his steel it skins…').

    Keeping folding in the contexts: in genetics, the Human Genome Project as the sudden appearance of expansive means to work directly on the human as raw material. How do I act in a society in which all the options that exist to act ethically I feel are compromised? Isn't thinking like that about ethics merely reactionary ethical thinking? Does me thinking *that* leave me in a Derridean transcendental aporia, 'in uncertain hope of annihilation' – hang on, that sounds ridiculous – at least when Elvis was there he made it sound good: – 'I'm caught in a trap / I can't go on…' 'put an end to it'

WADDLE: From Habit to Habitus – A Simulated Life

aesthetics as redolent of ethics ('Fisher to Mac Cormack #2')

At which time, in search of something to grab hold of, pull myself back up onto my feet with, I reach proprioceptively: –

> a movement that allows you to situate yourself through discriminating performance or narration as part of a process of aesthetic participation (opening of Fisher's summary of Olsonian proprioception – 'Notes…')

for WADDLE (and with acute awareness that by engaging in exegesis, I risk unethically blocking the poem with a belated tracing). Here's Fisher again to open the lock-up, writing of the lack in 'modern', and 'subsequent discourses' of: –

> an understanding of the heightened performance often made possible by the text that has its grounding in a rich complexity of resource, promotes a projective performance in simulation of the self – even a multiple self – delivered as larger than simple, at once and from a text that is itself a record of performance in itself. (Fisher, ibid)

WADDLE I propose as exemplary of such a text, and thus one whose performative action undertaken rhetorically on the aesthetic plane must be fully attended to, and not subsumed by 'semiotic analysis', which too quickly smothers the urgent task such action promotes: that of re-thinking what we've come to accept as our understanding (this following Fisher on Twombly in 'The Crowd'). More specifically, I would assert the importance of such an approach to this particular poem, given the acute awareness of its relationship to future readers that it manifests, and which is of a piece with its explorative performance of concerns regarding freedom and misery. It seeks to energise thinking ethics by using an aesthetic of collage that relates it distantly, but not irrelevantly, with medieval florilegia (a compositional aid and promptbook for memory made from choice extracts from past literature) and by introducing a compositional *ductus* which organises an array of rhetorical ornament "arousing emotions of fear or delight, anger, wonder and awe" by which the inventive memory practice of *meditatio* is catalysed. As such, the poem performs its active meditation on freedom in a way that maximally facilitates* its performance by others. As Carruthers says: –

> The presence of an audience would appear to be crucial to the making of the ethical action. This simply reminds us that a rhetorical conception of ethics requires its social and public nature to be stressed. (*Book of Memory*)

Which leads me, but without wanting to shove, that perhaps Fisher's concerns when writing WADDLE were shaped in some part by his awareness that it would be brought forth during his becoming-public collaboration / correspondence with Mac Cormack.

Carruthers' work, amongst others, has encouraged Fisher's thoughts on reception and facture to such an extent that they have recently been achieving their own shifting frame in his crowd-out theory, aspects of which hold out the potential for aesthetic action to become realised in processes of thinking's re-orientation, whose transformations become the reader's own. Carruthers describes how: –

> ...communal forgetting was also mastered by the Christians – not through some variety of amnesia, but by applying carefully the mnemotechnical principles of blocking one pattern of memories by another, through crowding or overlay, and by intentional mnemonic replacement ... Where two or more competing patterns exist on one site ... only one will be seen: the others, though they may remain potentially visible, will be blocked out or absorbed by the overlay... (*The Craft of Thought*, 54, 57)

This way indoctrination lies, but what if the overlaying is multiple to the extent that the action of overlaying is what becomes most prominent, is what the poem's each next frame from word up does, with no frame ever becoming fully blocked out? The development of *intentio* in medieval meditation Carruthers informs, achieved by rhetorical *ductus*, 'a way of meditation ... initiated, orientated and marked out by the schemes and tropes of Scripture', figured as 'a flow and movement' through a series of 'habituations' and 'common places' which gave 'choice for an audience about how to "walk" among them' (Carruthers 116-7) ... Carruthers's work is one that extends usefully Fisher's earlier researches in this area therefore: see, for example, his *The Topological Shovel* where he's linking 'consistent/inventive memory' (sourced initially from Minkowski's *Lived Time*, 1970) to the 'word-page dynamic'.

To focus back on WADDLE with this in mind, and to develop the sense of its design decisions being shaped by an ethically-enhanced desire for participatory engagement, I register the offering of a clearly identifiable *ductus* that is shot through all levels of the poem's multiplex field, and which can be distortingly seen at the whole-poem level as a movement from seizure to 'damage' to 'recovery' (the latter phrases from Fisher's discussion of 'crowd-out' during the *PhillyTalks* 19 event). This path, 'underlying thought', perhaps conceivable also as, to draw on another area of Fisher's thinking, a kind of fully positivised, supportive Waddingtonian 'chreod': a cord, or spinal chord (for Olson, the body's interior 'mt range' – (cited by Fisher in 'Notes...'), and also, reminding me of the horizontal line that runs with occasional breaks through the centre of Cornelius Cardew's huge visual score 'Treatise' – a commonplace for Fisher – with its myriad curves, circles, lines etc coming off it on either side marking the paths of aesthetic invention for the improvising musician, and we heard too Fisher's description during the *PhillyTalks* event of his own process as 'improvisation out of a structure').

A ground which feeds and supports the challenging *intentio / ambition* of WADDLE: to be (reaching back again) a 'source of ideas/ distribution of ideas/ to and fro the general flow' (Fisher, *Place* I) through the undertaking, in the formal acts of a guided (by crowd-out's *ductus*: 'damage' to 'recovery'), self-interrupting, collaged narrative, of a striving / energised recovery of the raw material of our thinking being's familiar, damaged modalities of freedom and misery, so that a means, a manner, a way to return to who we 'common individual(s)' are, and thus may multiply become, is shown 'to others'. Recalling again *The Secret of the Golden Flower*, which opens: – 'Master Lu-tsu said That which exists through itself is called the Way (Tao)', and describes the means of enacting the backward-flowing method of thought through which energy is conserved that it may engender further energy; so that the individual may 'live mingling with the world and yet in harmony with the light'. And de Beauvoir's criteria for ethical action: – 'We must try, through our living projects, to turn to our own account that freedom which was undertaken in the past and to integrate it into the present world' (*Ethics of Ambiguity*). This the demand the poem performs and offers, in all its difficulty potential, to the reader to realise for themselves.

(cut...)

To specify, and so show some of the ways in which the performative transformations I've been alluding to may themselves be enacted. The re-orientation being undertaken through WADDLE's 'way of meditation', I figure as the rescuing of 'immanence: a life' (I am calling on Deleuze's last short piece *Pure Immanence* [2001])* from that legitimised tropism of the Western mind: transcendence. Figured alternatively, I think of the poem becoming a transparent showing of a passageway (*ek-stasis*) from ontology to ethics, or rather, the opening of a reverberating passageway between the two; a tour de force against capitalism's transcendent agency theft…

Focusing closer, into the gap between stanzas one and two, the ongoing re-orientation process as yet invisible, but active. The performance of a damage-critique that, as two starts, crashes the transcendental subject down to earth after its crowded-out 'flight'-response ('a state of uplift / a new freedom…' – a limit state) to the perceptual seizure that so strikingly occurs in the opening stanza. Elsewhere, Fisher's description of this response as that 'path beyond the hut into a self-interested take-off, flight beyond syntax from joy characterised as an escape from suffering' ('Crowd-Out'). At this early stage, with the subject still framed within an 'I', a sense of loss is apparently engendered as it falls into the counter-trap of its own alienated interiority, Dante's 'dark wood' ('Fisher to Mac Cormack #2').

(magnifying further…)

I'll now focus on a particular transformation that maps the emergence of a self-organising aesthetic process within the poem. This occurs through the transition of 'loose metal bushes burn' to 'shell metal mossed wrath' to 'hector lime hash'. To link these is made deliberately easy through repetition and a shifting syntactic disruptiveness that works to effectively block the ongoing alienation-narrative. What they occur however does not become clear until the called-for etymological act at the final stage is undertaken. The earlier shifting four-word patterns now condensed into a three-word asyntactical charge, 'hector lime hash', where syntactic breakage is this time given an even more explicitly representative function: the bringing forth *as encoded* of an alternative aesthetic *intentio* being *imprinted* into the linguistic material of the poem itself (this the place and means of facture: between the words, a *ductus* resisting all 'flight beyond syntax' … ethics nearing the poem-surface … close enough to smell). My uncovering of an encoded representation of an ethical-aesthetic process prompts a rereading of the previous transforming chain and a growing awareness of a shift from external sensory experience to internal organisation of that experience. Key encouragement to re-focus is given by the collage mode of facture which maintains a simultaneity of modes of engagement which my returning / re-reading now works to uncover. A constant rewarding as previously masked layers now come swarming, forming new patterns of thought (not Bataille's general economy of waste/loss here, but not a return to a restrictive economy either; the 'reward' not a static meaning-value to be hoarded but more like an ongoing affirming investment into a 'general flow' of thinking-renewal whose relevance any reader's adding to). An enlivening complexity ensuing: the poem being experienced as what it's been waiting as: a liveable 3-D thinking-environment: '…a map that is always detachable, connectible, reversible, modifiable, and has multiple entry-ways and exits and its own lines of flight' (Deleuze & Guattari, *A Thousand Plateaus*)…

The pay-off?: – when the next phrase in the transformation occurs, I register it as also involving my own readerly experience. I am speeded up into this by my own re-reading of Benjamin's discussion through Freud, Valéry and Baudelaire in 'On Some Motifs in Baudelaire' of consciousness as shock defence, so that now when I read 'shell metal mossed wrath', I feel that my simultaneous act of re-collecting the earlier phrase is itself marked in that emergence of a protecting emerging thinking (shell metal…) which leads to the now sensed 'wrath', both of which establish the shock experience as distant; that which has been gone through.

I now also note more acutely the increasing syntactic disjunctiveness across the three 'phrases' as a clarifying means. The poem's surface as: I'm here thinking, making my re-reading of the sudden naming of the poem's ongoing process into a flash 'pink' of accumulating aesthetic affirmation: 'vivify flight indoctrination / through hector lime hash robbery's guise'. This time round I choose to overlay Carruthers here for further illumination: –

...Greek *charakter* means literally 'the mark engraved or stamped' on a coin or seal; by transference the word came to mean 'distinctive mark' and hence the distinctive quality of a person or thing....The Greek concept of *hexis* [habitual necessity], crucial to an understanding of moral behaviour is a predisposition that 'stamps' or 'forms' the embodied soul towards behaving in certain ways towards others... (*The Book of Memory*, emphasis mine)

I imagine a kind of self-encoding of the aesthetic action ... placing it in my memory by exploiting my heightened awareness of the increasingly uncluttered space made available by the asyntactical word-separation (a kind of made Coolidge-space), enhanced by the upcoming white space breaking the stanza here, and furthered also by my called-for etymological reading act that offers a shift into my own spacetime as I move from the transforming mobile poem collage to the stillness of the dictionary.

The etymological act not a fanfared one-step glory-stop unveiling of Author Name, but, in its uncovering of a process of material transformation, becoming my performance of a different act of material transformation which situates me as active amidst the poem's concerns off which I now improvise my own material thinking-chains (*catena*, Carruthers): a becoming 'copiousness' (*The Craft of Thought*) at the level of amplified thinkings' behaviour which this time goes: ...'word/ page dynamic' now the medium of exchange ... of thinkings' energy... through three words ... through coin/silver mark, barcode, to mark of aesthetic facture ... turning displaced power of currency's metaphysics, through aesthetic action, back into its materials' complexity now realigned for inventive thought facture ... Prynne's 'Note on Metal' (1968): 'it's how the power of displacement side-slipped into some entirely other interest which is difficult, not a simple decision that any one movement is towards ruin' (and it's precisely irrelevant whether Fisher's repetition of 'metal' in the poem is in part a gesture towards the Prynne text or not – working independently, I combine the word with the above Carruthers quotation to lead me to re-reading the Prynne and enhancing my sense of the poem's crowding out of Capital's currency by a currency / becoming affirmed pertinence of aesthetic action) ... so, no take-off ... back again: encoding ... sonic hedgehog (Shh gene) directing embryonic patterning (Fisher, note 8, *Ring Shout*) ... life's material emergence ... fresh thought bomb ... initialising multiplying subjectivities under "robbery's guise" ... stealing back free will, in under Banker's radar...

Holding fast as an openness to difficulty – I'm thinking again about how those three words when etymologised simultaneously mark the potential failure of process – factoring up: a failure that is apparent at any size of focus-frame I bring to the poem and which, as noted, is itself importantly re-orientated towards the end of the poem to release 'the reader'. This Fisher's ethical complexity, that risks the insistent re-engagement with those tendencies to stasis which most threatens the re-orientating process; positing this as the process' own engine of re-orientation ... In this, the method offered is that called for by Deleuze and Guattari: *'the tracings should always be put back on the map'* (Introduction to *A Thousand Plateaus*) where 'the tracings' in WADDLE include the stultifying redundancies of transcendence, of History as Fate, the power of Capital, and 'the map' being the poem's rhizomatic performance of those modes' complexing. Importantly, this is not, to address a Levinasian discourse, a return to the Same as the same, but rather one that returns to the 'Same' as mask to be lifted to expose its alterity (for Fisher, read 'complexity' here – a more material engagement?). As such, an ethical-aesthetic process which contrasts with the dominant ethical mode in Levinasian thought which takes the form of a traversal towards the radical alterity of the Other. A trajectory that WADDLE's performance would seemingly figure as a difficult continuance of 'flight indoctrination'. Interestingly enough, as Steve McCaffery in an Appendix to his chapter, 'The Scandal of Sincerity: Towards a Levinasian Poetics' (*Prior to Meaning*, 2001) has with welcome openness shown, Levinas actually does countenance this 'movement out of sameness into alterity' in his exegesis of the Talmud in *Nine Talmudic Readings* (1994), but as McCaffery then states, 'Such exegesis and narrative properly situate not on the ethical plane of Levinas's discourse but on the juridicial plane – in the active, disputative sphere of social interaction.' And here the radical difference with Fisher's ethical poetics becomes clear, for it is exactly in that 'active disputative sphere of social interaction' that Fisher is still situating his 'ethics as redolent of aesthetics'. An enduring promotion of an efficacious aesthetic function that saves ethics from ideology while catalyzing re-orientation of our commonplaces. A functionality that 'must be constantly won" (de Beauvoir, 'Fisher to Mac Cormack #2') by the difficult task of retaining a full engagement with exactly those habits that would suffocate it. The implication being that such necessary action can only be effectively performed within an aesthetic field due to that field's potential to simultaneously enact radical re-articulations and site the mode of such action in any engaged reader as a becoming singularity in a growing, radicalised community.

I've chosen a discrete section of a particular pathway to re-perform from among multiple (which, as one might now expect, is worked through increasingly higher-ratio transformations as the poem continues, demanding at each stage a vitalising re-thinking of all aspects of that pathway), as it eventually intersects one of the uses Fisher has for the kind of 'eclectic' discourses (in this case genomics) his work is often most easily recognised by. But, as Fisher suggests in the correspondence, such 'eclecticism' is an 'illusion' created, WADDLE adds, by the pointedly familiar Blakean 'snares of Reason, absoluteness and knowledge' our culture still remains trapped within. On this, I wanted finally to open out Nate Dorward's otherwise helpful review of some of Fisher's latest work in *The Gig* 9 ('The Harmony of Mutually Divergent Things', September 2001), in which he conjectures that Fisher's use of 'specialist knowledges' might "imply a kind of propositional or referential poetics which could be considered at odds with textual skews and shifts." Clearly, to de-link the knowledges from specific aesthetic modalities, factured for them by Fisher's and other readers' attention, is to block the aesthetic function that the poems institute. Rather, the specific uptake of certain information at particular moments in the poetry's projective performance creates shifts through blockage (at times, Fisher incorporates difficult material as simulations of impenetrability to instill a limit-status of numbness the poetic process and the attention it calls for is then activated against – look at those two horrific, directly-derived website (i.e. mainstream) downloads in 'Watusi' ... and then look again, and aren't they precise descriptions of the poem's aesthetic process that is therefore re-orientating genomics motivations?) and diffusion. These shifts hold up the knowledges that that information constitutes for critique and reorientation along performative parameters of liberatory action within the inventive sphere of the poem / reader's thinking.

I've chosen to show some of WADDLE's ground, and a glimpse of the intricately condensed, eidetic transformations of becoming subjectivities this helps Allen and other readers to perform, but hopefully no more. Clearly Karen's exploration of an 'ethics of memory' in the life-showing that is *Implexures* has informed my own thinking here, and I trust that my variable, Carruthers-led, focus on WADDLE, arising as it did during the correspondence, is also seen as registering of the energies she helped to generate at the time. I'd hope also that my rather intense focus on WADDLE has still managed to raise avenues for discussion that a more wide-ranging response to the *Philly Talks* 19 correspondence / event would have signposted more directly.

(1 February, 2002)

Contributors

Clive Bush is Emeritus Professor of American Literature at King's College, London, and former Head of the Department of English. His publications include *Out of Dissent: A Study of Five Contemporary British Poets* (Talus Editions, 1997) and the accompanying anthology, *World of New Measure: An Anthology of Five Contemporary British Poets* (Talus Editions, 1997). He has also published a number of books of poetry, including *Pictures after Poussin* (Spanner, 2003), *Lingerings of the Large Day* (Five Seasons Press, 2014) and *Arioso* (Five Seasons Press, 2019), all with drawings or paintings by Allen Fisher.

cris cheek is a multimodal poet, performance writer and professor at Miami University, Oxford, Ohio. His music and sound collaborations include *Slant* (1994) and *skin upon skin* (1996). Between 1999 and 2007, in collaboration with Kirsten Lavers, he produced a body of performance writing under the heading *Things Not Worth Keeping*. His poetry publications include *Songs from Navigation* (Reality Street, 1998), *part: short life housing* (The Gig, 2009) and *Pickles & Jams* (BlazeVOX, 2017).

Robert Hampson was Professor of Modern Literature at Royal Holloway, University of London, and is now a Research Fellow in the Institute for English Studies, University of London, where he co-organises the Contemporary Innovative Poetry Research Seminar (with Amy Evans Bauer). His publications include *New British poetries: The Scope of the Possible* (Manchester University Press, 1993), with Peter Barry; *Frank O'Hara Now* (Liverpool University Press, 2010) with Will Montgomery; and *Clasp: late modernist poetry in London in the 1970s* (Shearsman, 2016) with Ken Edwards. His own poetry publications include *Seaport* (Shearsman, 2008), *an explanation of colours* (Veer, 2010), and *re-worked disasters* (kfs, 2012), which was long-listed for the Forward Prize.

Mike Hart is the author of *Who's Who Vivid* (Slope Editions, 2006), *Wolf Face* (H_NGM_N BKS, 2006), *Light-Headed* (BlazeVOX, 2011), *Sermons & Lectures, Both Blank & Relentless* (Typecast Publishing, 2012), and *Debacle Debacle* (H_NGM_N BKS, 2013). He teaches at the Art Academy of Cincinnati.

Calum Hazell completed the MA in Creative Writing (Poetic Practice) and is now a research student in the Department of Media Arts at Royal Holloway, University of London. His poetry publications include *Tends* (Veer, 2017) and *Wung Chan e: The Preparations 1-7* (Red Ceilings Press, 2019).

Steven Hitchins completed a PhD on contemporary poetry at Aberystwyth University. He currently teaches Creative Writing and English at Coleg y Cymoedd. Through a series of publications – *Bitch Dust* (Hafan Books, 2012), *The White City* (Aquifer, 2015) and *Ilan (*Stranger Press, 2018), he has been conducting a non-linear mapping of the South Wales coalfield.

Rob Holloway is a London-based writer and teacher. His publications include *American Heroines* (Writers Forum, 1999) and *Permit* (Subpress, 2009) as well as various showings of his work in progress, *Flesh Rays*. He also hosted the radio show 'Up for Air' on Resonance 104.4FM.

Pierre Joris is a Luxembourg-American poet, translator, anthologist and essayist. In collaboration with Jerome Rothenberg, he has co-edited a number of volumes including *The Collected Writings of Kurt Schwitters*, the selected poems of Pablo Picasso, and the two-volume anthology, *Poems for the Millennium* (University of California Press, 1995, 1998). He has also published translations of Tristan Tzara, Rilke, Habib Tengour, Maurice Blanchot, Edmond Jabès and Paul Celan – as well as translations of numerous English-language poets into French. His essays have been collected as *A Nomad Poetics* (Wesleyan University Press, 2003) and *Justifying the Margins: Essays 1990-2006* (Salt, 2009).

Karen Mac Cormack is a Buffalo-based British-Canadian poet. Her publications include *Straw Cupid* (Nightwood Editions,1987), *Quirks & Quillets* (Chax Press, 1991), *Marine Snow* (ECW Press, 1995), *The Tongue Moves Talk* (Chax Press / West House Books, 1997), *At Issue* (Coach House Books, 2001), *Vanity Release* (Zasterle Press, 2003), and *Implexures* (Chax Press / West House Books, 2008). She also collaborated with Alan Halsey on *Fit to Print* (Coach House Books, 2003). *Tale Light: New & Selected Poems 1984-2009* was published by Book Thug and West House Books in 2010.

Paige Mitchell has taken a keen interest in Allen Fisher's visual art since encountering it in the early 1970s.

Will Montgomery is Reader in English Literature at Royal Holloway. He is the author of *The Poetry of Susan Howe* (Palgrave, 2010) and *The American Short Poem* (Edinburgh University Press, 2020). He co-edited *Frank O'Hara Now* (Liverpool University Press, 2010) with Robert Hampson and *Writing the Field Recording* (Edinburgh University Press, 2018) with Stephen Benson. He has also released several CDs of field recordings, sound art and music.

Redell Olsen is Professor of Poetry and Poetics at Royal Holloway, University of London, where she founded the MA in Poetic Practice. From 2006 to 2010, she was the editor of *How2*, the online journal for modernist and contemporary poetry, poetics and criticism by women. Her poetry publications include *Book of the Fur* (rempress, 2000), *Secure Portable Space* (Reality Street, 2004), *Punk Faun: a bar rock pastel* (subpress, 2012). She works with film and performance – and in the emerging critical space between academic and creative practice. Her film and performance projects include 'Newe Booke of Copies' (2009), 'Bucolic Picnic (or *Toile de Jouy Camouflage*' (2009), 'The Lost Swimming Pool' (2010). The texts were published as *Film Poems* (Les Figues, 2014). Her film, 'Now Circa (1918)' was shortlisted for the AHRC Research in Film award (2018). She was Judith E. Wilson Lecturer in Poetry at the University of Cambridge (2013-14).

Will Rowe was the Anniversary Professor in Poetics in the Department of Iberian and Latin American Studies at Birkbeck, University of London, and is now Emeritus Professor of Poetics there. He is an expert on poetry and poetics in Latin America, USA and Britain and is the author of numerous books on Latin American literature and culture, including a monograph on Cesar Vallejo (2010). He has carried out ethnographic research on Peruvian song and shamanic discourse. His *Collected Poems* was published by Veer in 2016.

Robert Sheppard was Professor of Poetry and Poetics at Edge Hill University, Liverpool. He is the author of several critical books including *The Poetry of Saying: British Poetry and its Discontents* (Liverpool University Press, 2005), *Iain Sinclair* (Northcote House, 2007), *When Bad Times Made for Good Poetry* (Shearsman, 2011) and *The Meaning of Form in Contemporary Innovative Poetry* (Palgrave, 2016). He edited *News for the Ear: Homage to Roy Fisher* and *The Salt Companion to Lee Harwood*. He has published numerous books and pamphlets of poetry: his long-running poetry project *Complete Twentieth Century Blues* was published by Salt in 2008; more recent work includes the sonnet sequence *Warrant Error* (Shearsman, 2009) and *A Translated Man* (Shearsman, 2013). Shearsman also published *The Robert Sheppard Companion*, edited by James Byrne and Christopher Madden in 2019.

Scott Thurston is Reader in English and Creative Writing at the University of Salford. He co-edits the *Journal of British and Irish Innovative Poetry* and was one of the organisers of the Other Room poetry reading series in Manchester. His publications include *Talking Poetics: Dialogues in Innovative Poetry* (Shearsman, 2011), critical essays on contemporary innovative poetry by women, and a number of volumes of poetry, the most recent of which are *Reverses Heart's Reassembly* (Veer, 2011), *Figure Detached Figure Impermanent* (Oystercatcher, 2014) and *Poems for the Dance* (Aquifer, 2017).

Marjorie Welish is a poet, artist and critic. Her poetry publications include *The Windows Flew Open* (Burning Deck Press, 1991), *Casting Sequences* (University of Georgia Press, 1993), and *The Annotated "Here" and Selected Poems* (2000), *Word Group* (2004), *Isle of the Signatories* (2008) and *In the Futurity Lounge / Asylum for Indeterminacy* (2012) – all from Coffee House Press. A collection of essays on her work and a selection of her writing and painting was published as *Of the Diagram: The Work of Marjorie Welish* (Slought Foundation, 2003). She has written widely on contemporary art. A collection of her essays was published as *Signifying Art: Essays on Art After 1960* (Cambridge University Press, 1999). She was the Judith E. Wilson Visiting Poetry Fellow at Cambridge University in 2005.

Shamoon Zamir is Associate Professor of Literature and Visual Studies at NYU Abu Dhabi and Director of Akkasah Center for Photography at NYUAD. His publications include *Dark Voices: W.E.B. Dubois and American Thought* (University of Chicago Press, 1995); *The Photobook: From Talbot to Ruscha* *and Beyond* (I.B. Tauris, 2012) with Patrizia di Bello and Colette Wilson; *The Gift of the Face: Portraiture and Time in Edward S. Curtis's 'The North American Indian'* (University of North Carolina Press, 2014); and *The Family of Man Revisited: Photography in a Global Age* (I.B. Tauris, 2018) with Anke Reitz and Gerd Hurm. He also co-edited *The Unruly Garden: Robert Duncan and Eric Mottram, Letters and Essays* (Peter Lang, 2007) with Amy Evans.

Allen Fisher
Bibliography 1969-2016

The bibliography covers the main single-author publications 1969-2016 (Group publications and single-page broadsheets have been excluded.)

Imperfect Fit: Aesthetic Function, Facture, and Perception in Art and Writing since 1950, Tuscaloosa, AL: University of Alabama Press, 2016.
Gravity as a consequence of shape, Hastings: Reality Street, 2016.
Fall air Sound, Hereford: Apple Store Gallery, 2015.
TIP REGARD, Hereford: Spanner, 2014.
SPUTTOR, London: Veer Books, 2014.
drawn rooms, Pontypridd: The Literary Pocket Book, 2013.
The Marvels of Lambeth. Interviews & Statements, edited by Andrew Duncan, Bristol: Shearsman Books, 2013.
PROPOSALS, Hereford: Spanner, 2010.
Birds, Hunstanton: Oystercatcher Press, 2009.
LEANS, Cambridge: Salt Publishing, Cambridge, 2007, 2nd edition 2013.
Confidence in lack, Sutton: Writers Forum, 2007.
Quietly Random, Manchester: Matchbox, 2007.
singularity stereo, London and Brighton: Barque Press, 2006.
PLACE, collected books, Hastings: Reality Street, 2005, 2nd edition 2016.
Stroll and Strut Step, Hereford: Spanner, 2004.
ENTANGLEMENT, Willowdale, ONT: The Gig, 2004,
GRAVITY, West Perth, Australia and Cambridge, UK: Salt Publishing, 2004,
   Gravity shapes, audio-cd 02, London: STEM, 2004.
Sway Back, London: Tolling Elves, 2004.
Vole Volespin, video-tape, Hereford: Root & Branch, 2003.
Traps or Tools & Damage, University of Surrey Roehampton, 2003.
VOLESPIN, Hereford: Spanner, 2002.
WATUSI, Hereford: Spanner, 2001.
Sojourns, Bray, Ireland: Wild Honey Press, 2000.
Woodpecker, Hereford: Spanner, 2000.
Winging Step, Hereford: Spanner, 2000.
Ring Shout, Cambridge: Equipage, 2000.
Topological Shovel, Willowdale, ONT: The Gig, 1999.
Emergent Manner, Hereford: Spanner, 1999.
PULLING UP/QUASI QUEEN, Hereford: Spanner 1996.
Philly Dog, Hereford: Spanner, 1995.
FIZZ, Hereford: Spanner, 1993.
Now's the time, London: Form Books, 1995.
FISH JET, Southampton: Torque Press, 1997.
DISPOSSESSION AND CURE, poems 1988-1991, London: Reality Street.

HORSE AND HUBBLE, Sutton: RWC, 1992
SCRAM, or the transformation of the concept of cities, selected poems 1971-1982, Peterborough: Spectacular Diseases, 1994.
CONVALESCENCE, London: Wiwaxia, 1992.
AMNESIC INSTANT, Hereford: Spanner, 1989.
CIVIC CRIME, Lowestoft: Sound and Language, 1995.
BREADBOARD, Hereford: Spanner, 1994.
BUZZARDS AND BEES, London: Spanner, 1986.
BRIXTON FRACTALS, London: Aloes Books, 1985 and Vancouver: Tsunami, 1999.
Necessary Business, London: Spanner, 1985.
BOOGIE BREAK, Southampton: Torque Editions, 1985.
BENDING WINDOWS, London: Spanner, 1983.
BANDA, London: Spanner jointly with Open Field, 1983.
AFRICAN BOOG *and miscellaneous poems,* London: Ta'wil Books, 1983.
STEPPING OUT, Durham: Pig Press, 1989.
Ideas on the culture dreamed of, London: Spanner, 1983 and Pontypridd: The Literary Pocket Book, 2016.
DEFAMILIARISING ....*, London: Spanner, 1982, and London: Veer Books, 2013.
CAREFUL ABSENCE, Derbyshire: Figlet Books, 1982.
Allen Fisher's Stepping out, a film by e.e. vonna-michel, video-tape, Balsam Flex, 1983.
'Thumbnail Lecture' and 'The Mathematics of Rimbaud', San Francisco, 80 Langton Street gallery, 1982
THE ART OF FLIGHT and *BLOOD BONE BRAIN,* audio-cassette tape, London: Typical Characteristics, 1982.
POETRY FOR SCHOOLS, London: Aloes Books, 1980 (issued 1982).
THE ART OF FLIGHT VI-IX, London: Writers' Forum poster, 1982.
BLOOD BONE BRAIN, Documents on nine microfiches in 7 booklets, London: Spanner 1981-2.
UNPOLISHED MIRRORS, London: Spanner serial format 1979-80, 1981. Republished in selected form, London: Reality Studios, 1986.
IMBRICATIONS, Cambridge: Lobby Press, 1981.
EROS : FATHER : PATTERN, Ashford, Kent: Secret Books, 1980.
Hooks, taken out of place 32, Baltimore: pod books, 1980.
INTERNATIONAL FAMINE, audio-cassette tape, London: Combat, 1980.
SOUTH THAMES STUDIOS, London: Spanner, 1980.
INTERMEDIATE SPIRIT RECEIVER, London: Zunne Heft, 1980, with a book of the same title by Ulli McCarthy, authors' names transposed.
Kessingland Studies, London: Spanner, London, 1979.
COMBS, London: Spanner, 1979.
REICH, London: Spanner, 1978.

SSSSPEECH, London: Writers' Forum, 1978.
atherapy studies group docket Q, London: Writers' Forum, 1978.
CHEST BREATH and Car Wash interview, cassette tape, with e.e. vonna-michell, Southend-on-Sea: Typical Characteristics, 1978.
THE APOCALYPTIC SONNETS, with etchings by Robert Clark, Durham: Pig Press, 1978.
BECOMING, Place Book Four and part of five, London: Aloes Books, 1978.
Convergences, in place, of the play, newspaper format, London: Spanner, 1978.
LONDON BLIGHT, Brighton: Tapocketa, 1978.
DOCKING, Bishop's Stortford: Great Works Editions, 1978.
THE PREPARATION, with David Miller, London: X Press, 1977.
doing, Maidstone, Kent: Twisted Wrist, 1977.
FIRE-WORK, including *FIRE-PLACE,* jointly with Pierre Joris' *HEARTH-WORK,* bound as a Z-book, Leeds: Hatch Books, 1977.
STANE, Place Book Three, London: Aloes Books, London, 1977, 2 editions.
‚Der Verlorene' Operation, Maidstone, Kent: Mugshots, 1976.
GRIPPING THE RAIL, Durham: Pig Press, 1976.
THE LEER, Philadelphia and London: Branch Redd Publications, 1976.
PAXTON'S BEACON, (selections from *The Art of Flight*) Todmorden, Lancs.: Arc Publications, 1976.
5 PLAGES 'SHUN! Wales: Prison Clothes Press, 1975.
PROSYNCEL, blueprint, Toronto and New York: Strange Faeces,1975.
long shout to kernewek, London: New London Pride Editions, London, 1975.
taken the days after we had beef curry…, Cullompton, Devon: Beau Geste Press, 1974.
PLACE, BOOK ONE, London: Aloes Books, 1974 and St. Paul, MN: Truck Books, 1976.
FIVE FOR GRAHAMS', London: Aloes Books, 1973.
SICILY, London: Aloes Books, 1973.
CREEK IN THE CEILING BEAM, London: Aloes Books, 1973.
CIRCLES LINES WHEELBARROWS, Germany: International Art Cooperative, 1973.
FFACECE, London: Aloes Books, London, 1972.
Shitwell Bernado, with Dick Miller, London: I.B.Held Books, 1972.
SPACES FOR WINTER SOLSTICE, blueprint, Cullompton, Devon: Beau Geste Press, 1972.
All Horses Have Feathers, with Dick Miller, London: I.B.Held Books, 1971.
My Bijou, with Dick Miller, London: I.B.Held Books, 1971.
Before Ideas, Ideas, London: Edible Magazine, 1971.
Thomas Net's TREE-BIRST, London: Edible Magazine, 1970;
BAVUSKA, London: Big Venus, London, 1969.

Index

abandonment 114, 207-8
Adorno, Theodor 18, 31, 106, 187, 191, 200
aesthetics 44-5, 56, 134-5, 147, 153, 156-9, 218, 236, 247, 261, 272
aesthetic function 101, 117-8, 126, 159-61, 202, 205, 236, 284, 285
Albers, Josef 218, 227
alienation 24, 30, 33, 49, 128, 142, 147, 167, 203, 251, 277, 281
allegory 25, 51, 139, 167, 235
analogy 42, 45, 87, 106, 168, 198, 272, 275
archive 70, 80
Aristotle 157, 185, 243, 247, 248, 249
assemblage 163, 174, 177, 182, 189, 196, 204
Attridge, Derek 115, 120, 133
auto-destructive art 8, 54, 65-6

Barry, Peter 7, 8, 12, 115-6, 117, 133
Bataille, Georges 31, 164, 282
Bateson, Gregory 265
Baudelaire, Charles 25-6, 108, 111, 182, 207, 274, 282
Baudrillard, Jean 94, 136-7, 161, 248
Becoming 27-8, 81, 204, 210
Benjamin, Walter 18, 31, 35, 182, 233, 261, 282
Beuys, Joseph 24, 30, 51, 56, 94, 106, 202, 203, 204, 231
Biopolitics 277
Blake, William 14, 25, 26, 30, 36, 37, 77, 110, 130, 131, 132, 135, 143-47, 151, 159, 161, 169, 177, 187, 189, 202-3, 211, 213, 285

blur 165, 254, 266, 267, 271
body 9, 24-5, 27-8, 33, 35, 45-6, 49, 124, 127, 164, 172, 230
Boltzmann, Ludwig 81, 266
Brixton riot 11, 98-9, 101, 105, 108-9, 110
Bunting, Basil 23, 28
Burroughs, William 66, 164, 172, 235
Bush, Clive 8, 20, 21, 71, 187, 219-22

Cage, John 20, 53-4, 55, 62, 203, 235
capitalism 10, 15, 37, 119, 129, 164, 166, 169-70, 172, 174, 175, 177, 180, 181, 254, 277, 281, 283
Carpaccio, Vittore 204, 216, 222, 232
Carruthers, Mary 243, 245, 247, 255, 279-80, 282-3, 286
catastrophe 17, 32, 35, 83, 86-7, 89, 92, 128, 234, 254, 265
cusp catastrophe 48, 86, 89, 94, 188
Chadwick, Helen 57, 58, 63
chance operations 15, 53, 61, 94, 164
chaos 30, 33, 83, 85, 87-8, 95, 203, 249, 271, 277
chaos theory 15
cheek, cris 105, 113, 121, 158
chreods 81-5, 88, 94, 96, 158-9, 243, 254, 280
Cicero, Marcus Tullius 135, 149-50, 151, 153, 155, 157, 161
city 24, 34, 41, 72, 241, 243
civic duty /civility 155, 204, 214, 221-2, 277
Clark, Robert 10, 121
Clarke, Adrian 14, 91, 114, 118

Cobain, Kurt 135, 139-44, 159, 161
Cobbing, Bob 7, 57
cognitive poetics 270
Coleridge, Samuel Taylor 56, 168
collage 15, 16, 20, 21, 91, 105, 109, 110, 118, 120, 134, 137, 138, 139-40, 142, 147, 150, 151, 155, 158, 161, 172, 173, 179, 180-81, 182, 189, 192-6, 203, 205, 213, 224, 228, 246, 258, 271, 278, 282
collective (see also community) 23, 25, 27, 34, 55, 112, 126, 140-41, 252
Collings, Simon 14
colour 30, 143, 145-6, 205, 218, 226-8, 229, 246, 266
commodity 24, 60, 166
commons 60, 67, 75
community 20, 51, 55, 285
Complexity Manifold 106, 154, 191, 193
conceptual work 7, 8, 28, 60, 112, 212, 234
'confidence curve' 39, 242, 266
'confidence in lack' 186, 198, 199, 207
connectedness 136, 159, 161, 178, 188, 205, 209-10, 228-9, 234, 236, 237, 247, 255, 257, 270-71, 273, 276
consciousness 30, 40, 68, 107, 160-61, 168, 172, 178, 183, 204-5, 236, 239, 247, 255, 257, 261, 282
Corbin, Henri 24
Crane, Hart 25, 33
creative linkage 118, 120, 131
crowd-out 42, 48-9, 78, 237, 239, 242, 244, 246, 247, 248, 254, 265, 266, 267, 271-2, 275, 279, 283

cultural memory 103-4, 106, 109
cultural resistance 99
cut-ups 8, 66, 120, 164

Dada 54, 107, 169
damage 13, 14, 24, 26, 34, 48-51, 80, 112, 186, 194, 196, 209, 226, 231, 242, 280, 281
David, Jacques-Louis 221-2
de Beauvoir, Simone 204, 216, 242, 244, 254, 257, 280, 284
Debord, Guy 137, 161, 165-9
decentring 65, 119, 126
decoherence 14, 15, 106, 186, 189, 197, 239, 242, 248, 252, 270, defamiliarization 159, 168, 180, 185, 189
deformation 214, 245, 273, 274
de Kooning, Willem 182, 208, 229
Deleuze, Gilles 21, 166, 169-77, 179-81, 182, 187, 240, 254, 257, 263-5, 270, 275, 281, 284
de Quincy, M. Quatremère 135, 156-7, 161
desire 170-1, 203, 257, 259, 264
detournement 137-8, 139-40, 158
dialectical image 18, 35
discontinuity 15-16, 21, 47, 81, 84, 86, 89-90, 96, 118, 158, 188, 250, 257, 270
documentary 65-82, 102, 104, 116
documentation 19, 59, 63, 65-6, 68-82, 185, 196, 238
dramatic monologue 24, 112, 132
dub poetry 100, 104, 108
Duchamp, Marcel 121, 127, 130, 236
Duncan, Andrew 7, 12, 18
Duncan, Robert 23, 28, 30, 233, 237
Dürer, Albrecht 10, 121, 122, 124-5, 126, 127, 129, 130, 131

ecology 11, 17, 41, 51-2, 126, 138, 163, 176, 184, 186, 270, 271
Edwards, Ken 7, 12, 104
  Reality Studios 83, 114
energy 10, 29-30, 33, 36, 37, 40, 113, 118, 129-31, 212, 217, 221, 257, 280
erotic love 10, 127, 164, 170
error 76, 243, 253-4, 274-6
ethics 52, 129, 161, 174, 176, 184, 205, 222, 231, 244, 245, 261, 276-86
Euclid 197, 216, 218
everyday life 56, 61, 70, 128-9, 137, 167, 202-3

facture 186, 187, 189, 202, 203, 209, 210, 217, 226, 227, 231, 237, 271, 279, 282, 285
Fanon, Frantz 101-3, 111
Faust 9-10, 120, 122-3, 126-7, 129-31
Feng Shui 40, 47
Fibonacci series 14, 83, 216
Fichte, Johann Gottlieb 242, 254, 257
figuration (see also iconography) 77, 205, 208-9, 215, 229, 231, 233-5
Fisher, Allen (poetry, performance, poetics)
  The Apocalyptic Sonnets 9-10, 18, 21, 112, 114-5, 120-32, 185, 234
  Blood Bone Brain 18, 20, 39, 46, 53, 59, 62-3, 112, 123, 185, 212
  Brixton Fractals 11, 29, 33, 47-8, 83, 92-6, 100, 104-10, 118-20, 132, 188
  Creek in the Ceiling Beam 19, 42, 53, 59, 62, 63, 65

Dispossession and Cure 11, 13, 212, 213, 215, 224
Gravity as a consequence of shape 8, 10-15, 21, 47, 83-93, 106, 112, 113, 117-20, 126, 131, 132, 134, 143, 163-84, 185, 196, 203, 213-17
Imperfect Fit 7, 20, 186-90, 198
'Milk in Bottles' 60, 61
Necessary Business 7, 20, 91, 101, 110, 113, 117, 158-60
Paxton's Beacon 9, 128
Place 8, 9, 12, 14, 19, 21, 23-38, 39, 49, 53-4, 63, 67, 100, 105, 112, 113-17, 196, 203, 207, 208, 213, 235
Proposals 15
Prosyncel 53, 60, 112
Sicily 8, 53, 59, 62, 63
Sputtor 15, 16-18, 21, 191-200
Thomas Net's Tree Birst 8, 65
The Topological Shovel 7, 83, 101, 236, 280
Unpolished Mirrors 8, 20, 24-38, 114-5, 120, 185
'Vole Volespin' 70-82
'Waddle' 249-54, 257, 276, 278-86
'Watusi' 285
Fisher, Allen (as painter) 20-21, 68, 71-9
Fisher, Allen (visual works)
  'Before the Pain of Return' 209, 224-6
  'Dispossession and Cure' 20, 205, 206, 210, 224-6, 235
  'Kessingland Studies' 20, 234
  'Landscape Studies' 218-22
  'Meditation Traps' 206-10, 213
  'Mr & Mrs Thubron' 209, 227-9
  'Scattered Studies' 218-23

'Views of the City' 203-4, 214, 215-8, 231-2

Fisher, Allen (as publisher) 19, 60, 68-9
  Spanner 20, 55, 58, 113, 114, 118
Fisher, Elaine 212, 233
Foucault, Michel 18, 94, 169-71, 187, 192-3, 200, 250, 277
Fluxshoe 7, 18-19, 53-5, 57-9
Fluxus 18-19, 21, 53-9, 61, 70, 79, 105, 181, 185, 203, 233, 243
fractals 11, 12, 21, 29, 43-4, 83-4, 88, 106
fragment 50, 135, 173, 183
freedom 40, 67, 77, 105, 204, 222, 248, 251-4, 277, 278-80
free will 40, 75, 243, 284
Freer, Ulli (see also McCarthy, Ulli) 118, 160, 205

Gödel, Kurt Friedrich 39, 242
Goethe, Johan Wolfgang von 9, 10, 39, 126, 130, 132, 133, 182, 242,
Giotto 225
Griffiths, Bill 20, 66
Gris, Juan 218
Guattari, Felix 21, 166, 169-77, 179-81, 182, 254, 257, 263-5, 275, 284

Hancock, Tony 72, 204, 216, 217, 232
Hart, Matt 237, 272-6
Harwood, Lee 23, 113
Health 8, 9, 10, 21, 30, 35, 39-52, 116, 204-5
Hegel, G.W.F. 156, 161
Heidegger, Martin 94, 128, 129, 133, 162, 178, 210
Heisenberg, Werner 176

Higgins, Dick 54, 55-6
Hilbert, David 11-12
historical time 23-5, 34, 269
Holloway, Rob 238, 276-86

Iconography 205, 210, 214, 228, 231-2, 233
Imagination 25, 32, 47, 180, 188-9, 204, 237, 247
imperfect fit 13, 120, 228-9, 236
improvisation 10, 70-9, 92, 113-4, 116, 205, 233, 236, 280
incident-set 136, 138-9, 142, 147, 149, 158
incompleteness 31, 33, 37, 75, 80, 82, 117, 151, 156-7, 237
instability of text 70, 79, 90, 150
intermedia 56
Invisible Committee, The 17

Jameson, Fredric 18
jazz-dances 11, 107
Johns, Jasper 212, 233, 237
Johnson, Linton Kwesi 21, 98-104
Jones, David 202-3
Joris, Pierre 9, 10, 20, 23, 66, 193, 196, 201
joy 25, 31, 41, 82, 127, 132, 295, 251, 281

Kandinsky, Wassily 218, 230
Katko, Justin 238-9
Keats, John 186, 198, 199, 201
Kitaj, R.B. 181-3, 214-5, 226, 232, 233
Klee, Paul 35, 218, 229
Knowledge 23, 27, 31, 36, 47, 114, 130, 164, 187, 191, 192, 196-200, 203, 249, 253, 254, 276, 285
Korzybski, Alfred 248-9
Kropotkin, Peter 135, 147-8, 149, 150, 155, 161

Lang, Doug 7, 58
Langland, William 75
Lawson, Andrew 107, 111
Lawson, Hilary 265-6
layers 30, 63, 73, 77, 79, 80, 174, 228-9, 258, 270-71, 276, 279, 282
ley line 39, 41, 46-7, 108, 116
linearity 11, 25, 43, 51, 80, 81, 250
linguistically innovative poetry 117, 118
Lopez, Tony 18, 20, 66

Mac Cormac, Karen 238-67, 269-86
Mac Low, Jackson 53-4, 55, 58, 62
MacSweeney, Barry 20, 66, 104, 113
Mandelbrot, Benoit 44, 84, 88, 106
maps / mapping 24, 33, 35, 41, 42, 44, 114-5, 165, 193-4, 241, 243, 248, 260, 262, 264, 270, 282, 284
Marcuse, Herbert 34, 244
mathematics 7, 11, 12, 14, 39, 149, 197, 203, 256
Mayor, David 57, 58, 60, 63
McCarthy, Ulli (see also, Freer, Ulli) 20
McClure, Michael 31
measure 29-30, 32-3, 37, 108, 237, 248, 251, 252, 266
meditation 206, 208, 279
memory 30, 48, 106, 164, 221, 226, 237, 245, 247, 255-6, 259, 266, 278, 285
 Inventive memory 94, 95, 244, 276, 279, 280
Memory Jars 30, 62, 68-70, 212, 243

mnemonics / mnemotechnics 34, 243, 245, 256, 279
Metzger, Gustav 56, 66
Michaux, Henri 43
migraine 41, 42-4, 123
Miller, Dick 9
Miller, David 17
mirrors 12-13, 14, 15, 24, 25, 30, 31, 64, 78-9, 105, 114, 130, 131, 132
misery 25, 248, 253-4, 277, 278, 280
Mitchell, Paige 21, 70-72, 80, 226, 236
momenergy 248
morphogenesis 84, 89, 234
Mottram, Eric 7, 20, 23, 39, 55, 58, 60, 66, 91, 105, 113-4, 117, 118, 121, 128, 133, 158, 163-5, 167, 177, 181, 235
Mukařovský, Jan 117, 159-60, 161, 244
multiphasic language 30
multiplicity 15, 120, 165, 170, 174, 177, 178, 179, 180, 182, 251, 257, 266
Musil, Robert 249, 250, 255, 257, 270

'Negative Capability' 186, 198, 199, 207
neo-Platonism 84
Newton, Isaac 15, 29, 36, 37, 144, 188, 235
Nietzsche, Friedrich 27, 43, 75, 177, 224, 226, 235, 247
nomadism 51, 170, 171, 174-5, 185

objects 55, 56, 57, 62-3, 68-70, 137, 172, 236, 256, 271
Olson, Charles 7, 20, 23, 25, 28, 31, 33, 53-4, 67, 84, 104, 105,

Index 299

113-4, 186, 187, 190, 213, 229, 233, 234, 235, 237, 280
open field poetics 7, 67, 113-5, 118, 122, 189
Oppen, George 187
Oram, Daphne 17-18
Oulipo 122

paradise 35, 75, 76, 109, 132, 186
parrhesia 18, 187, 189
pedagogy 54, 66, 106, 165, 179-80
perception 40, 48, 50, 95, 106, 168, 170, 203, 210, 215, 230, 236, 239, 242, 246-7, 251, 267, 273-4
performance 7, 10, 11, 18-19, 39, 53-64, 66, 70-9, 233, 264, 278
pertinence 19, 113, 117
phase shift 48, 188, 254
Phillips, Tom 16, 65
play 19, 59-60, 66, 225
Pliny 135, 151-3, 161
plurivocity / polyvocality 91, 106, 173-4, 197, 199
poetics 20, 28, 66, 104, 106, 112-3, 117, 134, 136-8, 154-5, 158, 180, 189, 198, 246, 269, 271
police / policing 99, 101, 102, 107, 108-9, 166, 181
Pollock, Jackson 230-31, 235
polyphony 106, 107, 108, 110
Pound, Ezra 7, 23, 113, 187, 217, 219, 235
Poussin, Nicolas 71, 218-23
power 17, 24, 29, 34, 164-5, 170, 176, 179, 184, 186
    power structures 33, 164
procedural poetry 7, 9, 19, 23, 53, 61-2, 67, 105, 131, 187
procedure showing 19, 54
process 23, 206, 213-4, 281-2, 284
processual poetry 9, 53, 61, 67, 131, 187, 199

process showing 19, 53-4, 188, 189, 213-4
proprioception 70, 186, 212, 220, 229-30, 232, 236, 278
Prynne, J.H. 91, 105, 113, 158, 244, 283
psychogeography (see also ley line) 41
psychosomatics 116, 122, 123-4, 126, 127, 132

quantum physics 11, 14, 15, 39-40, 106, 154-5, 163, 189, 197, 239, 242, 243, 254, 264, 265, 266, 271, 274

Raworth, Tom 54, 119, 122
reading 32, 40, 48, 80, 81-2
the reader 76, 84, 87-8, 89-92, 114-6, 117-8, 126, 136, 158-9, 189, 199, 255
reading strategies 77, 114-6, 136, 191, 199-200, 278-86
recombination 61, 62, 63
reggae 99, 100-3, 104, 105, 107, 109
Reich, Wilhelm 10, 25, 170, 173
re-narration 105-6, 134, 138, 140, 142, 144, 146-52, 156-7, 161
renewal 50, 78, 110, 131, 143, 161, 187, 205, 282
repetition 12, 106, 127, 132, 140-4, 206, 210, 213, 259, 281
research 134-5, 191-2, 195, 196, 197, 202, 204, 221-2, 238, 242, 254, 265, 276, 280
revolution 24, 26, 30-31, 35, 55, 99, 130, 167, 170, 175
rhyme 75, 122, 132, 136, 157, 182, 205, 214, 253, 255
Rimbaud, Arthur 33, 83
Rivers, Larry 231, 232, 233
Rothko, Mark 218

Sartre, Jean-Paul 166, 172, 174, 204, 216-7, 232, 244, 254, 257
scores 10, 121, 122, 131, 132
self-interference 14, 107, 131, 280
sequence / series 83, 89, 125, 193, 207-11, 218, 222, 255, 260, 267
sexual violence 25, 128
shamanism 204
Shelley, Mary 17
Shelley, Percy Bysshe 180, 187
Sheppard, Robert 8, 11, 21, 133, 159-60, 161
simultaneity 49, 118, 246, 248, 256, 270, 282
Sinclair, Iain 25, 29-30, 33, 34, 36, 113, 116
site 24, 256, 261
site-specific 20, 80
Situationism 73, 94, 136-7, 138-9, 167, 179
space 9, 107, 129, 256-7, 269
space-time 105-6, 110, 118, 120, 126, 129, 154-5, 165, 242, 247, 254, 260, 265, 266, 267, 274
Spectacle 166-7, 170
structure 125, 205, 220, 248-9, 254, 261, 262, 263-4, 270
Sufism 32-3
Surrealism 87, 90, 170
survival 47, 164, 165, 168, 205
syntax 94, 95-6, 189, 258, 281-2
   pseudo-syntax 119, 123, 131

technology 8, 9, 10, 17, 30, 36, 70, 78, 109, 122, 125, 127-32, 148, 188, 257
Thatcher, Margaret 26, 27, 34, 99, 122
Thom, René 50, 86, 87, 89, 90, 234, 254
Thubron, Elma 227-30, 234, 235

Thubron, Harry 160, 205, 227-30, 234, 235
Thurston, Scott 13, 14, 21
tools 50-1, 186
topology 8, 12, 28, 33, 56, 85-6, 89, 107, 112
transcendence 61, 130, 277, 284
transformation 13, 14, 15, 23, 24, 27, 32, 47, 50, 94, 109, 127, 163, 187, 188, 194-6, 202, 205, 206, 211, 216, 219-21, 223, 242, 256, 257, 273, 276, 279, 281, 283, 285
traps 20, 50-1, 71-4, 75, 76-7, 78, 170, 186, 198, 207, 212, 251, 266, 273, 277, 285
truth 18, 23, 31, 39-40, 77, 81, 128, 157, 167, 171, 176, 191, 192, 198, 242, 254, 273
truth claims 15, 18, 78
Twombly, Cy 237, 271, 278

use 39, 48
utopia 31, 24, 127, 130, 131

Vaneigem, Raoul 52, 56, 61, 73, 128, 137, 185
versioning 66, 79
violence (see also sexual violence) 10, 34, 36, 98, 101-4, 105, 108, 110, 119, 139, 164, 193, 197, 199,
Virtanen, Juha 18, 192, 199, 201
Vitruvius 153, 154-6, 161

Waddington, C.H. 50, 85, 158, 243, 280
Welish, Marjorie 238, 267-72
Whitman, Walt 177, 180, 184
Williams, Jonathan 10
Williams, William Carlos 23, 33, 128, 187
Wittgenstein, Ludwig 135, 160

Woods, Tim   107, 111
Wordsworth, William   8, 65, 168
Wren, Christopher   24-5, 29, 34-7, 114

Young, J.Z.   27

www.ingramcontent.com/pod-product-compliance
Lightning Source LLC
Chambersburg PA
CBHW022002160426
43197CB00007B/231